Planting Native

to ATTRACT BIRDS to YOUR YARD

SHARON SORENSON

STACKPOLE
BOOKS
Guilford, Connecticut

STACKPOLE BOOKS

Published by Stackpole Books

An imprint of The Rowman & Littlefield Publishing Group, Inc.

4501 Forbes Boulevard, Suite 200, Lanham, Maryland 20706

www.rowman.com

Distributed by NATIONAL BOOK NETWORK

800-462-6420

British Library Cataloguing in Publication Information Available

Library of Congress Cataloging-in-Publication Data Available

ISBN 978-0-8117-3764-7 (paperback)

ISBN 978-0-8117-6743-9 (e-book)

♾™ The paper used in this publication meets the minimum requirements of American National Standard for Information Sciences—Permanence of Paper for Printed Library Materials, ANSI/NISO Z39.48-1992.

Printed in the United States of America

Contents

Introduction

FOR SOME YEARS NOW, WE'VE HEARD DISTANT RUMBLINGS THAT WE SHOULD PLANT NATIVE. The very early murmurings seemed valid but not urgent, emanating from obscure voices that somehow smacked of unnecessary saber rattling. Still, some of us squirmed in the face of it, wondering if we were somehow bad people, maintaining landscapes awash with daffodils, tulips, and daylilies, giving nod to purple loosestrife, water hyacinth, and English ivy. We added butterfly bush, burning bush, and yews; and then we merged them with Amur honeysuckle and Callery pears. What could possibly be wrong with pretty plants with masses of pretty flowers? The vague answer always seemed to be something about their being nonnative, introduced species and that they didn't support wildlife. A few nonnatives apparently were even invasive, and somehow that was worse.

But the message that made us bird lovers squirm the most was the underlying and oft-repeated one that none of these introduced species support our native birds. While the allegation made sense—that native plants would somehow support native birds—the why and how remained vague. Why couldn't birds find a happy life among the lovely nonnatives? Besides, why change the yard now? It's worked for years, and lots of birds visit the bird feeders.

Recently, though, more numerous, prestigious, and resonating voices swelled the chorus of commands to plant natives, carrying the weight of the avian research community, including Cornell University's Lab of Ornithology, American Birding Association, American Bird Conservancy, National Wildlife Federation, National Audubon Society, The Nature Conservancy, and numerous affiliated and related organizations. The unrelenting voices repeatedly belted out the refrain: Attracting birds to the yard is not about feeders and feed. It's about plants. Native plants.

Some media picked up the message. Magazines offered pithy how-to articles recommending native plants for birds, usually a half dozen or so perennials that produce nectar or seeds birds love. In colorful spreads, we saw the potential for native plants in the yard. Nevertheless, we all had that niggling feeling that a couple of asters and a trio of purple coneflowers probably didn't answer the cry for native plants.

Books followed. The "why?" part of native plants became more insistent, more personal. And the books included exhaustive lists, boasting hundreds of native plants to make a yard a sanctuary. But which of the 500 natives work where? Which ones attract which birds—and why?

Websites also took up the charge and charted regional compilations that boggled the mind—hundreds of plants that, in theory, attracted hundreds of birds. Wading through the information and recommendations became time-consuming, exhausting, daunting, almost frightening.

Folks who really wanted to heed the call found themselves still with unanswered questions. What, exactly, is a native plant? Isn't "native" just a nice name for weeds? Why, exactly, do birds need native plants? Why don't nonnative plants serve them just as well? How many native plants must a yard have to satisfy birds? If the yard has one each of half of the top 10 perennials, will that suffice? Which natives work in a mini yard? How does a person choose among the hundreds of native plants? Which plants are the best of the best?

Here's what folks need to resolve the conundrum:

A concise and convincing explanation of why—and how—native plants support birds but nonnative plants don't. Until a clear understanding hits home, there's little motivation to move forward.

State-specific recommendations for native plants or suitable varieties that best attract birds. Every plant is native somewhere, and plants native in Florida may not be native in Wisconsin. Plants native to a bog aren't native to a prairie or mountain glade. So "native" depends on place. Still, no matter their native status, not all native plants are created equal in terms of how they support birds.

Recommendations for the full gamut of native plants, the best of the best, including trees, shrubs, perennials, vines, and grasses. Planting native extends well beyond coneflowers and asters. Prior to 1492, this continent was lush with its original—i.e., native— vegetation, from the tiniest orchid to the most magnificent oak tree. Planting native implies choosing from among the many plant families, not just herbaceous perennials.

Recommendations that detail which feature(s) of specific plants make them bird-friendly. A knowledgeable basis for choosing plants springs from knowing which plants provide seed, which ones support year-round shelter, which ones grow berries and when those berries ripen, which ones host bugs, and which ones meet all the other necessities of life for birds.

Recommendations limited to well-behaved plants, the best of the best, that function satisfactorily in specific landscape sizes. Many native plants are

rangy, aggressive, or unsightly. Many others are stunningly lovely. Some
tower to 100 feet; some need room only to vine and twine; some
hang out comfortably in pots on the patio. Guidance makes plant
choices easier, more satisfying, and more successful.

But no reference provides all the nuts-and-bolts information for folks who
want to heed the call to plant native. Until now.

If you're a bird-watcher, you may not feel you know as much as you'd like
about native plants and how they support the birds you love. And you may not
be a gardener, much less a landscape designer.

If you're a gardener, you may not be a birder. You no doubt want to garden green, but you may not understand clearly how native plants fit in your
landscape—or why you'd want them there.

If you're a botanist, you may not be either a birder or a landscaper. You know
plants, where they thrive, how they grow, how they behave. You understand
inside out and backwards why natives surpass nonnatives on every measurable
botanical scale. Conversely, you may not fully understand how plants support
birds—or, especially, which plants support which birds.

If you're a landscaper, you may not be a birder. Still, your clients request native
plants that attract birds. Even once you choose natives suitable for your area's
growing conditions, they may not fit ordinary landscape designs. And they may
not attract the birds your clients want. Still, you understand the ecologically
sound reasons for moving forward.

In short, there's an entire gamut of caring folks out there looking to enhance
biodiversity and protect wildlife, especially birds.

Here's the pivotal point for this book: Birders, gardeners, botanists, and landscapers together know more than any one of us alone, and this book has put
those folks together, pooling their areas of expertise and offering a set of solid
suggestions for transforming your yard and/or garden into a native paradise for
birds.

SERVICE AREA FOR THIS BOOK

Because this reference can't address the extraordinary range of plants suitable
for birdscaping yards across the entire US, we have limited our discussion to,
roughly, the eastern half of the country, states including and east of Minnesota,
Iowa, Missouri, Arkansas, and Louisiana to the East Coast, and from the Canadian border to the Gulf Coast. Thus, when we talk about the "eastern US," we're
referring to this broad 31-state area.

To reach the folks in the eastern and central US who want to heed the call to plant native for the birds, this book

> explains the relationship between birds, bugs, and native plants;

> suggests bird-friendly, state-specific native plants that support birds during the four seasons;

> recommends bird-friendly native plants that work successfully in attractive home landscaping, in spaces the size of a pots-and-patio garden to that of a mega estate.

As a hands-on, here's-how-you-do-it book, lavishly illustrated for inspiration and clarity, this reference should function as a handle for easily understanding why and how to plant which natives to turn your landscape into a biologically diverse and ecologically sound birdscape.

Let's do it!

Native tree blossoms feed native pollinator insects; and the insects, in turn, feed the birds, a seasonal rhythm especially important to spring migrants like this Blackburnian Warbler, foraging for bugs among pecan blossoms (*Carya illinoinensis*).

"Birds matter because they give us wings. And because if we save the birds, we will save the world."
—PEPPER TRAIL, USFWS forensic ornithologist

Chapter 1
TALLYING A YEAR'S BIRDS IN THE YARD

A few years back, I decided to do a Big Year in the Yard—just a little challenge to see what kinds of birds showed up over the course of 12 months. I wasn't looking for any earth-shattering results; I just wanted to know what's here.

So for 52 weeks I kept a spreadsheet on the kitchen table, ticking off the birds I saw each week. Some I spotted out the windows; more I caught sight of as I wandered the yard, standing all but motionless at strategic spots, spending hours being what I hoped to birds looked like just a lump in the landscape. A few birds I only heard; some I glimpsed as they flitted through undergrowth or foraged in treetops; most I watched at length, noting how and where and on what they foraged.

The resulting spreadsheet isn't very scientific because I didn't tally how many I saw of each species, only which species and how frequently they appeared in the yard. For instance, the tick marks show that every week I saw "regulars," like Northern Cardinals and American Goldfinches. But only during spring and fall migration did I log most of the warblers. A few rather unusual birds I saw only once over the 365 days, like Black-billed Cuckoo, Cape May and Blackburnian Warblers, and Yellow-throated and Blue-headed Vireos. A few migrants lingered multiple days but no more than a week, like the Orchard Oriole that settled in to feed during a single

A migrating Cape May Warbler stopped to fuel up in our bird-friendly yard during his spring journey north.

week in late May and the male Purple Finch that visited several days in late November. And so it went for the year.

Over the course of those 12 months, I tallied 114 bird species on our little three-acre property in southwestern Indiana. Did I miss any visitors? No way to know for sure, of course, but I'm certain I did. Still, the count is probably a fairly realistic summary of what's here—and when.

Okay, so my Big Year in the Yard is truly No Big Deal, at least not to anyone else. It's a slow game, certainly not one for those who bore easily, grow weary of repetition, get too hot or too cold in the great outdoors, or give way to cell phone distractions. Nor is it a game for those short on commitment. By mid-June, it would have been easy to quit. There's no competition, no reward, no prize. And basically nobody else cares.

Even with seemingly few rewards, however, I'm compelled to feel that somehow I did win something during this challenge—maybe not something tangible, but to me at least, something valuable. What I learned about birds that year can't be compared with any other birding activity in which I've been engaged—except maybe, of course, voluminous reading about birds and peeking in on the many authorities' observations.

Indeed, the year-long challenge brought home a few startling observations, most of them real kickers—the "Who would have guessed *that*?" kind of kicker. As a result, even without a degree in biology, I was forced, by the obvious conclusions, to quit rattling on and on about what to feed, what kind of feeders to use, and where to strategically place those feeders. I already had the ultimate bird feeders in my yard, and I needed to make those feeders even better.

Here's what I mean:

Kicker 1: Of the 114 species sighted in the yard that year, a mere 29 species came to my well-stocked feeders. That's only about a quarter of the species tallied. That kicker alone was enough to bring me to a full halt, taking stock of that number and what it meant.

And so: Given that 75 percent of birds never came to feeders, the conclusion seems clear: There's more to attracting birds than putting out feeders and feed. Attracting birds to the yard must have some other component.

Kicker 2: Of the 114 species sighted in the yard that year, 76—or a whopping 67 percent—visited only seasonally. About half of the 76—or about 33 percent of the total—only migrated through, showing up during a few weeks in April and May and/or for a few weeks in September and October. Only one of these migrants visited feeders, but many visited water features.

And so: Given that about one-third of the birds that visited the yard were migrating, headed farther north in spring to nest, maybe as far north as Canada, or headed farther south in fall, maybe as far south as central South America, the conclusion seems clear: To provide habitat attractive to migrants, the yard must offer the necessary nutrition to stoke the metabolic needs of long-distance fliers. That kind of nutrition comes in the form of insects (high protein) in spring and rich lipids (fats) in fall. Whatever offers those two in-demand nutritional foods will help build the ultimate feeder.

Purple Martins, which come from South America to the US to raise their families, feed their babies bugs, this female providing a cicada to her nestlings.

Kicker 3: Of the 76 seasonal birds sighted in the yard, a full one-quarter spent the summer here nesting before returning to their winter ranges. Think Summer and Scarlet Tanagers, Indigo Buntings, Baltimore Orioles—you know, the really bright neotropical migrants that come here to nest and raise their babies.

And so: Given that about 25 percent of birds came here to nest and raise babies, that our year-round resident birds also obviously nest and raise babies here, and that 96 percent of songbirds feed their

About 96 percent of songbirds feed their babies bugs, including year-round resident Song Sparrows, this one having snagged a mayfly for its nestlings.

babies bugs, the conclusion seems clear: To provide healthy, nutritious habitat for nesting birds, I must attract the bugs—the big-time ultimate feeder.

Kicker 4: Of the 76 seasonal birds sighted in the yard, about one-quarter spent the winter here. Relatively speaking, I suppose the winter-only birds consider southwestern Indiana a sort of Caribbean getaway, far less snow- and ice-clad than their breeding territories in the boreal forests of Canada and parts farther north. At my house, the winter-only visitors come in the likes of White-throated and White-crowned Sparrows, Dark-eyed Juncos, Pine Siskins, Yellow-rumped Warblers, and Purple Finches.

And so: Given that some birds come here only for the winter, the yard must provide significant winter forage and ample winter shelter. After all, it's not really the Caribbean here. So the ultimate winter feeder must also somehow, at least indirectly, include shelter.

Kicker 5: Of the 114 species sighted in the yard that year, some foraged only in the upper canopy, some foraged mid-canopy, and some foraged only on or near the ground; some hung out mostly in conifers; some stayed concealed in brambles; some visited the garden for seeds or nectar; and some focused their attention on berries or bugs. Just like people, they didn't all want to live or eat in the same kinds of places or from the same menu.

And so: Given that certain species were spotted only in certain specific types of habitat, and given the observation that varied birds favored a varied menu, the conclusion seems clear: The greater the diversity of habitat, the greater the diversity of birds. So the ultimate feeders must offer foraging high, mid, and low, and also present fodder in a wide range of offerings.

Kicker 6: Of the 114 species sighted in the yard that year, about 50—or roughly 44 percent—would likely be considered unusual yard birds, winged wonders like Mourning Warbler, Blue-headed Vireo, and Wood Thrush.

Each bird species demonstrates feeding-site preferences, some high in the canopy, some mid-level, and some, like Brown Thrashers, low on or near the ground.

And so: Maybe there's something about the habitat that drew these unusual birds to the yard. After all, for birds, life is always and singularly about habitat. The effect of habitat on birds comes down to three important and somewhat overlapping principles:

1. Change the habitat and you'll change which birds live there.
2. Diversify the habitat and you'll diversify the birds that live there.
3. Eliminate the favored habitat and you'll eliminate the birds that lived there.

WHAT IS HABITAT?

What do we mean by "habitat"? In short, good habitat offers suitable food, shelter, nest sites, nest materials, and water to sustain creatures' lives. The big wrinkle in that simple explanation is that for birds, everything except water (and even that, sometimes) comes naturally from plants. To survive, birds are irrevocably tied to the vegetation around them, for food, for shelter, for nest sites, for nest materials. In simple terms, then, to better serve the birds, we as hosts should add more plants, not more feeders. Let me be the first in this discussion, however, to admit it: Feeders are really for us, to attract some birds closer to our windows for our own selfish enjoyment, an activity that I'm betting every one of us truly enjoys.

THE ULTIMATE FEEDER

Now, back to that ultimate feeder. How we make the botanical habitat more suitable to birds is almost as far-ranging as the yards in which those habitats grow. The key element, however, the one common denominator for everything that makes habitat most suitable for birds, is not the addition of just any plants. Rather, it's the addition of plants that provide food. Furthermore, we're

Good bird habitat supports sheltered, secure nest sites, including those for cavity nesters like Great-crested Flycatchers, this one checking out a potential cavity in an American sycamore tree (*Platanus occidentalis*).

not talking here only about direct food production, like seed, berries, fruit, and nectar. We're also talking about indirect food production—plants that supply birds' protein, in the form of insects that themselves reside on or find support from plants.

Think, for example, about *Lepidoptera* host plants, those plants on which butterflies, skippers, and moths lay their eggs. To oversimplify the process, butterflies, skippers, and moths choose very specific plants as hosts for their eggs and, following, the larvae. Monarchs, for instance, while they nectar on a wide variety of blossoms, lay their eggs only on milkweed plants. Other *Lepidoptera* likewise nectar broadly but choose specific plant hosts for their eggs. When the eggs hatch, the larval caterpillars of all those butterflies, skippers,

A monarch butterfly nectars on the blossoms of swamp milkweed (*Asclepias incarnata*), one of the milkweed species on which she will lay her eggs.

and moths feed on the leaves of their host plants. The host plants get their food through photosynthesis, a process by which plants use energy from the sun to turn carbon dioxide and water into energy-rich glucose (sugar) and, as a by-product, release oxygen into the air. So, as the caterpillars munch the leaves and grow, they are converting the product of photosynthesis into protein. How clever is that!

The protein that caterpillars embody, along with that from other plant-eating insects and their eggs and larvae, is the single protein source for songbirds. No hamburger, grilled chicken, or pot roast—just plant-hosted protein. Bugs, their eggs, and their larvae offer the right amount of protein in just the right size and serve it up at the right place at the right time for birds and their babies to thrive. Think about it this way: The protein necessary for birds' survival ultimately comes from or is supported almost entirely by native plants. It follows, then, that if you want the viewing pleasure of birds in your yard, you'll need those protein-supporting native plants in your yard!

Here's the kicker regarding the symbiotic bug-plant world: In general, native plants support native bugs that feed our native birds. In many cases, in fact, the chemical composition of the leaves of nonnative plants makes many of those plant parts unpalatable—sometimes even toxic—to native bugs.

WHAT'S THE DEAL WITH NATIVE PLANTS?

So, who knew? The landscaping around our homes isn't just for decoration. It serves, or should serve, a purpose—in fact, a life-or-death purpose—for birds. But, since plants are not created equal, only if we have the right plants do we feed the birds! And how do we know?

Let's take a look at why and how and what we can do to meet birds' needs—whether they be birds that grace our yards year-round, come to nest in summer, visit only in winter, or sail through during spring and fall migrations. Following a few simple directives, you really can make a life-giving change for birds. Then think how good you'll feel knowing you helped some one-ounce feathered miracle survive its perhaps 5,000-mile journey home.

Meanwhile, you will have created the absolute ultimate bird feeder.

In spite of all that potentially life-saving bird support, however, here's betting that you have a zillion questions about what native plants are, what they look like, and how they would fit in your yard. Maybe you even have doubts about whether you really want native plants in your meticulously manicured yard. So, let's answer those questions with some down-and-dirty details to help you make an informed decision.

Before we do that, however, let's get to some other down-and-dirty details—about why and how birds use plants. And it's not just about food.

After a daunting migration from South America, a male Baltimore Oriole gleans nourishment from eastern cottonwood catkins (*Populus deltoides*).

"If homeowners used native plants in their yards—which would enable them to control pests without using pesticides—it would represent the largest habitat-restoration for birds ever taken."

—JOHN FLICKER, President, National Audubon Society

Chapter 2
UNDERSTANDING BIRDS' DEPENDENCY ON NATIVE PLANTS

What's all this chatter about birds needing native plants? At first glance, they seem to lead the simple life. They flit about, wing across the yard or soar above it, enjoying lovely days but hunkering down in bad weather. They breed in spring and summer, and otherwise lounge about.

That idyllic scenario, however, couldn't be further from the truth. Yes, they flit about, wing across the yard or soar above it; but when they do, it's purposeful. The flitting about is almost always part of their ongoing search for food, always foraging for the next tidbit—bug, berry, seed, or sap. But dining is not a single-feature event. While the food search is on, birds must ever and always be on guard against predators, usually sneaky, well-concealed, and speedy predators. Get too distracted foraging for a suitable meal, and the bird becomes a meal itself. But if a bird fails to find sufficient nutrition for even a day, it may not live to see the next. Birds live on the edge. Always.

And plants, specifically native plants—or the absence thereof—determine whether birds continue to live on the edge or fall off. To understand how that all plays out, how native plants can have such an impact, let's do a quick, seriously condensed review of a year in the life of a bird.

A YEAR IN THE LIFE OF A BIRD

Let's start the year in spring. Birds in the eastern US breed only during spring and summer, sometimes raising a single brood, sometimes several. Nesting females, however, are especially vulnerable, sitting quietly, presumably well concealed but nevertheless recognizable by hungry predators that can smell birds even when they can't see them. Even if the female escapes predation, her nest may not. The effect is not only a lost opportunity to reproduce—the only true purpose birds have—but also the loss of energy and effort.

I once took apart a failed Northern Cardinal nest. As I dismantled the nest bit by bit, I was overwhelmed by the immensity of it all. The woven masterpiece, a scant 6 inches in diameter, contained 314 pieces—leaves, a few sticks, small twigs, grasses, strips of grapevine bark, pieces of bald cypress tree bark. Each of the 314 pieces represented a search for the right piece of the right size and the right shape. Each represented a flight to the nest and placement in the creation. Each represented a significant expenditure of time

While building her nest, a female Northern Cardinal searches for, selects, and snaps off a twig from an American beautyberry bush (*Callicarpa americana*). Birds exert significant effort building a nest that might include 300 to 400 pieces of vegetation.

and a significant exertion of effort. What's more, during every moment of that now-deemed-fruitless effort, the bird remained vigilant to save her very life. Predators always lurk.

Nest completed, the female laid five eggs, together nearly equaling her own weight. Producing enough calcium to form the eggshells alone necessitated a loss of her own body's minerals, and producing the embryos dramatically challenged her physical strength and stamina. Incubating the eggs demanded unfailing attention to protect the nest, feeding only briefly and, we hope, successfully.

When the nest failed because a snake helped itself to her eggs, all of that time and energy was lost. Since the summer was young, she likely re-nested, but that further challenged her well-being. Of course, the snake fed to live another day. In that respect, the eat-or-be-eaten cycle represents, once again, Mother Nature's balance. She's not always sweetness and light.

When nesting is successful, a different challenge faces the adult pair, assuming both sexes raise the brood. (Male hummingbirds, for example, never support the nesting effort and never help raise the young.) Generally, breeding adults must feed their brood while they also feed themselves, a daily frenetic search that never slows even in rain, wind, heat, or humidity. The little ones, often noisy, now need protection against predators that can not only smell but now hear the ruckus that represents to them a life-giving meal.

Midsummer Crisis

Once the offspring fledge and scatter, off on their own, you'd think the adults could finally settle in for a much-needed rest. Well, not so fast. At season's end, adults molt, shedding and replacing

An American Goldfinch shows evidence of molting. During this time, when flight is compromised, birds seek safety in dense shelter.

faded, worn, and damaged feathers. They've had a rough summer, after all, scooting in and out of nests, rubbing against vegetation while foraging, and following an exhaustive routine, searching with single focus for bugs to feed demanding babies and themselves. Now, though, they must ready themselves for winter—maybe winter in a place as far away as South America.

The long, drawn-out process of molting takes up to 12 weeks, depending on the species, and leaves birds vulnerable. While they shed and replace their feathers systematically and symmetrically across their bodies (they can't go naked, after all!), a few missing flight feathers necessarily hinder flight—never a good thing with a predator on the chase. So molting birds tend to lie low, seek shelter, and hang out where an abundance of food allows them to forage leisurely and safely. You might well guess, however,

that growing new feathers—between 1,500 and 3,000 of them on small songbirds—requires unimaginable energy. Look at it this way: Feathers are 90 percent protein, primarily keratins. To put that in perspective, feathers contain 25 percent of the protein found in a bird's entire body. To meet the energy demands required to produce all those feathers, birds need diets singularly high in protein. Think bugs. To produce bright feather color, birds need diets high in lipids. Think fats. Think berries.

If birds molt in your yard, then, they need safe habitat, lots of protein (bugs), and lots of fats (berries). Birds weakened already by the heavy demands of the breeding season often struggle to survive the nutritional demands—and the safety crisis—that accompany molt.

Winter Nears

By this time in the annual cycle, winter nears. The many-faceted challenge of surviving winter brings about the demise of many birds. The simple truth, however, is that many birds do stay. And they do survive. Those tough little winter-bird dynamos earn my respect. Big time.

Where I live in southwestern Indiana, and to the north, winter hits stay-at-home birds with a four-way whammy. First, severe cold demands birds consume more calories in order to survive. Logically, finding more calories takes more time. But short winter days slash foraging time in half, from 16 hours of daylight to a mere 8—less if you live farther north. There's a double whammy already.

Next, add snow, maybe a foot or more, depending on where you live, and birds need their own snowplows to find sufficient food. Foraging in protected patches, under dense vegetation, they hunt for open spots that may offer up a few morsels. They check cracks and crevices of tree bark for hidden delicacies. They rely on their caches, those stealthily concealed tidbits hidden in the fall. They glean buds. They scratch into the snow to reach leaf litter, hoping to discover nourishment there. Now, a bird's only goal is finding food to sustain body heat and shelter to gain protection against the elements.

Finally, as winter drags to an end, birds face a direct hit from the fourth whammy. Food grows more and more scarce, gobbled up, crushed, or spoiled, dwindling more quickly in years when summer's drought renders seed and berry crops short. It's a tough go for overwintering birds. Still, they can survive the cold if they can find enough to eat. Think plants—seeds and berries— and the things plants harbor—eggs and larvae in tree trunks and under leaf litter. Even as we mere humans see trees and other vegetation as bare sticks and skeletal silhouettes, for birds the grocery store doors remain open, even if shelves hold scant supplies. Life continues, still and always, only because of plants, including those that may be in your yard.

Migrants on the Move

Then there are the birds that migrate after raising their broods—not a bad plan if you don't mind the commute. Gone, for instance, are Gray Catbirds, House Wrens, Ruby-throated Hummingbirds, Scarlet and Summer Tanagers, Indigo Buntings, Rose-breasted Grosbeaks, and Yellow-billed Cuckoos; all the flycatchers and gnatcatchers; all but one of the warblers; all the swifts, swallows, and martins; all the nighthawks and whip-poor-wills. They're gone, snapping up bugs in places as far south as Brazil. Sounds tropically delightful, until I think about a single tiny creature, weighing perhaps less than an ounce, flapping its way more than 9,000 miles to Brazil and back—and living to tell about it. Indeed, various GPS, radio, and satellite tracking systems do the telling, proving what seems unbelievable.

During spring and fall, migrants like Black-throated Green Warblers need reliable migratory stopovers where they can refuel and rest before continuing their journey the next night.

How do they survive? Again, think plants—for on-the-road food and shelter.

We call those places where migrating birds pause for food and shelter "migratory stopovers." Migrants prefer that these patches be thick with protective shelter, rich with nourishing bugs and berries, and refreshing with water for drink and bath. In many ways, migratory stopovers parallel our interstate highway rest stops, where we grab a snack, perhaps take a nap, and fuel up for the next leg of the trip. Since most songbirds migrate at night, by early dawn they're ready to alight, refuel, rest, and refresh. By sunset, they're off again.

Sounds simple, right? Just stop when the sun is about to rise and hang out for the day. We humans, however, have created a problem, a life-or-death problem, for birds. We've bulldozed and paved thousands and thousands of acres that were once migratory stopovers for thousands and thousands of birds. Those feeding stopover spots, hardwired in birds' brains over millions of years of genetic tweaks, disappeared.

Compare their plight to yours: You've traveled for hours, your fuel gauge says "empty," and you're hungry. You've traveled this way before, many times, so you know (equivalent to the bird's genetic hardwiring) that there's a rest stop 23 miles ahead. When you arrive, however, you're shocked. The rest area is closed, the gas station out of business, the restaurant boarded up. You try to struggle on, but the car sputters, and you're stranded alongside the road. For you, a simple cell phone call can do the trick. For birds, not so. Surely I need not explain the result. I will explain, however, that over the long haul, migratory bird populations have declined dramatically, and lost migratory stopovers are in large part to blame.

Our yards, however, can become migratory stopovers. Every single berry-producing bush may make the difference for some bird's migratory survival. This platitude is not just something I read about, thought sounded good, and decided to pass along. I've counted migratory birds in my own yard, and I know it to be true.

The Year's Wrap-Up

So, there you have it—a condensed version of a year in the life of a bird. By now you know that birds never have time to "lounge about."

No matter what they're doing, however, be it eating, choosing nest sites, building nests, caring for their broods, molting, overwintering, or migrating, birds depend on the vegetation around them. Well, no, let's put that more emphatically: They're *irrevocably tied* to the vegetation around them—especially native vegetation.

Next, then, let's take a close look at exactly how that plays out, beginning with plants as food.

The Eastern Meadowlark, shown here at its on-the-ground nest, is one of the top 10 avian species in serious decline because of habitat loss, including its grassland nesting habitat.

PLANTS AS FOOD

Before humans invaded birds' territories, the birds survived quite nicely without us. Mother Nature's plan for perfect balance availed the birds of food, and the fittest survived. They didn't rely on decorative or sometimes elaborate feeders delivering sunflower or safflower seed, nyjer seed or peanuts, suet or mealworms.

Given today's dramatic loss of habitat, perhaps we should, out of guilt, feel compelled to help however we can. After all, we've destroyed so much of many birds' habitats, especially their breeding habitats, that their populations have plummeted—Eastern Meadowlarks, Bobolinks, Evening Grosbeaks, Northern Bobwhites, Field Sparrows, and Grasshopper Sparrows, to name a few of the top 10 in decline. As a kid, I listened to Eastern Meadowlarks sing "spring of the a-year" most every summer day. Now, I'll jam on the brakes to come to a screeching halt if I detect one while traveling—just to hear that song again. In every case, the plummeting populations have been the result of the loss of habitat. Think "loss of vegetation."

Bird Feeders at the Ready

These days, it's common practice for folks to mount feeders, with some feeding stations more expensive than my own set of dinnerware. We worry about the quality of the feeders and feed; we worry about protecting the feeders from scavenging rascals like raccoons and squirrels; and we spend more money feeding birds than what families in third-world countries earn in a year.

We do it in the name of helping birds. Don't misunderstand—I do it, too, although perhaps to a more modest extent than some. But let's be perfectly honest here: We really mount and fill feeders in order to draw in the birds for our personal enjoyment. It's a selfish habit that we enjoy. And after all, who doesn't enjoy watching a brilliantly

*B*eyond the dollars we pay outright for feeders and seed, what about the hidden costs—especially to the environment? As far as we know, no research or even sound estimates tally the indirect environmental costs for producing, packaging, and shipping commercially marketed wild-bird seed. But consider these questions:

Are those sunflower seeds harvested from vast monoculture fields that have stolen away yet more natural habitat from the birds? What kind of and at what cost are fertilizers applied? Are the fields or crops treated by herbicides, fungicides, and/or insecticides? Is there result-ing pollution, including runoff, from the use of fertilizers or pesticides? What are the CO_2 emissions resulting from planting, harvesting, and transporting seed? How much nonrenewable fuel is used to transport wild-bird seed from field to feeder? What environmental issues are involved in the production of packaging? Do the inks used in package printing pollute air or water? Were trees that birds rely on cut down to make paper to bag the seeds? What are the CO_2 emissions for that? At what energy cost are plastic containers produced, those little throwaway cartons for suet?

Since most nyjer seed is grown in places like Ethiopia and India, are lands used for wild-bird seed production replacing land needed for human food production? And since any shipment of nyjer seed from Africa or Asia to the US requires, by government mandate, that the seed be sterilized to prevent germi-

Adding an oak tree (*Quercus* spp.) to the yard feeds more birds than any other tree. Early-spring bugs attracted to oak catkins (shown here), summer's host of *Lepidoptera* eggs and larvae, fall's acorn crops, and winter's leaf-liter provisions of eggs and larvae feed birds during all four seasons.

nation and kill weed seeds, at what cost to the environment does that process occur? Who can ignore transportation costs from the opposite side of the world to US backyards?

Listing similar questions about feeders themselves would take pages, since the environmental concerns depend on feeder construction—like size, materials, and manufacturing process, plus packaging, label printing, and transportation.

So here's the ethical issue: Are we using natural resources wisely by artificially feeding birds? What if we took all those direct and indirect dollars and used them to purchase native plants, restoring habitat that would naturally feed the birds? Buying feeders and seed is an effort with only short-term effects; planting for birds is long-term, maybe even a once-and-done effort. And—need we mention?—plants reduce CO_2 from the air and add oxygen; their roots help retain moisture and prevent runoff; and their fallen leaves fertilize and revitalize the soil. All these advantages exist above and beyond feeding the birds.

Something to think about, isn't it?

colored Northern Cardinal cracking sunflower seeds and, during mating season, feeding one to his equally lovely if more subtly colored mate? Who doesn't thrill to an Eastern Bluebird pair snatching mealworms to feed a growing brood in that specially designed nest box mounted at garden's edge? And who could ignore the gloriously tiny Ruby-throated Hummingbird feeding on syrup just inches from the kitchen window, his brilliant namesake ruby-colored gorget flashing in the light? We love 'em. So we feed 'em. So we love 'em even more!

And that's okay. Mostly.

Some researchers have tried to prove we actually cause harm by artificially feeding birds, that we increase population density in feeder areas and thus encourage the spread of disease. Then we further spread disease through unwashed and untended moldy feeders. By attracting unusually high numbers of birds to an unnaturally small feeding area, maybe we also attract predators that then kill off the very birds we hope to enjoy. A few researchers suggest we even give birds a false sense of the natural availability of resources, encouraging too many birds to nest near the artificial source of feeder food, none of which is suitable for feeding babies. Babies eat only bugs. By keeping mess cleared away, feeders cleaned, and resources consistent, however, we can likely avoid the doomsayer problems. Avoiding the serious problems, though, requires making a serious commitment.

Still, that leaves the babies without bugs.

The real kicker here, though, is not from the doomsayers who would nix entirely the idea of feeders and feed. No, the real kicker, and the more disheartening part of this feed-the-birds exercise, rests in this unsettling statistic: Fewer than one-quarter of birds in my yard ever visit feeders. And therein lies the rub. To ignore the needs of more than 75 percent of birds seems carelessly wrong.

Fortunately, it's a wrong that's easily righted.

Imagine this land in the time before 1492, before Europeans arrived on the continent carrying from home the plants they loved. Prior to then, what did birds eat? It's perhaps oversimplified to say that they ate what they found, but in fact, that is the singular truth.

So let's take a look at what birds eat in the old-fashioned way, without commercial feeders and bagged seed. We're thinking here especially about the 75 percent of birds that never come to feeders. Altogether, songbirds' diets include nectar, sap, berries, bugs, buds, blossoms, and seeds—all from native plants, those growing here prior to 1492.

Plants—Not Just Flowers—for Nectar

Among nectarivores—that is, birds that eat nectar—hummingbirds likely jump to the front of the line. Everyone knows they habitually visit blossoms for nectar. Their amazing memories allow them to remember which flowers they have already visited and which flowers are newly opened. They remember which flowering patches have produced good blossoms in previous years, and they return to those patches in

A hatch-year migrating Ruby-throated Hummingbird nectars at jewelweed (*Impatiens capensis*), a native plant rich in nectar and attractive to insects.

Hummingbird
FLOWERS

H ummingbirds, with their long bills and even longer tongues, can reach nectar in long-necked native flowers like trumpet honeysuckle (*Lonicera sempervirens*) and trumpet vine (*Campsis radicans*) and thereby feed without competition from bees and butterflies. It's a myth, however, that they nectar only from red flowers. They nectar at any good source, including blue, orange, yellow, and white blossoms.

Again to avoid competition, hummers often nectar at plants with little or no scent. Because scent attracts bees and butterflies, hummingbirds can better feed in peace while nectaring at sites that other pollinators and nectar-feeding critters miss.

following years. They actually establish routes from patch to patch, anticipating what they'll find where. Over the millennia, hummingbirds became hardwired to recognize the flowering plants that evolved with them, those that supported them for thousands of years. During fall migration, for instance, hummingbirds throughout the entire eastern half of the US depend on jewelweed (*Impatiens capensis*) for nourishment. They know to look for those flowers, the ones we call "native."

Of course, hummingbirds aren't the only birds attracted to nectar. Orioles, both Baltimore and Orchard, turn to nectar for quick energy in spring (although they abruptly abandon nectar once breeding begins, switching to protein-rich diets). Orioles always make me chuckle when I watch them in tulip trees, upended and face-first into the blossoms, only their backsides visible as they sip the rich native nectar. Tulip trees bloom just as orioles arrive during spring migration, a mutually perfect timing for both the birds and the trees, as birds pollinate the flowers while gorging on sweet energy. The clearly symbiotic relationship between bird and tree has coevolved

over millennia but is now threatened by climate change, causing the tree to blossom earlier than the nectarivores arrive.

Woodpeckers likewise enjoy a sip of nectar now and then, although they tend to glean their sweet sips from fruit rather than from flowers. Warblers also occasionally sip nectar from native sources, especially in their winter ranges.

As we consider the importance of plants as nectar sources for birds, it's worth noting that flowers aren't the only nectar sources for hummingbirds and other nectarivores. Hummers have been documented sipping sweetness from ripened fruit already pierced by another bird or insect. Early literature claims a hummingbird hovered long enough to sip from an apple while a young girl was paring it. And it's a fairly common observation to catch hummers making early-spring visits to Yellow-bellied Sapsucker wells, especially those in maple trees. The accumulated sap in the little rows of holes provides hummers much-needed nourishment, especially when flowers are scarce or washed free of nectar from heavy rains. It's yet another example of Mother Nature's plan to provide for all.

Yellow-bellied Sapsuckers drill sap wells into tree bark, visiting them repeatedly to dine on both sap and insects the sap attracts. In early spring, returning hummingbirds visit the sap wells for the same carbs and proteins.

Okay, so birds eat nectar. Nectar comes from plants. You knew all that. The loose cannon in the nectar business is timing. Native plants offer nectar at just the right time (assuming climate change doesn't race the clock). Introduced non-native plants, though, may fall short, pineapple sage (*Salvia elegans*) a case in point. By the time it blooms, offering up its rich nectar, hummingbirds—prime candidates for the nectar's use—have long gone, back to their winter homes.

Hummingbirds' Protein Diet

As surprising as it may be, however, hummers eat lots of protein. Biologists have long understood that hummingbirds eat a certain number of bugs, but it's tricky to figure out exactly how many bugs or in what proportion to nectar. By necessity, of course, hummers can snatch only tiny bugs, including flies, gnats, wasps, aphids, beetles, leafhoppers, and especially spiders. If you watch closely, you'll no doubt witness hummers bugging. They perch, watching, then dart out, snatch a bug midair, and return to their perches. Some ornithologists would argue, in fact, that hummingbirds visit certain flowers not for the nectar at all, but for the tiny insects the flowers attract.

Some rather startling research suggests that hummers actually consume a lot more protein than most people think, perhaps way more protein than they do nectar. In 1980 a reputable research team reported that one female hummingbird tracked for over two weeks was never seen nectaring. In fact, she seemed to have sustained herself (and, we assume, her young) during those 14 days on a 100 percent protein diet she gleaned primarily from arthropods.

Here's what all this means to those who want to attract hummingbirds (and who doesn't?) to their yards: If hummers—especially breeding females—require a protein-rich diet, no nectar feeder or even sets of nectar feeders will completely satisfy their needs. But there's a corollary to this demand for protein: The bugs that hummers prefer depend themselves on plants one way or another, including the plants that host bug eggs and/or larvae. So, for hummers, it's plants for nectar and plants for bugs. To potential hummingbird hosts, that translates into a simple formula: Plant plants. Just be careful which ones!

Seeds for Sustenance

Most bird-watchers would agree that a high proportion of birds eat enormous amounts of seed. These backyard hosts cite the pounds and pounds of commercially produced sunflower, safflower, and nyjer seeds they supply to birds visiting their backyard feeders. There's a caveat, however: Only certain birds eat seed. So if we offer nothing more than seeds, either in feeders or in the wild, we'll attract only the certain birds that eat them. In truth, the explanation is fairly straightforward: Not every bird has a bill structure that enables it to crack open even the smallest of seeds. So hummingbirds never eat seeds. Nor do swallows, swifts, martins, or creepers. Raptors don't eat seeds. Shorebirds don't eat seeds. While Eastern Bluebirds have been known to eat sunflower seeds, they eat only chips; they cannot crack open the whole seed.

Here's the law of the land when it comes to what birds eat: Bill structure determines diet. By extension, bill structure also largely determines whether or not a bird migrates. If a bird's bill structure limits it to eating entirely, or at least mostly, bugs—like those of warblers, swallows, swifts, martins, vireos, nighthawks, and flycatchers, among others—those birds obviously must migrate in order to find wintertime bugs.

On the other hand, year-round avian residents in the eastern US tend to rely on seeds to survive the winter. Their bill structures allow them not only to crack open seeds but, in the case of Red and White-winged Crossbills, for instance, to dig those seeds out of spruce, fir, and pine cones. Northern Cardinals, Blue Jays, Carolina and Black-capped Chickadees, Tufted Titmice, American Goldfinches, House Finches, Hoary and Common Redpolls, and White-breasted and Red-breasted Nuthatches readily survive on winter supplies of seeds.

Again, from the old-fashioned perspective, apart from backyard bird feeders, seeds come from plants. Period.

Even birds recognized as primarily seedeaters, however, rarely rely solely on seeds. Summer-nesting Indigo Buntings forage in grasslands and along roadside edges for grass and weed seeds, but they feed their babies bugs. Northern Cardinals forage on a range of flower seeds, fruit, and insect larvae, but they too feed their babies bugs. Carolina Chickadees glean small seeds from flowering plants and other small-seeded vegetation but supplement their diets with insects and spiders gleaned from twigs—and feed their babies bugs. Only two songbirds fall outside the pattern: Mourning Doves forage on the ground for dropped seeds and feed their babies "milk," a slurry of digested, regurgitated seeds. Likewise, American Goldfinches, which are 100 percent

Like this male Indigo Bunting with a beak full of seeds, most mature grassland birds feed on tiny native grass seeds but feed their babies bugs. In the fall, most migrate to Central America.

vegetarian, glean grass and weed seeds and then feed their babies regurgitated seeds.

Perhaps one group of birds best known for their dependency on seed are the many kinds of native sparrows. Common backyard sparrows like Chipping Sparrows and Song Sparrows readily glean grass or flowering plant seeds. That gives us reason for planting something other than lawn wherever space permits. Birds we traditionally refer to as "winter sparrows"—those sparrows that breed in the northern US and well into Canada but move into the central, eastern, and southern US for the winter—represent one of the largest populations relying on small winter seeds for survival. Winter sparrows include such species as White-crowned, White-throated, Lincoln's, Fox, Swamp, American Tree, Savannah, and Vesper Sparrows, as well as our largest sparrow, the Eastern Towhee. With only a few exceptions, notably White-throated Sparrows and occasionally White-crowned Sparrows, winter sparrows generally don't visit feeders. They need natural native seed supplies.

Finches, of course, expand the list of seed lovers—House Finches, Purple Finches, American Goldfinches, and their cousins, Dark-eyed Juncos and Pine Siskins. All love seeds, tiny seeds. Thus, only if these mostly wintering birds find sizable patches of native grasses and other small-seeded plants will they stay for any length of time or even make an appearance in your yard. If yours is a mini or even mid-sized yard, enticing more than one or two of these sparrows or finches into window view may be a challenge in winter. On the other hand, if you have acreage, planting an expansive meadow will help maintain populations and reverse the loss-of-habitat crisis, at least for some winter sparrows and finches.

Other, larger birds more successfully find a variety of seeds appropriate to meet their needs. Even mast crops as large as acorns and pecans

Caching a pecan (*Carya illinoinensis*) in a broken snag, a male Red-bellied Woodpecker prepares for lean winter days to come.

feed the likes of Blue Jays, Red-bellied and Red-headed Woodpeckers, American and Fish Crows, Wild Turkeys, and Northern Bobwhites.

Some clever species, like chickadees, jays, woodpeckers, and nuthatches, engage in a sort of secret caching of seeds in preparation for lean times. Their tiny brains somehow have sufficient memory to find the hundreds, sometimes thousands, of seeds, nuts, and mast that they bury in the soil or tuck into bark or other crevices. What's more, their thought process is keen enough that they even watch to see if they're being watched as they cache their horde. But ironically, the birds that have stolen other birds' caches are the most secretive—and vigilant—in hiding their own. Telling, isn't it!

Meeting the Needs of Many

So seed-bearing plants have to meet the needs of many. From tiny seeds for tiny birds to chunky seeds for chunky birds, only a wide variety of native plants can produce the wide variety of needed seed.

Again, why native? First, if birds didn't evolve with the plants, they may not recognize the food source. For example, I happen to love crape myrtle bushes (*Lagerstroemia*), native to Asia and Australia. My father took a slip from his grandmother's plant and presented it to me as a house-warming gift some 50 years ago. Every year it produces oodles of seed heads, but rarely do any birds ever look at it twice. Because it's not native, almost no bird recognizes it as food. To the extreme, however, some introduced plants, as well as most hybrids, are sterile and/or produce no seed at all. The lesson: Know what you plant.

This beak-designated seed-eating business, however, poses some interesting exceptions, including the following examples:

Rose-breasted Grosbeaks sport hefty beaks that allow them to crack the most stubborn seeds and are regular visitors to seed-stocked feeders during migration and, farther north, during breeding. Yet come fall, they depart for Central and South America.

Summer Tanagers boast hefty-looking beaks but really prefer bees and wasps for lunch. Scarlet Tanagers, with equally hefty-looking beaks, don't like seeds either. Come fall, they too head south, to Central and South America.

On the other hand, Eastern Towhees and Brown Thrashers don't eat seeds ever—at least not that I've observed—nor do they ever visit my feeders. Yet they hang out in my Midwestern yard year-round. How do they survive?

You'll soon see.

Birds, Bugs, and the Plants They Love

Biologists agree that about 96 percent of songbirds feed their babies bugs, Mourning Doves and American Goldfinches being the two notable exceptions. Just to feed a single brood of babies, a pair of adults will feed, conservatively, about 300 caterpillars a day. By the time the brood fledges, the babies will have consumed roughly 4,000 bugs, including a high percentage of caterpillars.

Extrapolate the numbers: Most pairs produce more than one brood, probably at least two, maybe even three. Now we're at 8,000 to 12,000 bugs. Across several acres, there would likely be multiple pairs breeding. Within my own three acres this spring, I've confirmed nesting House Wrens (3 nests), Eastern Bluebirds (3 nests), Carolina Chickadees (2 nests), Northern Cardinals (2 nests), and Carolina Wrens (2 nests), as well as Tufted Titmice, House Finches, Song Sparrows, Great-crested Flycatchers, Yellow-throated Warblers, Northern Parulas, White-breasted Nuthatches, Downy Woodpeckers, Hairy Woodpeckers, Pileated Woodpeckers, and Red-bellied Woodpeckers (1 nest each), for a total of 23 nests by 16 pairs of birds. Leaning toward the conservative side, let's say each brood required only 3,000 bugs. That gives us a total of 69,000 bugs. But there's more. Adult birds themselves also feed on protein-rich bugs during breeding season. That's another 32 birds. I have no way of knowing how many other bug-eating birds roam the property,

Rose-breasted Grosbeaks (male shown here) have beaks adequate for cracking large seeds; but they never winter here, instead making the arduous journey south through Central America and into northern parts of South America.

so those must be left uncounted. Even so, we're looking at a demand of around 75,000 bugs over the course of about two months.

Foraging for Bugs

Where do these birds find so many bugs? You guessed it: on or supported by native plants. Maybe the bugs were adults, or maybe they were in egg and/or larval stages. Call me a bit whacky (oh, surely not!), but because I'm fascinated by this plant-bug-bird phenomenon, I sit watching—and photographing—what adult birds bring their babies. Many tidbits remain unidentifiable, but the recognizable list includes little green caterpillars (likely larval stage of some sort of moth), striped brown caterpillars, millipedes, centipedes, katydids, spiders (lots of spiders), crickets, leafhoppers, beetles, spider egg sacs, and some unknown eggs sacs I saw birds plucking from behind the rough edges of tree bark. All these bugs depend

on plants for their very lives—and by extension, so do birds.

The flip side of this question, obviously, is how do birds find that many bugs within our three acres? Of course, I'm not at all positive that they do. Birds, after all, have wings—and, as Roger Tory Peterson was fond of noting, they tend to use them. But the yard and garden apparently supply sufficient bugs to be worthy of note. Within the confines of my 90-by-40-foot garden, this spring Northern Cardinals, Eastern Bluebirds, House Wrens, and Song Sparrows nested simultaneously. Native plants make up about three-quarters of the garden. And we never, ever use insecticides anywhere on the property.

Still, I hear you saying, "Oh, my. I don't want to be in your yard—ever—with 75,000 bugs!" That's a valid response, but here's the error of that logic: Bugs hatch daily, and birds eat daily. Let's do the numbers again: If birds take 75,000 bugs over two months, say 60 days, that's 1,240 bugs disappearing per day!

Somehow, without my being able to prove it, the birds seem to eat the bugs about as fast as they hatch and/or mature. If I were to go out right now and try to find a dozen bugs, I'd likely fail. We're outside folks and enjoy our yard, lounging under the pergola with a full view of the garden or sitting under the dogwood trees, catching the sunset across the neighbor's hayfield—all without buggy comrades. Because my garden houses mostly native plants, mulched heavily with shredded local leaves or pine straw and free of insecticides, and because the remainder of the yard and our little half-acre patch of woods house trees and shrubs, also mostly native and also free

Top: House Wrens, like most other songbirds, feed their babies high-protein caterpillars, the majority of which are found only on native plants.
Bottom: Conducting a safety check before approaching his nest cavity, a male Eastern Bluebird brings a caterpillar to his nestlings.

While *Lepidoptera* species (butterflies, skippers, and moths) will nectar on almost anything, host plants are often specific to the species. Although not every one of these plants appears on our "best choice" tables in the following chapters, and although butterflies, skippers, and moths are only an indirect focus of this book, it makes sense that if these native plants host butterflies, then they attract birds to the caterpillars. Here are a few plant-butterfly relationships:

Red-spotted purple butterflies generally lay their eggs on the leaves of their preferred native host plant, wild black cherry trees (*Prunus serotina*).

ASTERS (*Aster* spp.) host pearl crescents.

CHERRY TREES and their close cousins (*Prunus* spp.) host red-spotted purples, tiger swallowtails, and spring azures.

FALSE INDIGOS (*Amorpha* spp.) host dog-face butterflies and silver-spotted skippers.

HACKBERRIES (*Celtis* spp.) host American snouts, eastern commas, mourning cloaks, hackberry emperors, tawny emperors, and question marks.

MILKWEEDS (*Asclepias* spp.) host monarchs and queen butterflies.

PASSION VINES (*Passiflora* spp.) host gulf fritillaries, zebras, and variegated fritillaries.

PAWPAWS (*Asimin triloba*) host zebra swallowtails.

PIPEVINES (*Aristolochia* spp.) host pipevine swallowtails and polydamas swallowtails.

SASSAFRAS (*Sassafras albidum*) and SPICEBUSH (*Lindera* spp.) host spicebush swallowtails and tiger swallowtails.

TULIP TREES (*Liriodendron tulipifera*) host tiger swallowtails.

VIOLETS (*Viola* spp.) host greater and lesser fritillaries and variegated fritillaries.

WILLOWS (*Salix* spp.) host viceroys and mourning cloaks.

of insecticides, bugs here do what bugs do best: reproduce—probably to the tune of thousands a day.

While camouflage is any wild creature's best defense, keen-eyed birds are driven to feed their babies and are hardwired to know where and how to target even well-concealed bugs. Though I can't find many bugs, obviously birds do. But then, of course, their lives—and that of their babies—depend on it. That's called high-level motivation. The bugs don't have a chance.

For instance, when Eastern Towhees flip leaf litter until they virtually cover themselves, I know the undulating leaves conceal a well-satisfied bird gleaning invertebrates, insect eggs, and larvae. For birds in general, flipping leaf litter equates to a do-or-die food search. For females, however, leaf litter equates to breeding success. How so? To produce eggshells, their bodies demand a super-calcium-rich diet. And where do our feathered friends find calcium? Primarily in land snails, little critters that overwinter in—guess where—fallen leaves. If you rid your yard of leaves, you also rid your yard of snails—and the calcium for next spring's egg-laying birds.

Lots of sightings clarify how keen-eyed birds, other than leaf-flipping towhees, find bugs. When Carolina Chickadees swing upside down at the ends of northern hackberry tree twigs (*Celtis occidentalis*), I'm fairly sure they're plucking spiders from leaf undersides. When Song Sparrows alight repeatedly on pure, untreated hardwood mulch, I see them snag tiny bugs for their babies. When Eastern Bluebirds drop-catch from the utility wire to garden's edge and then dash to their nest box, I know full well they've snared yet another morsel for the brood—from a border of lawn untouched by any herbicides, insecticides, fertilizers, or other lawn treatment. It's that mantra again: To feed the birds, we must first feed the bugs—or at least provide a happy home for insects in all their forms.

Dangling upside down for a better look at the undersides of leaves, a Carolina Chickadee, bug in beak, forages for insects in a hackberry tree (*Celtis occidentalis*).

Here's the rest of the story from a different perspective: If the bugs weren't readily available, I would have no nesting Yellow-throated Warblers, Northern Parulas, Great-crested Flycatchers, White-breasted Nuthatches, or any of the rest. Nor would I awaken each spring and summer morning to their chorus of songs.

A Bit of Bug Biology

What makes bugs so important to birds? There's a bit of biology—well, really, quite a lot of biology—involved. So here goes: As insects, in whatever form, eat plants, they're converting plant tissue, produced by photosynthesis, into animal tissue. Think protein. Birds can't eat plants directly (except for seeds and berries), so ingesting the bugs that ate the plants gives the birds the essential proteins they need. Bugs in general contain more protein than the ground beef we pat into burgers—not that I'm recommending a diet of ground caterpillars for you and your family.

Neonicotinoids
BUG KILLERS EXTRAORDINAIRE

*A*nother issue has raised its ugly head when it comes to bug biology and bug host plants. Ongoing research regarding the use of a group of systemic insecticides called neonicotinoids gives gardeners, landscapers, and now birders cause for serious concern. Here's the how and why:

In order to produce perfect, unblemished plants that show well and therefore sell well in the marketplace, many growers indiscriminately treat their products with neonicotinoids, usually shortened to "neonics" (pronounced "nee-o-nicks"). Because the insecticide is systemic, every part of the treated plant is toxic—roots, leaves, stems, nectar, seed, berries, everything. Any bug—or bird—that feeds on the plant automatically and unwittingly consumes the toxins. The toxins affect the nervous system, and ultimately cause death. The smaller the critter, the quicker its demise. So a caterpillar eats the toxic leaves; a bird carries the now-toxic caterpillar to its babies; the nestlings absorb the toxins from the caterpillar. After maybe a half-dozen toxic caterpillars, nestlings essentially suffer damage to the nervous system and die. The problem is exacerbated by the long half-life of neonics in the plants, from 2 up to sometimes 10 years.

So if you introduce these treated plants in your garden, you introduce long-term bug and bird killers. We'll discuss this more in Chapter 9, but be on the alert.

But wait! Where do native plants fit into that picture? The vast majority of native bugs specialize in eating native plants, and 90 percent of bugs are plant-specific, breeding and feeding on sometimes a single native plant species or only a few native plant species. In fact, sometimes those introduced, nonnative plants contain toxins that our native bugs find fatal. Remember reading labels on nonnative plants touting that this plant "repels insects"? Now you know why. So planting nonnative plants won't produce or promote bugs that birds can eat. Back to that old mantra again: To feed the birds, we must first feed the bugs. And the vast majority of native bugs eat mostly native plants.

Now you may be scratching your head, puzzled. You have only a small space, maybe a mini-yard. How can you possibly add enough native vegetation to make a difference? Don't despair. We'll get you set up with a number of strategies to improve—and even expand—your native habitat, all without buying more land. Just hang with me here.

Fruit- and Berry-Loving Birds

We've explored the fact that plants provide nectar (and sap), that plants serve up seeds, and that plants support bugs. Nectar lovers and bug lovers obviously can't survive eastern US winters except, perhaps, in the Deep South, and most nectar and bug lovers don't eat seeds. They're left with really only one choice: They migrate.

A few bug lovers, however, stay the winter, Eastern Bluebirds, American Robins, and Northern Mockingbirds included. How do they survive? They switch from bugs to berries. Think along the lines of American holly berries (*Ilex opaca*), wild rose hips (*Rosa carolina*), native bittersweet (*Celastrus scandens*), and gray dogwood berries (*Cornus racemosa*). Cedar and Bohemian Waxwings would, if they could, chow down on nothing other than berries and more berries. And waxwings need an abundance of berries. A single waxwing eating flowering dogwood fruits (*Cornus florida*), for instance, needs 230 berries a day. While we humans can't eat dogwood berries, we do love blueberries. By comparison, then, if we ate the same amount of blueberries relative to our weight of, say, 140 pounds, as do waxwings, we would have to eat 46,577 berries—a whopping 215 pints—per day! Does your yard or neighborhood stock the needed provisions? Oh—and that's for just one bird! Need more plants?

Here's another consideration: Since not all birds eat berries the same way, berry size also matters. Birds like cardinals and native sparrows can manage large berries because they crush both fruit and seed, somewhat like chewing before swallowing. They're called "seed predators" because they crush the seeds. When eliminated, then, the seeds are no longer viable and will not sprout. Other birds, however, like robins and bluebirds, require small berries because they gulp the fruits whole and then eliminate the smaller seeds or

Berry eaters are often bug eaters, and vice versa. This Gray Catbird feasts on red mulberries (*Morus rubra*) in late May but will switch to protein—in the form of bugs—for the breeding season.

spit up the larger ones. These birds biologists refer to as "seed dispersers" because as they eliminate the seeds, they end up spreading and regenerating their own favorite plants—a sort of self-gardening for the future.

While many bird species eat fruit—both our resident birds and seasonal migrants—their table manners vary. Robins, mockingbirds, cardinals, and Rose-breasted Grosbeaks seat themselves politely and pluck one berry at a time, but gulp it down whole. By contrast, others like House Finches and Downy Woodpeckers seat themselves and then nibble daintily. Some birds, perhaps feeding nestlings, elbow their way to the table, grab a berry, and flee. Some notables flutter around the table, too rude to be seated, snatching berries on the fly, particularly birds like Great Crested Flycatchers, which snatch bugs the same way. Finally, like household pets, some patiently patrol under the table, scouting for chopped berries, notably those that the pluckers and snatchers dropped. Look for grackles, starlings, Blue Jays, and robins with these under-the-table manners.

Once again, then, a variety of berry sizes will host a variety of bird species—something to keep in mind as you select native berry-producers for the yard.

High Fat, High Carbs

Mother Nature's grand plan, however, as always, best feeds birds. While we humans usually choose low-fat, low-carb foods, birds in fall, especially those undergoing thousands-of-miles-long migrations, need just the opposite: high-fat, high-carb foods, a diet that meets their autumn high-energy demands. Curiously, about 70 percent of native berries that birds love ripen in fall and contain high fat, helping birds replace all those worn feathers, chunk-up for migration, or ready themselves for winter.

By contrast, late spring and summer berries rank high in protein and carbs that promote growth, ripening to coincide with the end of nesting season when fledglings first seek food on their own. While fledglings might prefer a fat tasty bug, berries sit still and are much easier to catch! At the other extreme, winter berries have small amounts of fats; but as a result, they don't spoil readily, thus lasting through the winter and even into very early spring in time for the first returning migrants. It's a grand plan, don't you think?

Still, even within a season, not all berries are created equal. Late summer and fall native berries contain higher fat levels than either nonnative or invasive berries. In the Midwest, according to Cornell University's Lab of Ornithology research reports, black raspberry (*Rubus occidentalis*) and elderberry (*Sambucus* spp.), fruiting from July through early August, and chokecherry (*Prunus virginiana*) and rough-leaf dogwood (*Cornus drummondii*), fruiting August through September, all contain 30 to 50 percent fats, ranking them among the most nutritious of all berries.

Other nourishing berries include those of viburnums (*Viburnum* spp.), other dogwoods (*Cornus* spp.), American holly (*Ilex opaca*), American beautyberry (*Callicarpa americana*), chokeberry (*Aronia melanocarpa*), spicebush (*Lindera benzoin*), common winterberry (*Ilex verticillata*), pin cherry (*Prunus pensylvanica*), red cedar (*Juniperus virginiana*), and Virginia creeper (*Parthenocissus quinquefolia*). More about these plants later.

By contrast, however, nonnative invasive berry producers like multiflora rose (*Rosa multiflora*), Amur honeysuckle (*Lonicera maackii*), and autumn olive (*Elaeagnus umbellata*) contain no more than 3 or 4 percent fats. That's significant, right? Three or 4 percent compared to 30 to 50 percent? It's like feeding your kids a diet of nothing but potato chips. The poor-quality nonnative berries (like

Get rid of it! Highly invasive Amur honeysuckle (*Lonicera maackii*) shades out native plants and produces berries that lack the nutrition birds need, filling them up but providing little food value—like kids eating nothing but potato chips.

potato chips) fill them up but give them such lousy nutrition that they're unlikely to thrive.

But here's another problem with nonnative berries: While some birds gorge on the nonnative berries of Amur honeysuckle and autumn olive—much to the detriment of the birds' health—sometimes birds don't recognize nonnative berries as food at all. Most wildlife biologists believe that's because the birds and the plants didn't evolve together. Thus, birds can starve to death amid an abundance of nonnative berries.

To put it bluntly, given a shortage in your yard or neighborhood of native plants providing nutritious berries, you'll have an equal shortage of birds.

Buds and Blooms

Early-spring menus available for birds read something like after-season produce lists: Items are unavailable, out of stock. In March and April in the central US (earlier or later if you're farther south or north), seeds and berries are gone. Grasses, forbs, and brushy plants that formed seed heads last fall have probably long since lost their seed to wind dispersal, pelting rains, weighty snows, and foraging birds like sparrows, cardinals, goldfinches, chickadees, and titmice. What few seed-bearing stalks remain now lie broken, likely "planted" by rain and snow, mudded in, no longer viable food for birds

Tree seeds last a bit longer. If tulip trees (*Liriodendron tulipifera*) and American sweetgum trees (*Liquidambar styraciflua*) produced sizable seed crops last fall, seedeaters sort through what remains. Still, in March, seed supplies have all but disappeared, and our tiniest birds seeking the tiniest seeds often come up short.

New seed, however, is on the way, right? Well, soon. But we must think in terms of months, not days or weeks, before new seeds appear. Plants have to green, grow, bloom, and produce seed heads. Then seed must mature before most birds find anything edible or nourishing. Among native grasses, maturity peaks more quickly than among some other plants. Still, edible seed production is a month or more away. As soon as spring buds form, however, some birds will gorge on petals and flowers, desperate for anything nutritious in the absence of seed. Buds, after all, contain the plant shoots and flowers and offer high food value. Cedar Waxwings munch their way through clusters of apple and crabapple blossoms. Chickadees bounce through maple trees, dangling upside down, devouring tree blossoms. Tufted Titmice scramble through the pecan tree blossoms. Mockingbirds follow suit.

Sometimes, though, when early-spring birds perch on or dangle from blossoms, I have no way of knowing for sure whether they're dining on buds or bugs. For instance, as soon as the migrant Blue-gray Gnatcatchers arrive, I find them frequenting the bald cypress tree catkins. But in this case, I know they're really foraging on the buds—because cypress trees are pollinated by the wind,

Top: Blue-gray Gnatcatchers, among the first migrants to arrive in spring, forage on bald cypress tree catkins (*Taxodium distichum*).
Bottom: A female Eastern Towhee, foraging amid leaf litter for bugs or buds, finds a nutritious plant sprout, vital late-winter sustenance when food grows scarce. Leaf litter harbors life-saving morsels.

By planting a wide diversity of natives that bloom and thus produce seed and/or berries at different times, your yard will host a wider diversity of birds.

PLANTS AS SHELTER

Okay, it's obvious in every way that songbirds rely on plants for food. But perhaps it comes as a bit of a surprise that food is only a fraction of the habitat equation that calls also for shelter, nest sites, and nest materials. Since shelter, like food, is a year-round necessity, let's look at that next.

Birds always have one eye on shelter. Yes, I'm talking 24/7, year-round. Surprised? You thought shelter was necessary only at night? Or only during bad weather? Or maybe only in winter? Would you believe, even while eating, even while drinking or bathing, birds always have one eye on shelter. They're always vulnerable. They always need an escape route, always need a safe place. Once I saw a Sharp-shinned Hawk pluck an American Goldfinch off its tube-feeder perch only inches from my kitchen window. The finch probably never saw the little hawk come jetting in. Certainly, it never had a chance to even lift off its perch. Still, to give birds at least half a chance, they need shelter even close to feeders or baths. Most authorities recommend that feeders and baths be within 20 feet of shelter. Otherwise, birds are lured into a compromising situation.

Just what, exactly, then is shelter? It's a place where birds find protection—all kinds of protection. Here's the idea: Typically, birds find shelter in shrubs, trees, brambles, patches of tall grass, or other vegetation, especially anything dense and/

not bugs. Mystery solved! And their behavior shows that the little Blue-grays have a fondness for catkins. Interestingly enough, though, they sometimes tuck catkins into their nest constructions as well. Still, among other birds and some other blossoms, it's always a matter of curiosity about whether the birds are foraging for buds or bugs. Maybe both!

But the sobering part about birds' seeming early-spring love affair with blossoms and buds boils down to this: With March being the most desperate month of all for birds, their foraging ingenuity marks the difference between life and death—and only the fittest, or the smartest, survive.

Planning so that some of your native plants will blossom early and provide some semblance of survival for struggling birds will surely give you satisfaction. And therein lies yet another lesson:

For the Barred Owl, "shelter" means a day roost, this one apparently commandeered from a gray squirrel. High demand for limited cavities makes for no-holds-barred competition.

Shelter 24/7

Why do birds need shelter 24/7? Obviously, birds seek shelter against inclement weather. Most of us think of bad weather as coming in some form of precipitation—rain, sleet, hail, snow. A hail stone the size of a nickel, for instance, can easily kill a bird not much bigger than three or four nickels. Sleet and snow can freeze to birds' feathers, even freeze them to the ground. More than one bird made its appearance at our feeders minus a tail the morning after an ice storm. Driving rain can destroy a bird's nest or hinder its escape flight from predators.

Inclement weather also includes wind, a violent obstacle during migration, killing birds exhausted but with no land in sight. Severe winds can toss birds with deadly force and rip nests from their anchors. After a heavy storm, I often walk the yard, looking for tree damage, flattened flower stalks, or scattered debris, picking up as I patrol and making whatever fixes I can. Sadly, though, when I find an empty nest tumbled upside down many feet from any possible anchor, I'm left with no recourse. Whatever eggs were snuggled inside are scattered, broken, spoiled; and whatever baby birds were cradled inside have met their demise. Stout wind rips birds' lives apart.

Shelter is also important for a surprising number of other reasons over the course of the 24/7 demand. During nesting, for instance, when direct sun would bake an incubating female, a well-concealed nest survives best situated in a sheltered shade-providing spot. Even birds

or thorny—anyplace where a hawk can't penetrate, where a cat can't hide, where a snake can't lie in wait.

unoccupied by incubation suffer from extraordinarily hot weather and seek shelter in shady spots.

After breeding season ends, most bird species molt. During that time, when they lose wing or tail feathers, their flight is somewhat compromised, even impeded, making the birds susceptible to attack. Shelter becomes the equivalent of a rehab center, a safe place to hang out. Because the extreme energy demands of molt can make the bird susceptible to ill health or predation, protective shelter frequently means the difference between life and death. And protective shelter in the proximity of an ample high-protein food supply gives birds a significant advantage. Your yard can offer that advantage.

At night, however, every bird needs a safe roost. Owls have a hungry habit of plucking sleeping songbirds from their perches, so roosting in hiding means surviving the night. Raccoons, skunks, foxes, and other nocturnal mammalian raiders also prey on birds at night. Sleeping with one eye open is not a joke among our avian friends. Don't try this while driving, but believe it or not, at least some birds have two parts to their brains, each side connected to one eye, so they can, literally, keep one eye open while the other side sleeps.

How Birds Use Shelter

Okay, so birds need nesting cover, escape cover, thermal cover, roosting cover, molting cover, storm cover, wind cover, rain cover, snow cover, ice cover—all grouped loosely into the term "shelter." But exactly how do birds use "shelter"? During storms and strong winds, birds perch on the lee side of tree trunks, very near the trunks themselves. If you're only 5 inches long from tip of bill to tip of tail, a tree trunk is huge by comparison. Even a sycamore leaf is big enough to serve as a body-sized umbrella. At night, many birds dive for dense thickets. Take a walk past

A basic-plumaged Chestnut-sided Warbler shows that a sycamore leaf (*Platanus occidentalis*) can serve as a full-body umbrella for a tiny bird during inclement weather.

thick vegetation at dusk and note the commotion as birds vie for positions.

The later the season, the colder the weather, and the more likely birds roost in groups, mostly to avail themselves of the best protective vegetation, out of the wind. The few birds that nest in cavities may also use cavities in winter as nighttime sheltering group homes. Togetherness helps maintain body heat, and coziness may mean survival.

In biting cold weather, look for a Tufted Titmouse or Carolina Chickadee with a bent tail—a sure sign it's overnighted in tight cavity quarters. Count the number of bluebirds or Carolina Wrens exiting a nest cavity at dawn. I've seen seven Eastern Bluebirds pop out over the course of six or seven minutes, each greeting the early dawn almost as if with a stretch and a yawn. Surely sleep is tough piled atop one another. Likewise, I've counted six Carolina Wrens tuck into a nesting gourd hanging under the awning at our front door, each scolding the next arrival, as if to say, "Go away—the beds are full." But after a short absence, when the poor thing returns, admission is granted, until every family member finds a place to settle in. It's five-star-rated overnight shelter. Incidentally, biologists call this behavior "huddling."

To put it simply, though, winter's best shelter is evergreen. Even a clump of thin needles offers more protection than a winter-bare twig. So as cover, evergreens—like pine, cedar, hemlock, holly, juniper, and fir—should stand as staples in every backyard bird habitat. Tall or dwarf, round or conical, they fit any yard and stand ready to shelter birds—summer or winter—against weather and predators. Evergreens also embrace secure nest sites. Early-season nesters find the best protection in evergreens. Later, for a second brood, those same birds can—and usually do—move house and home to then-leafed-out deciduous trees.

Offering dense vegetation in your yard means birds feel safe to stay with you. Even without towering evergreens—which obviously take time to grow—you can still offer shelter. For many species, vegetation as simple as dense clumps of grasses, brambles, or shrubs will meet the demand. Only with adequate shelter 24/7, however, will birds find the habitat they need. Otherwise, they're off to safer homes.

Layers of Shelter

Shelter needs vary. Think of it this way: Everyone lives somewhere—even birds—but we don't all live in the same kinds of places. Just as some people prefer the seashore or plains while others prefer the forest or mountains, birds too have specific preferences—even within the same locale. For instance, some birds, such as tanagers, vireos, orioles, and many warblers, forage and shelter in lofty treetops. Other birds—catbirds, thrashers, jays, and cardinals—hang out mid-level. Still others, like towhees, thrushes, and native sparrows,

seek the lowest levels of vegetation, including ground level. Ultimately, however, almost everything must come to ground level to drink and bathe. (We'll talk later about good ways to offer water.) Consider, though, what all this says about suitable bird shelter: To welcome a variety of birds, your yard's habitat needs ample vegetation from the ground up, the understory blending into the mid-story blending into the upper story. And water sources need safe zones, quick escape routes to nearby protection against predators during after-bath preening. You'll want to design your birdscape accordingly, bottom to top.

Ice Storm Tragedy

So let's try to pull all of this "shelter" business together. One of the best ways I can illustrate the impact of shelter—or lack thereof—on birds' lives is to share an admittedly unsettling experience. Even after all these years, memories of January 2009 grip my mind like ice grips the land. They're hard memories. A widespread ice storm hit with brutal force in our three-state area. We humans huddled in power-outage cold but nevertheless had fireplaces and wood burners. Birds, however, faced the elements with nothing more than their feathers and instincts—and whatever our backyard habitat offered for food, water, and shelter.

At first dawn, after the tree-crushing night, birds struggled to feed. Berries hung ice-coated, seeds drooped ice-coated, feeders stood ice-coated. Some birds flew into the backyard awkwardly, ice stuck to their heads and tails, skidding where they couldn't grip. Who knows how many never flew at all that morning.

Wildlife biologists agreed that the widespread damage would affect birds and other animals for years to come. Den trees downed by heavy ice left thousands of creatures homeless. Creation of new cavities would take years. Shrubby growth at forest edges, flattened, crushed by ice, no longer protected roosting or nesting birds. Old-growth forest canopy, devastated by ice and wind, no longer offered potential homes to treetop-loving birds migrating here to nest.

The ice storm dramatically altered food supplies. Berry eaters probably starved when ice-covered fruits remained encased for days. Foods cached in tree bark, in cavities, and in other niches were lost or exposed to rot. As the harsh weather continued, starvation worsened.

Mother Nature isn't always kind. She sometimes makes me very sad because I know, deep down, that other severe storms—hurricanes and tornadoes—create equal havoc for wildlife. But wildlife—including birds—is generally resilient. Although habitat was altered by that January ice storm, some good came of much bad.

The loss of shrubby vegetation, crushed and left to rot, attracted insects the following spring and summer, supplying hordes of tasty morsels for birds and their babies. Fallen limbs that collapsed into natural piles flooded the market with house-and-home sites for ground-dwelling birds. So, in the short term, birds that prefer large trees, continuous cover, and upper tree canopy lost their homes and moved out. But species that prefer early successional forest or tree gaps found a buyer's market of choice home sites. In forests ripped bare of limbs and with canopy shade gone, new vegetation replaced the old oaks and other hardwoods. The entire forest community took on a new composition with new inhabitants and new visitors. Sort of like massive urban renewal—out with the old, in with the new.

The ice storm, devastating as it was, taught us about natural habitat change. And it taught us about our own backyard habitats. In our yard, the Great Ice Storm led to the Great Thaw followed by a months-long Great Clean-Up. Like other area residents, we struggled to put our lives

Because owls don't build their own nests, snags often serve as the only suitable sites for Great Horned Owls to raise their babies.

and yards back in order. Three of our 40-year-old trees were nearly destroyed—seriously disfigured, jagged stubs jutting from trunks, the result of broken tops which were once themselves the size of respectable trees.

The tree guys would need days, they said, to down the disfigured trees, haul out logs, and shred brush—at a major cost. Or not. The broken trees threatened nothing—neither life nor property, neither ours nor our neighbors'. What if we left the trees, allowing stubs to rot back, creating nesting and roosting cavities for woodpeckers, owls, bluebirds, flycatchers, creepers, nuthatches, swallows, chickadees, titmice, wrens, even Wood Ducks in the right location? All desperately need

Mother Nature's Nursery
AND GROCERY STORE

*I*f a tree must come down, perhaps because it threatens life or property, consider leaving the largest log to rot, maybe somewhere out of the way, like along the back property line. A rotting log, Mother Nature's nursery and grocery store, supplying fresh food in the form of bugs and their eggs and larvae, guarantees a feast for many bird species. Plant native shrubs, perennials, or grasses around it, or let a native vine crawl over it. You'll dramatically enrich your birdscaping. In addition, as logs disintegrate, they enrich the soil for future growth. As for surplus debris, consider shredding the small stuff for next year's mulch. Natural mulch, another shelf in Mother Nature's grocery store, harbors a feathered friend's feast.

cavities. In fact, populations are limited by cavity availability: few cavities, few cavity nesters. By leaving the disfigured trees, we had nothing to lose and everything to gain. Maybe, after all, "disfigured" is in the eye of the beholder. Maybe ragged trees that enhance bird habitat alter the eye of the beholder. Or so it is with this beholder.

We kept the snags.

Decaying logs serve as a nursery for bugs and a grocery store for birds. A migrating Gray-cheeked Thrush forages in this log for bugs to fuel another leg of its journey.

Hindsight Magic

Now, years after the Great Ice Storm, we reap the rewards of the still-living but disfigured trees. This year, a pair of Great Crested Flycatchers raised their brood in one of the snags. Our woodpecker population has probably doubled. Just this morning, both a Hairy Woodpecker and a Downy Woodpecker appeared simultaneously in the backyard, on opposite sides of a big seed cake.

Yes, bird populations changed somewhat because the habitat changed. We have different birds—and also more of them. As we learned, then, change isn't always a bad thing. When it's all said and done, in spite of the drama and months-long work, sweat, and tears, the outcome of the Great Ice Storm has caused us to reevaluate what "habitat" means, what birdscaping can do, and how—sure enough—a change in habitat brings a change in bird populations. Simply put: Whatever we can do to add native plants to our yards—including their disfigured and perhaps rotting remnants, all a part of Mother Nature's plan—will enrich habitat, including more food, increased shelter, additional nest sites, and added building materials, improving life for the displaced and uninsured. It's rather like magic.

PLANTS FOR NESTS—LOCATIONS AND BILLS OF MATERIALS

For most songbirds, nesting season peaks in early summer. Depending on where you live, breeding season can begin as early as February or as late as mid-June. Some resident birds in southerly regions may manage to produce three or four broods a season; others attempt only a single brood (although they may re-nest if the first attempt fails early). Migrants, on the other hand, face a time crunch. In spring, they rush to reach their breeding range, find mates and establish territories, and get right down to business. Still, if the adult pair migrates from, say, South America to the northern US or even into Canada, travel time restricts breeding time. Given the delayed start, by the time the couple builds a nest, the female lays eggs and incubates maybe two to three weeks, and the brood is fed maybe another two or three weeks until the babies fledge, midsummer has passed. In addition, of course, fledglings must mature sufficiently to migrate on their own before winter weather threatens their food supplies. So bingo! The summer is gone. One brood is it for them.

Regardless of the frequency of nesting attempts, before birds choose nest sites, they look for three prerequisites: available suitable sheltered building sites, adequate suitable building materials, and ample food supplies for a growing family—the latter two required within close travel distance.

Incredibly, bird nests look as different as the birds that build them. In fact, each species' nest displays characteristics so distinctive that field guides readily detail location, materials, size, and construction—all of which are irrevocably tied to plants and plant materials.

For instance, orioles build meticulously woven 6-inch-long pouch-like nests suspended from the tip of a branch by a few long, fibrous strands. They like sycamore trees (*Planatus occidentalis*) near or over water. Vireos likewise build pendulous nests, suspended between two twigs near their fork, situated low, amid dense vegetation. Hard-wired to know how to weave, orioles and vireos also instinctively know which grasses, rootlets, plant down, and leaves will be pliable enough to weave but sturdy enough to hold them and their clutches of babes.

Brown thrashers, towhees, and song sparrows situate their nests on or near the ground, protected only by stealth and dense undergrowth. But the nests themselves, sometimes cushioned with moss, rootlets, fine grasses, and hair, take shape with dead grasses and weed stems, bald cypress or wild grape bark shreds, and bits of dead leaves. Using similar materials, Carolina Wrens shape closed nests with a side entrance. Chickadees

Bird-friendly habitat includes a ready supply of suitable nesting materials. Since Carolina Wrens rely heavily on leaf litter to shape their nests, raking up all the leaves in fall means you won't have nesting wrens—or other leaf-loving nesters—next spring.

From top: Male and female Blue-gray Gnatcatchers work together for almost two weeks to weave a delightfully compact little nest using plant down, plant fibers, bark, fine grasses, and catkins, bound together with spiderwebs and covered with camouflaging lichen flakes.

Gathering nest materials takes an inordinate amount of time in a bird's life, and this female Golden-winged Warbler illustrates the methodical one-blade-of-grass-at-a-time construction. Golden-winged Warblers are in sharp decline and have the smallest population of any bird not on the endangered species list.

By the time Ruby-throated Hummingbird nestlings are about to fledge, they've outgrown the stretchy nest made of plant fibers, fastened together with spiderweb and glued down with tree sap.

Pileated Woodpeckers (male shown) excavate nest holes and winter roosts for one-time use. Afterwards, the cavities serve other species, like Tree Swallows, Wood Ducks, and Northern Flickers.

The only cavity-nesting warbler in the eastern US, Prothonotary Warblers occasionally accept man-made boxes, illustrating the high demand and limited availability of cavities for the 85 or so species of US birds that require cavities for breeding.

choose cavities for nesting and lay foundations of moss on which they construct neat cups of plant down, hair, and plant fibers. If you insist on your yard being obsessively tidy, will birds be able to find construction materials?

Most flycatchers build cup-shaped nests in tree forks. Blue-gray Gnatcatchers, for instance, build a neat little nest using plant down, bark and plant fibers, fine grasses, and catkins, bound together with spiderwebs and covered with camouflaging bits of lichen flakes. Typically their nests aren't far from water. Brown Creepers stuff their nests behind loose tree bark. American Goldfinches tuck their tiny cup nests in forks of shrubs, small trees, even sturdy weeds—cups woven of plant down, plant fibers, and catkins so solidly compact that they feel wood-hard when tapped.

Female Ruby-throated Hummingbirds assemble lichen-covered nests built with dandelion and other plant down, fastening them with spiderweb to the limbs they straddle. Tree sap "glue," mostly from pine trees, is "painted" on, with the hummers using their long bills like brushes, making nests snug.

Think about the required locations and necessary bills of materials for all these various nest constructions. No bird can build a nest somewhere where it can't find needed materials within carrying distance. Conscious effort on your part may mean they will find the necessary plant materials in your yard.

Cavity nesters, however, demand special plants—dead ones. Woodpeckers, for instance, carve out tree cavities in which to raise their young, but they don't build nests inside. And since woodpeckers use a nest cavity for only a single brood, the following year may bring a whole flock of species that can't hammer out their own cavities. Look for Wood Ducks, Great Crested Flycatchers, Prothonotary Warblers, House Wrens, titmice, chickadees, or nuthatches to take over the ready-made abodes.

Filling Cavities

Humans have made life tough for cavity nesters. Most folks see dead or dying trees as unsightly; so at the first sign of decay, they fire up the chain saw, even when there's no imminent danger. Multiply the chain-saw mentality by growing human populations, and dead trees, often called "snags," all but disappear—along with potential nest-cavity sites. Woodpeckers and other cavity nesters like chickadees, titmice, nuthatches, bluebirds, and wrens all suffer.

About 150 years ago, though, we committed an irreversible crime against our native birds: We introduced House Sparrows and European Starlings from Europe, and these exotics multiplied beyond anyone's wildest dreams. Problem? Both nest in cavities. Every cavity used by these millions of introduced birds robs our natives, like bluebirds, kestrels, owls, and, nationwide, another

82 species. Here we have yet another example of the dramatically negative impact of nonnative species on natives.

Let's make an essential point clear: Birds that require cavities in which to nest simply don't breed if they can't find the necessary cavities. If they don't breed, over time their populations plummet. Case in point: Red-headed Woodpeckers, which compete with starlings and Red-bellied Woodpeckers for the same habitat, have seen populations dramatically decline. Or Eastern Bluebirds—they nearly went extinct because they lost nesting cavities to starlings. Fortunately, the North American Bluebird Society organized, fought the fight—and won—to bring them back.

Nationally, about 85 bird species nest in cavities. Most cavity nesters use "found" cavities in rotting snags because their beaks aren't designed for chiseling. Woodpeckers, on the other hand, can hammer out their own cavities, and then other birds rely on the former woodpecker cavities for their own. Unfortunately, very few cavity nesters accept man-made nest boxes. Your snag—assuming it's not a threat to people or to personal property—will make a difference.

SO PLANT PLANTS!

Amazing, isn't it, that vegetation supports birds so completely? Providing for birds is almost like saying, "Plant. And add water." That's the sum total of habitat: food—in the form of nectar, sap, seeds, fruits, berries, and bugs—water, shelter, nest sites, and nest materials. Every habitat component comes from vegetation—plus water! Later, in Chapter 8, we'll offer suggestions for efficient water sources—more than water on a pedestal—that can meet your preference for grace and elegance or add a rustic touch to your bird sanctuary.

So now you have it—how birds use plants, and how they are irrevocably tied to the plants around them. Now onward!

"When one tugs at a single thing in nature, he finds it attached to the rest of the world."

—JOHN MUIR, environmental philosopher (1838–1914)

Chapter 3
ANSWERING QUESTIONS ABOUT NATIVES

Okay, it's obvious. Birds rely on plants—heavily. Birds are irrevocably tied to the plants around them and must find adequate vegetation of the right kind in order to survive. We all get that. But when it comes to figuring out the right kinds of plants for the home landscaping, most of us drag our feet at making a switch to what we understand to be "native" gardens and yards.

Above: By including native host and nectar plants for butterflies and moths, a bird-friendly yard dramatically increases its *Lepidoptera* species (and thus caterpillars), therefore feeding the bugs that feed the birds. Here, an eastern tailed-blue butterfly nectars on native rattlesnake master (*Eryngium yuccifolium*)—also a host plant for black swallowtails.

Furthermore, most of us didn't start our landscaping or gardens thinking "native." We planted what we were taught to love. Both of my grandmothers had favorite flowers and shrubs. I'm fortunate to have those same plants, including shrubs my father slipped from his mother's originals. Some of my grandmothers' plants came from their mothers, so they're loaded with sentimental value. I'd never do away with them. My paternal grandmother's crape myrtle (*Lagerstroemia* sp.), her very thorny flowering quince (*Chaenomeles speciosa*), and her spectacular triple-flowered roadside lily (*Hemerocallis fulva*) as well as my maternal grandmother's schnitzelbloomen—cowslip primrose (*Primula veris*)—hold places of honor in my yard and garden, and my heart. They bring fond memories of my grannies because I remember those plants in their yards where I played. Likewise, my dad's daffodils and daylilies were all transplanted into my yard after his death. I'll never get rid of them either. They're easy care, need no water or fertilizer, and rarely need pruning or separating. And they were Dad's.

Hummingbirds occasionally visit the crape myrtle and flowering quince, and Northern Cardinals and Brown Thrashers sometimes nest in the quince. Otherwise, my heritage plants mostly just sit there, looking pretty. In short, they fail, of course, to serve a biological purpose.

As I've become more knowledgeable in my ripening years, I'm replacing less-sentimental flowers with natives and adding natives where there once was nothing but lawn. (I really don't like to cut grass anyway.) The transition has been a years-long process and remains a work in progress. Of course, gardening and landscaping are always works in progress. There's always something we want to add, replace, improve, or reduce. But the more native plants I add, the more birds take up residence with us, treating us with their color and song, rewarding me for the effort,

eating our bugs. With a new total of 167 bird species in the yard—not to mention 53 documented butterfly species—I'm grateful for the education others have given me. Now I'm eager to pass it along so that others may share the joy.

For most folks, though, the transition is wracked with fear and trepidation. So, here are the questions I had early on, and I'm betting they're many of the same questions you have. And for each question, there is a sensible, honest answer that sets the record straight. Let's go!

Q: *What is a native plant? Isn't "native" just a nice word for "weed"?*

A: Native plants are those that grew here prior to 1492. In other words, native plants were here prior to the arrival of settlers toting with them seeds from their favorite can't-do-without plants from home. Some plant seeds provided a colorful flowering memory of European gardens; others offered an opportunity to grow favored foods and season them with familiar herbs and spices.

That leaves us with the usual assumption: Aren't natives just plain weeds? Let's think about that. What's a weed? Properly, a weed is anything growing where you don't want it. So even a colorful fall aster (*Aster* spp.) blossoming in a cornfield, by definition, is a weed. Likewise, cornstalks popping up in a bed of asters, by definition, are weeds. In fact, however, most of those so-called weeds that we love to hate are not native. Think dandelions (*Taraxacum officinale*) and chickweed (*Stellaria media*), both native to Europe; bull thistle (*Cirsium vulgare*), originating from Eurasia and northwestern Africa; Johnson grass (*Sorghum halepense*), a gift from the Mediterranean; Queen Anne's lace (*Daucus carota*) and crabgrass (*Digitaria* spp.), both from Eurasia—all introduced after 1492. Or,

Vining Japanese honeysuckle (*Lonicera japonica*), a noxious nonnative invasive, grows with vigor and is exceedingly difficult to eradicate.

worse, think kudzu (*Pueraria montana*), from Southeast Asia; Japanese honeysuckle (*Lonicera japonica*) and wintercreeper (*Euonymus fortunei*), native to parts of east Asia, including China, Japan, Korea, and the Philippines; and purple loosestrife (*Lythrum salicaria*), native to Great Britain through Europe, Russia, India, and much of Asia—also all introduced. Maybe introduced by accident, but nevertheless introduced.

So are native plants weeds? Well, are oak trees weeds? What about flowering dogwood? Who could want a lovelier shrub than bayberry? Or witch hazel? Wouldn't a cottage garden of black-eyed Susans, columbine, coreopsis, garden phlox, blue sage, and rose mallow, all backed by tall clumps of liatris, make a stunning magazine cover? Native, all of them.

But, of course, some native plants have the reputation of "weeds" because they look rangy, grow tall, flower in a lackluster manner, or tend to be too aggressive for the garden. In fact, many of them wouldn't be invited into

my yard or garden either. On the other hand, many native plants are well behaved, tidy, and quite lovely. We'll give you the lists later.

Q: *Isn't a so-called native garden about the same thing as a wild thicket, an untended mess?*

A: Let's be honest here. Any garden, untended, will eventually become a wild thicket, regardless of what's in the garden—native or not. "Native" doesn't mean "untended," and only untended gardens become eyesores or wild thickets. I'm always irritated by folks who transition to "native" and use the transition as an excuse for laziness, creating an eyesore for the neighborhood and giving "native" a bad rap.

Q: *Natives are sometimes labeled as varieties or cultivars. What's a variety? What's a cultivar? Is a variety or a cultivar of a native still native? How are they different from a hybrid? If I want to plant natives to attract birds, does it matter which I plant? I'm confused!*

A: Sometimes terminology gets in the way of practicality, and confusion reigns. But since the big voices out there are telling us to plant native to attract birds, let's figure out what each of the terms—native, variety, cultivar, and hybrid—means. We'll rank them in terms of their benefit to birds and refer to them as "best choices," "better choices," "good choices," and "poor choices."

Purists insist that the only **truly native plants** are those grown from local seed gathered from local native plants. They're not just those plants that were growing somewhere in the US prior to 1492. Rather, they were then and are now growing in specific locales and are thus native only to those specific locales. It's worth noting that plants grown

In a late-July Midwestern native garden, wood-chipped paths wind among, left to right, short-toothed mountain mint (*Pycnanthemum muticum*) in front of liatris (*Liatris spicata*) with background compact button bush (*Cephalanthus occidentalis*) and ninebark (*Physocarpus opulifolius*). Joe-pye weed (*Eutrochium purpureum*) blooms center front with a wash of black-eyed Susans (*Rudbeckia hirta*) behind and right, and rattlesnake master (*Eryngium yuccifolium*) far right. To keep plants weed-free, shredded leaves mulch the garden.

from seed are genetically distinct individuals, while plants grown from cuttings are clones. Thus seeds promote genetic diversity and are preferred by purists for that reason. They strengthen the gene pool, so to speak. These seed-grown plants rank as the best choice possible for attracting birds. Unfortunately, finding the obviously limited supplies of these best-choice plants turns into a nearly impossible challenge for most of us. The purists resolve the challenge by raising their own plants by seed.

An alternate and less-strict interpretation of "native" accepts native **plants from a broader general region,** perhaps miles away but in nearly identical eco-regions. Those plants too pass muster to fit the **best choice** ranking.

If the challenge of raising your own plants from locally collected seed seems more daunting than you're likely to pursue, consider purchasing species and their naturally occurring varieties. Most of us do.

Species is the "typical" form of the plant as we know it from the wild. What differentiates it from the previous category is that when you purchase it, you will likely not know the geographic origin of the plant. For example, you might buy purple coneflower that is of the wild type at a local nursery but the original stock plants may have been collected and grown several states away. **Varieties** grow in nature without any human interference and are true to type, which means the offspring will share the same characteristics. For example, a population of white-flowering redbud was discovered in nature. Seedlings grown from them produce—true to type—mostly (but perhaps not always) white-flowering redbuds. Still, nothing about these natives was altered through selection or breeding; the genotype remains the same. The variety is merely an unusual natural variation of the standard. Often these "found" varieties are named for some attribute of the plant. We'll rank species and their varieties as **better choices** for attracting birds.

Next come **cultivars**, a shortened term for **cultivated variety.** Unlike varieties, cultivars have been bred—or cultivated—by plant breeders who intentionally select for desired characteristics that are different from the parent plant. The differences may present as brighter autumn foliage, smaller size, or different flower color than the parent. Consider, for example, purple coneflower (*Echinacea purpurea*) again. Let's say for the sake of argument that a grower planted seed from the standard plant but each year chose seeds only from the plants bearing the most intensely purple blossoms. Using those seeds, the grower then produced the next season's plants. After years of selection, the grower may come up with a consistently intensely purple-blooming coneflower. That's a cultivar. The grower selected the plant. Often, however, cultivars propagated by seed don't come back true to type. As a result, many cultivars are reproduced asexually through cuttings (making them clones). Thus, from an ecological point of view, cultivars lack diversity. Because the genotype remains the same, however, cultivars still rank as **good choices** for attracting birds.

Be aware, though, that sometimes cultivars have had bred out of them the real reason we birders seek the plant. For instance, a serviceberry cultivar, selected to grow more compactly, was found to produce almost no berries. So cultivars merit caution. Furthermore, don't let the new term **nativar** fool you. Plant breeders are trying to tap into the growing interest in native plants. But nativar is just a fancy term for a cultivar of a native—not a variety, not the real thing, and likely little different from any other cultivar. Nativars, like cultivars, may rank as **good choices.** Some native plant enthusiasts avoid cultivars entirely—by any name.

That takes us to **hybrids.** In short, a hybrid is the result of cross-pollinating two different plant species, thereby producing a new plant. Many of our vegetable crops and ornamental flowers are the result of artificial hybridization. But nothing is ever simple when we start categorizing plants. Here's why: Hybridization occurs in the wild as well as purposefully in the garden. Oaks, for instance, hybridize broadly in the wild, sometimes rendering an individual tree almost impossible to pin to a specific species. Because these hybrids are part of a natural process, they can be used in landscape with almost the same level of confidence as the species from which they originate. So a hybrid that occurs in the wild can be rated as better choice.

This brings us to **man-made "fancy" hybrids.** These are generally developed only for their aesthetic value. If you trace a hybrid's lineage, you can find out which species were cross-pollinated—and perhaps

A lovely but apparently useless hybrid purple coneflower (*Echinacea purpurea* hybrid) appeared to be sterile: Nothing nectared on its blossoms, and birds never looked for seed at its spent blossoms. And, unlike the standard purple coneflower, it did not survive our mild winter.

re-cross-pollinated—to create the hybrid. Sometimes such hybrids are sterile, producing no nectar, no seed, and thus no food value for birds or pollinators. They're all about appearances. These man-made hybrids rank as **poor choices** for attracting birds.

In the years before I began focusing on the importance of maintaining a native garden, I used to plant zinnia seed, a plant broadly cultivated and hybridized. While some zinnia species are native to some parts of the US (but more so in Mexico), they're certainly not native where I live. Still, I loved the flowers, knowing that by July, I'd delight to nectaring butterflies. One spring I discovered a packet of zinnia seeds that advertised multicolored 4-inch-diameter blooms on 4-foot-tall stems. Lovely! I planted the seed; it germinated well, the plants grew tall, and the flowers were bright, a full 4 inches in diameter. I was thrilled. Then I watched. A tiger swallowtail touched down, a spicebush

swallowtail flitted through, a spangled fritillary paused, two silver-spotted skippers alit—and every single one left immediately, never to return. The action told me what I needed to know: The hybrids had no nectar. The thrill was gone. But I learned a mean lesson. Yes, the flowers were lovely, and they were obviously developed purely for aesthetics. What a waste of space in my birdscape garden that year. Bummer.

So the difference between a cultivar and a hybrid boils down to parentage. Man-made hybrids cannot be categorized as native plants, even when produced by two native "parents." But varieties or cultivated varieties that maintain the native plant's integrity can, at least in a liberal sense and for the purposes of this book, thus be loosely deemed native.

In short, what we're concerned about here is whether a given plant is a poor, good, better, or best choice for attracting birds to your yard and garden. Although it's a bittersweet conclusion, what may be a best choice for your personal taste may be a poor choice for the birds. We'll revisit this matter again later.

Q: *My yard is planted with numerous flowering plants and berry producers. They're not native, but birds sip the nectar and eat the seeds and berries and seem to relish them. So what's wrong with that?*

A: It's true: Birds sip nectar and eat at least some seeds and berries from introduced species. However, some nonnative plants cause serious harm to both birds and their habitat.

Research by Ohio State University ecologist Amada Rodewald uncovered some surprising effects of nonnative plants. For instance, nonnative Asian honeysuckle (*Lonicera maackii*)—which produces lovely flowers, dense foliage, and abundant red

Sterile Plants *and How* THEY CAME TO BE

Why are sterile plants on the market? Why would anyone want them? In short, blame consumer demand. Here's an explanation:

First, let's clarify that hybrids aren't always a bad thing. Horticulturalists may hybridize plants to improve fruiting—maybe for quality, maybe for quantity. Sometimes hybridization intentionally eliminates seeds—think seedless watermelons. Or hybridization may reduce susceptibility to disease, thus improving crop yields. For the produce and other agricultural industries, these qualities, brought about by hybridization, improve crop quality, enhance business, and apparently cause no harm to whoever eats the products.

When it comes to forest and landscape trees, shrubs, and perennials, however, hybridization is typically all about aesthetics. Sadly, perhaps out of ignorance, a good many homeowners consider their landscaping to be pure decoration. To the uninformed, plants should merely look pretty. They forget Mother Nature's primary purpose for vegetation—to feed and otherwise support critters. In the yard, that translates into landscape plants that support everything from insects to mammals.

If you're a savvy nursery person and an even more savvy businessperson, however, you'll jump on the decoration bandwagon and provide homeowners with the showy vegetation they want. Quite simply, you meet consumer demand. And bingo! You sell bunches of nursery products. And make money. After all, why else would you be in business if you weren't trying to make a living?

While there are a few notable exceptions, most hybrids serve no other function in your birdscaping except to sit there in the garden or yard, look pretty, and demand lots of water, fertilizer, and TLC. They take space away from equally attractive plants that require little or no care and that will provide nectar and nutritious seeds, and simultaneously support insects, insect eggs, and larvae. The notable exceptions have mostly occurred in the wild and end up functioning essentially as natives. Case in point: Red maple and silver maple trees have cross-pollinated in the wild, and the popular result is marketed as *Acer × freemanii,* accepted now by most as native.

We homeowners tending yards and gardens have a choice. If we choose to request native plants, our consumer demand will affect the marketplace in a very similar way. Nursery staff, horticulturalists, and landscapers all aim to please their customers. And they're very good at what they do.

berries—actually creates an ecological trap for birds. Because nonnative plants leaf out early, they're attractive to male Northern Cardinals eager to establish early territories. Unfortunately, the situation creates predator targets, most likely because these early nests are easier to find and prey upon. A 20 percent reduction in nesting success is attributed particularly to the introduced Asian honeysuckle.

But the problem is actually more complicated than nesting success or lack thereof. The rest of the problem has to do with birds' health. Here's why:

The brilliance of his red plumage is the measure of a male Northern Cardinal's health and vigor. All female Northern Cardinals understand that. According to Rodewald, Asian honeysuckle berries "contain abundant pigments but are poor in the protein and fat birds need for energy and fitness." Thus, red-colored birds like House Finches or Purple Finches that eat Asian honeysuckle berries during molt may wear brilliant plumage, but in fact suffer from poor health. Other nonnative berries, however, lack the abundant pigments, so red-colored birds that dine on them during molt produce plumage more orange than red, thus rendering them, at least in the eyes of potential mates, as less healthy, less vigorous.

Further, as difficult as it may be to believe, some nonnative berries can kill. Nandina, sometimes called heavenly bamboo (*Nandina domestica*), contains cyanide and is a well-documented killer of Cedar Waxwings. There's little other research about the effects of introduced berry-producing species on birds' health, but why take the chance?

Perhaps an equally serious problem, though, is that the early leafing out and the dense shade produced by introduced species

Healthy male Purple Finches (shown here), Northern Cardinals, and House Finches wear brilliant red plumage, and females judge potential mates by their brilliance. Birds that eat certain nonnative berries, which contain significantly poorer nutrition than native berries, may look orangey, even yellowish, thus reducing or perhaps eliminating their opportunity to breed.

like Asian honeysuckle is literally destroying native plants. Ecology researcher David Gorchov of Miami University of Ohio reports his findings this way: "Tree seedling survival was reduced by up to 70 percent, and herb growth and reproduction rates plunged by up to 80 percent, primarily because of the shade cast by [Asian] honeysuckle."

Finally, and probably most serious of all, nonnative plants affect insect populations—dramatically. Because warblers and most other songbirds rely on insects, especially caterpillars, for 90 percent of their nourishment during breeding season, it's significant that nonnative plants do not support as many insects as native plants. So what? Well, entomologist Douglas Tallamy, University of Delaware, provides this startling statistic: A family of chickadees fed 4,800 caterpillars raising a single brood. That in itself is rather astonishing, but think about the ramifications.

Without caterpillars, the chickadees couldn't have raised their babies. And 96 percent of songbirds feed their babies bugs. If nonnative plants don't support or provide the food birds need to survive, isn't the result obvious?

And there's one final kicker that ought to render Asian honeysuckle illegal. It spreads its own poison, effectively rendering soil in the immediate area toxic to any other seeds or sprouts and killing any plants that may be growing nearby. Bad stuff, this Asian honeysuckle. And that's only one of the nonnatives that can taint your yard.

Q: *Well, okay, I admit that I have some seed- and berry-producing plants that birds ignore. Why?*

A: That question may best be answered by example. Birds seem not to recognize certain berries as food. For instance, while birds thrive on the red berries of most native winterberry and its cultivars (*Ilex verticillata*), they completely ignore the yellow berries of the golden winterberry cultivar. Apparently, it's for a simple reason: Birds don't recognize yellow berries as food. Likewise, birds leave seeds from some hybrids to rot while they struggle to survive the winter. Seeds from many hybrids are not viable; they have no food value. Somehow, birds seem to understand that. They're smarter than we are.

In some cases, though, we have to say we simply don't know why birds eat some things but not others—native or not.

Q: *So, how do native plants attract birds to my yard?*

A: By now, you no doubt understand that somehow native plants function to feed birds. How is it that native plants feed birds while nonnative plants don't? Yes, we've

Top: A breeding-plumaged male Magnolia Warbler, a morsel in his beak, does what most migrants do: He forages almost entirely for bugs, plucking insects as well as insect eggs and larvae from favored hiding places such as beneath loose bark.
Bottom: Willow trees (*Salix* spp.), recognized as moth and butterfly magnets, are thus also warbler magnets, the birds foraging for caterpillars. A Prothonotary Warbler snagged a little green caterpillar among these willows.

acknowledged that birds nectar on and consume seeds and berries from some nonnative plants. But the real issue here is about bugs—a term I use loosely to refer to all kinds of insects in all forms: egg, larval, and adult.

Here's the answer in a sentence: Because 96 percent of songbirds feed their babies bugs, without bugs, we'd have no birds.

And now the explanation: Native bugs, birds, and plants evolved together; and Mother Nature, when left alone, has always had a magical way of making everything balance out. Bugs lived on and reproduced via plants. Birds ate a hefty portion of the eggs, larvae, and adult bugs. And plants were pollinated by or reseeded by both bugs and birds. It's a handy and reliable balance of nature. Then we started messing around, introducing bugs like the Japanese beetle, emerald ash borer, gypsy moth, Asian praying mantis, cabbage white butterfly, and several kinds of aphids, sawflies, whiteflies, and beetles. They didn't evolve here, so they mostly have no predators to keep them in balance. Then we made a bigger mess by introducing plants like multiflora rose (*Rosa multiflora*), native to China, Japan, and Korea; garlic mustard (*Alliaria petiolata*), native to Eurasia and northwestern Africa; water hyacinth (*Eichhornia crassipes*), from the Amazon Basin; English ivy (*Hedera helix*), from Eurasia; tree of heaven (*Ailanthus altissima*), native to China and Taiwan; and autumn olive (*Elaeagnus umbellata*), from eastern Asia. When that happened, we threw things out of balance big time. With all these vigorous nonnative plants encroaching on and replacing natives, many native bugs had trouble finding native plants on which to feed, lay their eggs, and grow caterpillars.

So why don't the bugs just use nonnative plants for their dinner tables and nurseries? Because nonnative plants have such a dramatically different chemical composition than natives, they not only often can't support a good many of our native bugs, but sometimes actually poison them. In short, the vast majority of native bugs can't eat nonnative plants—or live on them. Then the plants are gloriously advertised as plants that are "insect resistant." We need to add that they're also "bird resistant"—perfect for keeping birds out of the yard.

So if you actually want birds in your yard, you'll need to support bugs in your yard—and that requires native plants.

Q: *But I've always been taught to keep bugs out of the yard and garden—for all kinds of personal and aesthetic reasons. Now I'm being told that to feed the birds, I must first feed the bugs. I'm a bit uncomfortable about that. How do you respond?*

A: Well, to put it simply, it turns out we've been taught to do the wrong things! More and more prestigious organizations have confirmed the error and are trying to help us change bad habits, with the National Audubon Society, Cornell University's Lab of Ornithology, National Wildlife Federation, The Nature Conservancy, American Bird Conservancy, and American Birding Association all pointing the way to saving birds' lives.

Here's why: First, not all bugs are created equal. Some bugs are indeed serious pests, but less than 1 percent of bugs found in the yard and garden cause any serious harm. Second, most bugs are actually beneficial. Remember

A spider gleaned from the foliage makes a quick but high-protein meal for a female American Redstart.

Mother Nature's balance-of-nature thing. Third, when birds discover the bounty in your yard, they'll join you—and eat those bugs. Then, finally, your yard will serve as a lifeline for migrating birds, making up in some small way for the major loss of habitat we've yanked from birds' use for survival.

Think of it this way: Aphids eat plants. Ladybug larvae eat aphids. And birds eat ladybugs. One simple example we can all understand. Balance of nature.

And here's my personal take on the entire issue: I've not used insecticides in my yard in over 25 years, but nevertheless, I have virtually no problem with bugs. My yard list of 167 bird species explains why.

Q: *What is a plant that "supports bugs"? How does that plant then feed birds?*

A: A plant that supports bugs provides insects a place to live and feed during all parts of their lives. Initially, of course, bugs need suitable places to lay their eggs. Each insect species chooses the site most likely to perpetuate the species, but many choose some specific plant part on which to raise their families, like under tree bark, under leaves, or maybe drilled into stalks and stems. These typically well-hidden eggs become the target for many birds' lunches. Nuthatches, for instance, forage upside down on trees to best see the eggs hidden in bark. Downy Woodpeckers know to drill open the galls that bulge on goldenrod stalks to lunch on the gallfly inside.

Of course, birds don't find all the eggs, so when the remaining eggs ultimately hatch, the larval form needs a place to feed, perhaps on leaves, stems, roots, nectar, seed, or some form of fruit/berries. This insect form also becomes a lunch target for birds. As a rule of thumb, most songbirds feed their babies

Top: Native goldenrod species (*Solidago* spp.) attract bugs to their fall blossoms, making the plants especially beneficial to fall migrants, including this female Common Yellowthroat with a bug in her beak. *Bottom:* White-breasted Nuthatches forage upside down along tree trunks, the better to find hidden insect eggs and larvae other birds miss. The foraging technique obviously worked for this bird.

caterpillars, an insect larval form. To test the rule of thumb, watch common backyard nesters like Eastern Bluebirds, House Wrens, or Carolina Wrens carry meals to their nests.

Again assuming birds don't find all the larvae, when the larval form becomes an adult, that critter also needs specific food supplies, including a vast range of delectables like nectar, plant sap, roots, grass, and other insects, including those insects' eggs and larvae. These adults also become part of a bird's menu for breakfast, lunch, and dinner.

So plants support bugs that in turn feed birds.

Q: *Do all native plants attract birds? How do I know what ones do?*

A: All native plants somehow fit into Mother Nature's balanced plan, but of course we can't plant everything in our yards. So in this book we've attempted to identify the native plants that best serve birds (and bugs) to provide the lifeline birds so desperately need.

Q: *Replacing plants can be expensive. Are native plants more expensive than introduced plants?*

A: Unlike most introduced species sold in pots at nurseries and big-box stores, native plants come in additional stages of growth. Yes, you can buy sizeable plants in sizeable containers, but you can save money by buying plugs, usually small plants in individual cells, some as small as 1½ by 2 by 4 inches. Typically, plugs are sold by the flat, thus providing more plants for less money. Additionally, in spring, you may consider bare-rooted stock, or even seeds. Depending on your need for instant gratification, purchasing these smaller plants, even in large quantities, saves money.

But to directly answer your question: No, native plants tend to cost about the same as introduced species, assuming you're choosing similarly sized pots and/or plants.

Q: *I live in a tidy neighborhood where the landscaping is lovely. Like my neighbors, I like a tidy, formal look. If I plant natives, won't I have to compromise my own aesthetics, become the eyesore of the neighborhood, and upset my neighbors?*

A: That's an excellent question and one that almost everyone considering native gardens asks. The short and sweet answer is that native gardens can be just as tidy and formal as any other. Folks who think planting a

native garden is an excuse for not tending the garden make the rest of us look bad.

But here's the rub: Not every native plant that birds love is a tidy, well-behaved plant. The aim of this book is to suggest natives ("best" choices) or their native varieties or cultivars ("better" or "good" choices) that not only attract birds but look good in landscapes. Since yard size determines which plants will best serve your landscaping purposes, we've categorized the plants we suggest according to where they'll best perform—in yards and gardens from super-sized to pots-and-patios.

Q: *What's different about the look of a yard or garden planted with natives and one planted with introduced species?*

A: If you like a yard or garden crammed full of blue and pink blossoms, for instance, you choose natives the same way you'd choose nonnative species—by blossom color. On the other hand, if you like a yard or garden entirely in shades of green—trees, shrubs, ferns, vines—again, you'd choose natives the same way you'd choose nonnative species—by their foliage. Granted, natives may not provide colors as varied or intense as do nonnative or hybrid plants, but if you plant natives, you can instead enjoy the color of birds!

Q: *What can I do to make my native yard or garden look more perfectly groomed than do some other native landscapes I've seen?*

A: You'll use the same techniques to make your native yard or garden look classy as you would for any other yard or garden. Maintaining carefully edged paths; adding sculpture accents, garden art, and benches; setting off plantings with lovely sections of fencing or other inorganic borders; tucking in ornate

A native garden can be as lovely as a nonnative garden. This early-July garden displays three washes of purple coneflower (*Echinacea purpurea*), one partially hidden by the trellis, along with two masses of wild bergamot (*Monarda fistulosa*), one partially shown far left, another far right. Golden common yarrow (*Achillea filipendulina* 'Gold Plate') and blanketflower (*Gillardia* spp.), front right; white-blooming narrowleaf mountain mint (*Pycnanthemum tenuifolium*), middle right; and the towering giant coneflower (*Rudbeckia maxima*) fill in with interest. The trellis supports crossvine (*Bignonia capreolata*) with upright prairie coneflower (*Ratibida columnifera*) standing tall, back left, and common milkweed (*Asclepias syriaca*) and nonnative fennel (*Foeniculum vulgare*), back right. A native catalpa-wood bench serves as a companion for a rustic fence of the same wood and invites visitors to amble the winding wood-chipped paths and sit a spell.

trellises or elegant birdbaths; structuring a stonework terrace or rock garden; adding an accent boulder; and establishing plantings that reach a variety of heights—all can make any garden more formal, native or not. Again, planting native is not an excuse for an untended eyesore.

Q: *How do I arrange native plants in my yard or garden to host the most birds?*

A: Birds hang out in places that provide ready food, safe shelter, moving water,

and—in season—secure places to nest and raise young. For years, people have focused only on feeders and feed to attract birds; of course, we're now professing that plants provide the ultimate bird feeders—nectar, sap, seeds, berries, and bugs.

But there's more. Folks who consciously set out to evaluate the availability of avian shelter in their yards may suffer tally shock. Up high, for instance, birds need an escape from soaring hawks; and down low, they need a place to tuck in when ground-level threats pursue. Birds visiting a birdbath need shelter within several feet of the bath where they can safely preen and dry off, enjoying protection during the few minutes they can't fly well or have become distracted by the task at hand. You see the general idea: They need dense, they need high, they need low. And if the distance between spots of shelter is more than 20 feet, they need shelter to break up the distance.

In short, think drifts of perennial plants, not twos and threes. Think a mass of shrubs, not ones and twos. Think a little grove of trees, not a single specimen. Of course, many yards can't accommodate drifts, masses, and groves, so approach it this way: Instead of planting landscape in the lawn, plant little patches of lawn in the landscape. In other words, reduce lawn to a bare minimum—or to none at all. It's useless to birds—maybe even toxic if Mr. Green Grass dumps pesticides on it.

Q: *Using 50 as a hypothetical number, would it be better to plant one plant each of 50 perennials or plant 10 plants each of five species? Or some other combination?*

A: Instead of aiming for a "zoo" of plants—one or two plants of 50 different kinds—think in terms of masses. You'll best attract birds (and bugs) by planting washes of a few species; so consider setting out 25 perennial plants of two species that bloom at different times—maybe in a mixed mass. Even 10 plants of five species each would, after a few seasons, create a decent wash of color since most native plants will multiply over time. Just choose these masses according to bloom time in your region. That not only varies the appearance of your yard or garden but also keeps pollinators happy over a longer period of time. As seeds ripen, the birds also enjoy an

Plants arrayed in masses like these fall-blooming New England asters (*Aster novae-angliae*) attract more birds—and butterflies and insects—than do only two or three plants of a kind.

extended buffet. Having only a plant or two of a few given species, however, may mean that nothing—bees, insects, or birds—finds the hidden gems.

Q: *My lot is tiny (or I have only a pots-and-patio place), so I can't plant washes and masses of trees, bushes, and perennials. How can I possibly plant native?*

A: One simple solution for expanding habitat space without buying more land is going vertical, thus expanding birdscape surface. Shrub layers work best for attracting birds in small lots because shrubs are where most birds nest, find shelter, and roost in winter. Even folks who can offer nothing more than a window box or a couple of containers on a 10th-floor balcony can plant natives that help foraging birds. We've included in this reference lists of plants that will serve every situation. With the right perennials, for instance, your 10th-floor balcony can host hummingbirds on a regular basis!

Q: *Planting native sounds like additional work. Is it?*

A: Actually, planting and tending natives is less work than doing the same for nonnatives. Native plants rarely need water—they're accustomed to the regional growing conditions. Natives don't need—or want—fertilizers. In fact, it's easy to burn plants when fertilizing adjoining lawn (maybe another reason to get rid of it). Natives don't need spraying—especially since you're hoping they support the bugs birds need. Natives don't need deadheading—especially since you want birds to enjoy the seeds. Natives don't need pruning—unless your yard or garden space demands it.

In short, natives provide more advantages than nonnatives with less work.

Q: *How are native plants better for the environment?*

A: Let's answer this question by first looking at the effect of lawns on the environment. According to a recent NASA study done in collaboration with Mountain West, US lawns blanket about 63,000 square miles, about the size of Texas, making it the largest irrigated crop by area in the country. Unfortunately, it's a crop that produces nothing that we can eat or wear. To birds, lawn is the second-most-desertlike place on earth—second only to pavement. The study further determined

Every plant helps! Even if you can plant only two small trees, such as a male and female American holly (*Iles opaca*) or one of their compact cultivars, you will support an amazing number of birds, including American Robins, desperate for winter berries.

that 50 to 75 percent of the total residential water use goes to the outdoors, mostly for irrigating lawns.

In 2002 a Harris Survey estimated that homeowners spent $28.9 billion on professional lawn care. That number has likely doubled by now. While a well-manicured lawn can function as a carbon sink, the advantage is typically lost by the use of fertilizers and pesticides that pollute runoff and by the use of gasoline-powered lawnmowers, weed whackers, and leaf blowers that, according to the EPA, account for 5 percent of summertime air pollution. Audubon.org claims that homeowners use 10 times more fertilizer per acre on lawns than farmers use on crops, thus compounding runoff pollution. And, finally, if homeowners bag grass clippings and send them to the landfill, that's another environmental red flag.

Many states, however, are encouraging homeowners to replace lawns with alternatives, namely native plants. Eliminating lawns reduces the carbon produced and the water used to maintain them. Natives that replace lawns need no fertilizer, little or no water, no pesticides, and no mowing or blowing. The landscape-instead-of-lawn scenario makes good environmental sense, for humans and, by the way, for birds. As the National Audubon Society notes on Audubon.org, "Native gardens also help birds be as strong as possible in the face of the climate threat—by providing food, shelter and protection. Native plant patches—no matter how small—can help bird populations be more resilient to the impacts of a warming world."

Q: *Where do I find native plants? How do I know they're native?*

A: Finding native plants is admittedly a challenge in some parts of the country. When nursery folks realize, however, that there's a demand, they'll carry more and more native species. Until then, check with your local and state native plant societies (every state has at least one) or go online to find a reputable supplier.

Q: *Okay, I'm convinced. So, in order to include plants that support the most insects and feed the most birds but still look terrific in my landscaping, what should I plant?*

A: That's what the rest of the book is about!

Fall migrants like Blackpoll Warblers rely on lipid-rich berries, including those of roughleaf dogwood (*Cornus drumondii*), to refuel along their arduous journeys.

"In nature, there are neither rewards nor punishments; there are consequences."

—ROBERT GREEN INGERSOLL (1833–1899)

Chapter 4
MAKING DECISIONS ABOUT ADDING NATIVES

The previous chapter ended with a question we promised to answer: In order to include plants that support the most insects and feed the most birds but still look terrific in your landscaping, what should you plant? It's no simple question, and so of course, it has no simple answer. If you're starting your landscape or garden with a blank canvas, you have the world at your feet. Go for it! But if, like most of us, you already have some degree of landscape in place (although probably not entirely native), you may be puzzled about how to proceed.

We have a plan, however, to take you through the decision-making process so that the answers will be specifically appropriate for your yard, your situation, your birdscape. That means, of course, that we'll take into consideration the size of your yard or garden—super-sized, mid-sized, mini-sized, or a pots–and–patio space.

Here's the plan. In this chapter:

1. We'll inventory your yard and immediate neighborhood, recording bird habitat assets—tallying up what's there that birds need—and drawing your yard's layout to scale on graph paper.
2. We'll analyze what the inventory says about bird habitat liabilities—tallying up what's missing that birds need. We'll also analyze your yard's growing conditions since they directly affect what can thrive where.
3. We'll help you organize a plan to eliminate the liabilities—zeroing in on the habitat components birds need but that are lacking in your yard. The plan will pave the way for deciding what kinds of plants—trees, shrubs, vines, perennials—and how many of each you can consider.

As we walk you through the inventory, analysis, and organization, however, we'll keep three promises:

1. We will *not* suggest planting natives for the sake of planting natives.
2. We will suggest native plants that fill the gaps in your bird habitat.
3. We will recommend native plants that expand the biodiversity in your birdscape.

So, let's get going. To begin, you'll need to take an inventory of what you have, both in your yard and in your immediate neighborhood, remembering that birds don't recognize property lines.

TAKING INVENTORY OF YOUR SPACE

Let's start by making a yard map that inventories what's in your space. As we progress through inventory, analysis, and organization, we'll continue building on this map, so start with a large piece of graph paper—maybe several sheets taped together, depending on your yard size. Since

space matters—both what space is in use and what space is available for use—you should verify dimensions with a tape measure, translating the measurements to scale on your map. The resulting "picture" of your yard will serve you well in making planting decisions later—decisions about not only what kinds of plants and which specific plants but where they can be planted. Important stuff!

Follow these steps:

1. On graph paper, outline your property boundaries.
2. Sketch in the footprints of your house, patio, sidewalks, garage, storage shed, driveway, pool, and any other permanent structures.
3. Graph tree canopy diameters.
4. Along property boundaries, graph neighboring trees.
5. Mark the locations and space taken up by shrubs.
6. Sketch in other plantings, including vines, perennials, brambles, ornamental grasses, etc.
7. Designate any other landscape elements, like trellises, arbors, pergolas, terraces, boulders, fences, sculptures, or permanently placed fountains and other water features.

Analyze what's in your yard as well as what's in the neighborhood. No need to plant eastern red cedars (*Juniperus virginiana*) if the adjoining neighbor already has a lovely stand.

8. Identify the locations of utility wires, both overhead and underground.

9. Make note of gas lines, water lines, and drain lines. If you're unsure about underground utilities, make the call before you dig—or even plan to dig.

10. Determine any rights-of-way that adjoin your property that might allow another party to disrupt anything you plant in or near that space.

The inventory takes some time, but in the overall scheme of things, it's essential. Your graphic to-scale map becomes the basis on which most other decisions will be made.

The next step is to analyze what's there, what it means, and what's missing—rather like measuring assets and liabilities.

ANALYZING ASSETS AND LIABILITIES

Begin your analysis with the bare space on your graph. I'm guessing that space likely represents lawn. For the most part, lawn is a liability. How much of that space now occupied by lawn can you use—or are you willing to use—to plant something else instead?

Here's a thought to mull over: Lawn is the second-most-desertlike place in the ecosystem. Second to what? Pavement. So if you're mowing grass, you have room to change directions and replace lawn with natives, turning a liability into an asset.

What about All That Lawn?

Let's rethink lawn. Historically, humans felt compelled to maintain low, open vegetation around their abodes in order to better spot approaching tigers, lions, bears, or other serious predators. These days, most of us don't have vicious, life-threatening predators lurking in the thicket, watching our every move, awaiting the perfect moment to attack. Still, we continue to plant and mow lawn, using mostly exotic grasses from a half a world away, creating vast, desertlike places. To birds, lawn is a wasteland. It's risky business flying across open spaces. And lawn treated with pesticides becomes, for birds, a toxic dump.

With homes enlarging their footprints and with more and more homes paving the landscape, we would be smart to change our ways—for the sake of the planet. If we added landscape, not lawn, we would also improve our personal living conditions. Further, by rethinking the proportions of lawn and landscape, we can actually help birds survive. Terrific asset, don't you think?

Try this: Instead of tucking landscape into vast lawns, consider making lawn a spot or two tucked within the landscape—an edge of lawn along the front walk, perhaps, or next to an outdoor dining area. Period. Skip the gargantuan gas-guzzling, pollution-spewing lawnmower. Think five minutes with a weed whacker! Or plant native low-mow or no-mow grass or sedge or perhaps

Mowing only paths and borders in super-sized yards gives a parklike appearance and permits natives to grow naturally among understory vegetation. "Letting the yard go natural," however, requires careful oversight since most "volunteers" will likely be nonnative, usually Asian species, maybe even invasives.

a bee lawn (more on these later) and pitch the weed whacker, too. Would you really miss all the work—and expense—of caring for a lawn?

Okay, maybe you can't quite give up lawn entirely—yet. Maybe another option will better work for you. Try this goal: Cut the grass in half. Use the other half to improve bird habitat with trees, shrubs, vines, and perennials—maybe even a clump or two or three of native ornamental grasses. Just think about all the oxygen you'll be putting into your personal atmosphere! Cutting the lawn in half reduces its liability by half and increases assets by 50 percent. Good step!

Before we get ahead of ourselves, however, consider this caveat: Even if you're willing to eliminate all lawn, don't take the step in one giant leap. The more you do at once, the more potential you have for mistakes. While landscaping mistakes can almost always be undone, usually within a year or less, the fix can be expensive. So analyze the space for the entire property and make plans for meeting your final goals, but ultimately focus on only a portion at a time. Most

Fragrant sumac (*Rhus aromatica*), its pollen and berries attractive to wildlife, serves as an attractive 2-foot-tall ground cover that adds to the biodiversity of the habitat.

WHAT IS Biodiversity?

*B*iodiversity is a portmanteau of "biological diversity," referring to the variety of life in a given location. In its broadest scope, examining biodiversity takes into account all living organisms, down to the microbes, found within a given area—in the air, on land, and in water. For our purposes, of course, we're talking about the diversity of plants in your yard and the critters they attract, from bugs to birds.

In general, we would expect that the more native plant species in a given space, the more animal species the space supports. Within my own plot, since I've added many more natives, I've noticed a big uptick in the number of not only birds but also other critters scooting about, like frogs, toads, and skinks. They all love bugs, and my habitat now gives them ample places to live. I never used to see them. It's another measure of the habitat's increased biodiversity, which has also led to an increase in biomass. Hooray!

Since birds don't recognize property lines, however, neighborhood diversity is as important as yard diversity. Take into account this broader tally of plant diversity as you analyze your yard, including its composition in your larger neighborhood.

landscape transfigurations are longtime works in progress. The more we do to expand the biodiversity, the more benefits we see as more-diverse birds discover the habitat. Then we want to do even more!

Analyzing What's There

Okay, so let's take a look at what else your inventory shows and analyze what's there, in your yard and in the neighborhood yards. Just as a note of comfort, no one can have everything in a single yard, but adding to the neighborhood's biodiversity serves as a reasonable goal.

Use the following questions as a guide to your analysis. As you identify plants, mark their identities on your yard map, perhaps listing neighbors' plants in the margins. Here we go with 20 questions:

1. What kinds of oak trees are in my yard and/ or my close neighbors' yards?
2. What kinds of deciduous trees, other than oaks, are in my yard and/or my neighbors' yards?
3. What kinds of evergreen or semievergreen trees are in my yard and/or my neighbors' yards?
4. Do any of the trees offer winter shelter for birds? Which ones?
5. Do any of the trees produce nectar for birds or pollinators? Which ones and during which season(s)?
6. Do any of the trees produce seeds, berries, or fruit suitable for birds? Which ones? During which season(s)?
7. Which shrubs or tall understory plants do I and/or my neighbors have? Are they deciduous, evergreen, or semievergreen?
8. Do any of the shrubs or tall understory plants offer winter shelter for birds? Which ones?

9. Do any of the shrubs or tall understory plants produce nectar for birds and pollinators? Which ones and during which season(s)?
10. Do any of the shrubs or tall understory plants support bugs in any form—adult, egg, or larval?
11. Do any of the shrubs or tall understory plants produce seeds, berries, or fruits for birds? Which ones? In which seasons do the seeds, berries, or fruits ripen?
12. What kinds of vines do I have on my property?
13. Do the vines offer winter shelter?
14. Do the vines produce nectar for birds and pollinators? When?
15. Do the vines produce any seeds, berries, or fruit for birds? When?
16. What herbaceous perennials are growing either on my property or adjoining my property boundaries?
17. Which of these perennials support bugs in any form—adult, egg, or larval?
18. Which of these perennials produce nectar for birds and pollinators? When?
19. Which of these perennials produce seed for birds? When do seeds ripen?
20. Do I have any clumps of native grasses that produce seed for birds? When?

When Identities Evade You

Let's face it: Identifying unknown plants can be frustrating. If you find yourself struggling with some of the IDs, check plant guides, available at local libraries, nurseries, and online. If "keying out" a plant's ID, however, was never part of your biology education, using such guides can be painstakingly slow. Consider contacting a local authority, perhaps your county extension agent, maybe your local botanical garden personnel, or possibly a Master Gardener, native-plant-society member, local botanist, or horticulturalist.

Once you've identified a plant, if you're unsure whether or not it's native, check the USDA Plant Database online (www.plants.usda.gov), where you can use either the common or scientific name to check a plant's native status. If you wish, by zooming in on the maps, you can verify a plant's status in your specific county.

Analyze Native vs. Nonnative vs. Nonnative Invasive

Let's say, in the course of your yard analysis, you've (very likely) found some nonnative plants. Of course, not all nonnative plants are created equal. Some nonnative plants are completely benign and cause no overt harm. They don't emit toxins or spread like wildfire or threaten birds or other wildlife. Their only fault is that they just sit there taking up space that a more productive, more bird-friendly native plant could use. So they're not really assets, but they're not serious liabilities.

Other nonnative plants, however, are just plain trouble. They're invasive, some extremely so. An invasive is defined, via a 1999 presidential executive order, as "a species that does not naturally occur in a specific area and whose introduction does or is likely to cause economic or environmental harm or harm to human health." It's fairly obvious, then, that invasives deserve your special attention. And it's fairly obvious that invasives are liabilities—sometimes extraordinarily serious liabilities.

One plant behavior that should rouse your suspicion is that the plant is very early green or very late green, sometimes even an all-winter green. Of course, we certainly have evergreens and semievergreens that are delightful, much-loved natives, so this early/late green or winter-long green habit isn't a rule. But let your suspicions be resolved. Many nonnative plants, especially the

Top: Many nonnatives, like daylilies (*Hemerocallis* spp.), are generally benign but take up space that could be better used for natives that support wildlife. Still, some nonnatives provide a certain minimal sustenance, such as pollen for bees.
Bottom: Invasive nonnative flowering pears have escaped yards and gardens, creating a monoculture along this highway, crowding out, as they multiply, everything else in their paths. Unfortunately, flowering pears are still being sold, usually touted as "sterile," but when crossed with other Callery pears—by birds, bees, or breeze—they reproduce prolifically.

more troublesome ones, tend to possess the quirky early-green, late-green habit. Unfortunately, their early green-up gives nonnatives a distinct advantage over natives, allowing them to form dense shade before native competitive sprouts can leaf out and gain a foothold. The result? The nonnatives can readily and quickly take over an area, crowding out any competition in the way. This behavior alone labels them as invasive.

From the point of view of a homeowner, nonnative invasives dramatically affect the environment. They crowd out native species, sometimes by toxins emitted by the plants themselves. In doing so, they create a monoculture that is friendly neither to our native insects nor to our native birds—nor to any other form of native wildlife. In some cases, in fact, the nonnative invasives cause the demise, or at least general decline, of wildlife, including birds. These troublesome plants deplete natural wildlife forage, deplete native bugs, deteriorate surface and ground water and aquatic habitat, and deteriorate the soil. One result of all these bad habits is that the invasives further stress—and often extirpate—endangered native plants. Further, they hybridize with natives and thus deteriorate the native plants' gene pools. They're the true bad guys of the plant kingdom. Those are all serious liabilities in your landscape.

There are dozens and dozens of nonnative invasives, but even some of the bad guys are worse than others. So if, in the course of identifying plants in your yard, you discover any of the following Disaster Dozen invasives, you will do well to eradicate them. For the present, put a big red X through any of the Disaster Dozen you've identified on your yard map. Later, we'll tell you how to deal with them and then provide an array of excellent native alternatives with which to replace them.

Keep in mind that even a single additional native plant adds to the natural biodiversity in your yard. It's preferable to nonnatives and supremely superior to nonnative invasives. In fact, even a blank spot in the yard is preferable to any of the plants in the Disaster Dozen.

The Disaster Dozen

Invasive Bradford/Callery pear (*Pyrus calleryana*). Having escaped gardens and yards and hybridized with other Callery species, Bradford pears have spread to form miles-long monocultures along roadsides and in disturbed areas, disrupting the ecosystem and destroying biodiversity.

Invasive princess tree/royal paulownia (*Paulownia tomentosa*). A highly invasive Asian ornamental, it grows rapidly in disturbed places. Its root system is fire resistant, so it's highly aggressive.

Invasive tree of heaven (*Ailanthus altissima*). This Asian invasive threatens sewers and structures and quickly forms dense groves, annihilating natives as it spreads. Elimination is a long-term goal; be diligent. It can, however, be confused with desirable native staghorn sumac (*Rhus typhina*), ash (*Fraxinus americana*), or walnut trees (*Juglans nigra* or other *Juglans* spp.). Use caution when controlling it. Its sap is toxic and can cause cardiac issues.

Invasive bamboo (*Phyllostachys* spp.). Technically a giant grass, bamboo is one of the most aggressive of Asian introductions. Because bamboo can grow a foot a day and readily spread 20 feet in every direction within a short time, it's a nightmare to control.

Invasive nandina/heavenly bamboo (*Nandina domestica*). Colonizing via underground roots and seeds, nandina bush produces berries toxic to animals—and birds. Because the berries contain cyanide, flocks of Cedar Waxwings have perished after gorging on them.

Invasive privets (*Ligustrum* spp.). Ligustrum privets form dense shade that prevents native seedlings from sprouting. Leaves are toxic to native bugs.

Invasive autumn olive (*Elaeagnus umbellata*) and invasive Russian olive/oleaster (*Elaeagnus angustifolia*). Dense growth from both root and a single plant's 200,000 seeds per year allow these bushes to crowd out natural selection and natural diversity. Difficult to eradicate since highway rights-of-way plantings keep reproduction at peak.

Invasive winged burning bush (*Euonymus alatus*). Burning bush has spread into woodlands, escaping gardens and yards, and has replaced the understory with vegetation deer refuse to browse, giving it an advantage over natives and ultimately replacing natives and reducing biodiversity. It forms a "seed shadow" around the original plant, spreading rapidly. Note that there is a native burning bush (*Euonymus atropurpureus*), sometimes called eastern wahoo. Check before you act.

Invasive Amur honeysuckle (*Lonicera maackii*) and related Tartarian (*L. tatarica*), Morrow's (*L. morrowii*), and dwarf honeysuckles (*L. xylosteum*). Now spread through most of North America, invasive honeysuckles crowd out native vegetation with their deep root systems and dense shade, providing nutrient-poor berries that birds eat and then eliminate to further spread the bushes.

Invasive Japanese honeysuckle (*Lonicera japonica*). This invasive vine has no enemies. Since it's evergreen or semi-evergreen, it has the advantage over any competing natives. Its tightly twisting vine strangles saplings and other new native growth in its path. A deep root system makes it tough to control and markedly resilient.

Invasive winter creeper/creeping euonymus (*Euonymus fortunei*). Shade-tolerant, this vine forms thick evergreen mats and climbs trees to bloom and reproduce. It covers, smothers, and strangles other plants. Waxy leaves limit the effectiveness of usual herbicides on this tough plant.

While hundreds of nonnatives have sprouted in our yards and gardens, some might be acceptable. I've already clarified that I'm not a purist, that the heritage plants from both of my grandmothers and my father as well as from close friends will always be a part of my garden, a part of my life. Perhaps you have the same nostalgic parts to your yard. I'm betting, though, that you'd want to eliminate noxious plants that wreak havoc on Mother Nature's plan.

So revise your yard map accordingly. Add red Xs to your yard map, crossing out invasive plant(s), liabilities that you surely need to eradicate before you add natives.

Analyze the Map—What's Missing?

Given your location in the eastern US, your yard or garden size, and the number of native, nonnative, and nonnative invasive species there, you have a good inventory of what's what. You know your assets and liabilities—the good stuff, the bad stuff, and the missing stuff. Perhaps most significantly, you know how much space remains for planting.

So, what to plant? The answer to that question is the same as the answer to this question: What's missing? Review your answers to the 20 questions. Do birds need more bug sources—trees, shrubs, vines, perennials, or grasses that host bugs? Do birds need more winter shelter, particularly

If your habitat lacks trees that host bugs, like oaks, willows, black cherries, and maples (red maple, *Acer rubrum*, shown here), birds like Black-throated Green Warblers won't be stopping by for lunch.

additional evergreens? Do birds need more shelter for nesting? Can they find suitable nesting materials? Can birds find nectar in your yard during at least two seasons? Will seedeaters find sustenance during all four seasons? What about berries? Are they available during summer, fall, and winter, including through late winter? Can birds find water?

Make a list of your yard's liabilities. That list will serve as your set of goals for filling in what's missing. Once it's obvious what's missing, you can zero in on the changes that will make the biggest difference in your yard.

Analyze Growing Conditions

With that set of goals in mind, you'll need to take into account some natural elements of your plot of land.

Sun and Shade

In the course of figuring out what you can and cannot plant where, you'll need to determine certain growing conditions over which you have little or no control, beginning with where sun and shade serve up their own form of assets and/or liabilities.

Since some plants grow best in full sun while others prefer part or full shade, you should make some careful observations about how sunlight passes across your yard. Some sunshine paths are obvious: The north side of structures will likely have full shade all day, while the south side will probably get full sun all day. The east side will get the cooler morning light, while the west side takes the brunt of hot afternoon sun. But trees and bushes—yours or your neighbors'—may shade some surprising places, and structures themselves cast shadows.

Check every two hours during the course of a full day to see what's what in your yard, perhaps recording on a graph how sunlight and shade play across your property. If possible, record the sun's path in mid-June and again in mid-December, on or near the dates of the summer and winter solstices when the sun reaches its northerly and southerly extremes. The graph will become a guide for choosing which plants go where.

The Down-and-Dirty

The tongue-in-cheek definition of soil says that soil is the medium in which you plant, and dirt is what's under your fingernails afterward. So let's talk about soil. While professional agencies will do a soil analysis for you, local nurseries or county extension agents can likely identify predominant soil textures in the area. In simple layman's terms, soil texture falls into five groups:

1. Clay soil is composed of tiny particles, so it holds water better than other soils. Since it holds on to water, it also holds on to plant nutrients, making it a rich soil for good growth. Wet clay is slippery but sticky, so it

will easily form a ball when rolled in your hand. Dry clay is smooth to the touch. In spring, it's slow to warm; and when dry, it's heavy to work. Anything planted in clay soils needs to tolerate wet feet.

2. Silty soil is composed of particles slightly larger than that of clay. When wet, it's soapy slick. Silty soil is slow to drain, so it compacts readily. To help reduce compaction, avoid walking on wet silty soil.

3. Sandy soil is composed of the largest particles of the three most common types of soil, so it holds practically no moisture. Since moisture runs through almost immediately, plant roots have little opportunity to gather nutrients. Only certain drought-tolerant plants will survive in sandy soil.

4. Peaty soil is found almost exclusively in boggy areas, so it's unlikely to be in your yard. Formed from decaying organic material, it's rich in nutrients and an excellent growing medium. As a result, peat has been used as an additive to some other soils to improve quality.

5. Loam is the gold-star standard for fine soil and what every gardener would die for. It contains about equal amounts of clay, silt, and sand, along with humus or peat. Given that combination, you can probably guess it's a rare commodity. Almost all of us add compost to our yards and gardens to make the soil more loamy, so don't despair if you think yours is less than the best. Fortunately, though, native plants find themselves at home in native soils.

If you're really concerned, you can do a simple home soil-texture analysis. Scoop up a pint-sized representative sample of soil, put it in a glass container (like a quart jar), add enough water to liquefy the soil, shake well, and let it sit overnight. The soil will separate into bands with sand at the bottom, silt next up, clay following, and loam on top. The wider the band, the more predominant the soil-texture type. Remember, however, that native plants grow in native soils, so unless yours is a suburban lot that has been significantly altered by construction—excavated to remove topsoil or filled to cover topsoil—you can guess it's close to right for natives.

Sometimes, though, distinctive small areas stand out within the larger yard. For instance, you may find a relatively rich patch of soil left from a previous owner's having heavily composted a vegetable garden spot. Chances are you will find routinely poor soil abutting

A low wet spot in the yard is not a detriment, but rather an opportunity to plant natives that like wet feet, like cardinal flower (*Lobelia cardinalis*), a hummingbird favorite.

building foundations—typically a target for after-construction backfill. Since foundation plantings are popular starting points for landscaping, you'll want to check.

In addition, you may find a low spot somewhere in the yard or garden that tends to stay moist—or maybe just plain wet. That's not a negative! Such a spot can host a good many specialty plants that significantly enhance your habitat. Maybe you'll choose to turn the spot into a rain garden. On the other hand, you may discover a sandy patch, soil that drains or dries more quickly than the rest of the yard or garden, again identifying special planting conditions. Maybe you'll want to consider xeriscape landscaping there. In any case, the more varied the soil, the more varied your plantings. The resulting plant diversity enhances the bird diversity!

Pull out that yard/garden map again and note special areas that may qualify for special plants, or at least special attention. You'll more easily improve your assets and decrease your liabilities by understanding soil conditions in your plot of land.

Slippery Slopes

Some yards are flapjack flat. Berms of varying size and shape have become popular means by which to convert flat to undulating, adding interest to the topography and an alternate soil texture to the overall surroundings. Since soil introduced to form the berm will likely be quite different from soils elsewhere in the yard or garden, be alert to how those differences affect what will readily grow there.

In addition to soil differences, be alert to the probability that, regardless of soil texture, berms will drain more quickly than the remainder of the flat yard. Thus, anything planted on the berm should probably be either drought tolerant or a target for heavy irrigation. Creating a need to

irrigate, however, seems to me to defeat one of the purposes of planting native. To put it simply, since one of the goals of a native garden is to reduce water use, a berm needs special consideration. Its primary use may be to direct rainwater into a rain garden!

If you're lucky, however, you'll have some change in elevation across your yard or garden that will accommodate layered plantings and a variety of wet- to dry-loving plants. Steep slopes, however, offer opportunities to select plants that have especially deep root systems and a reputation for holding soil. Certainly folks don't want their backyard slope to slide down into the neighbor's yard. While rock or soil terracing often becomes the go-to solution, native plants may resolve the issues with far less work and far less expense.

Add notations about these matters to your map.

Plant Restrictions

Given your yard analysis, you will most certainly face a few restrictions when you get ready to select your native plants. If you live in Michigan, for instance, you're too far north for rose mallow (*Hibiscus lasiocarpos*). No matter where you live, if your plot of land is fully shaded, blue sage (*Salvia azurea*) won't bloom there, no matter what you do to it or how badly you want to attract hummingbirds. If you have heavy wet soil, beard tongue (*Penstemon digitalis*) won't survive, so don't waste your money. And if you have a spot that's always wet, a heat-loving, drought-tolerant common yarrow (*Achillea millefolium*) won't thrive there.

But keep the faith! The next chapters of this book give you all the information you need to make the right choice for the right location in the right conditions. Even if your yard is tiny or contains only a few pots arranged on a patio, you'll find natives that work in your situation.

ORGANIZING YOUR PLAN

With the nitty-gritty work of inventory and analysis behind you, you have the background information necessary to plan the birdscape of your dreams. I'm betting that right now, though, you have a whirlwind of ideas in your head. You may feel confused, even overwhelmed, wondering where and how to start. Begin by envisioning your ideal birdscape. Here's how.

Envision the Plan

You know which of your current landscape assets you want to keep and which liabilities you want to eliminate or at least reduce, so roll out that yard map and think about your options. What do you envision for your birdscape? Something casual or formal? Dense shrubs beside the garage? A flower bed along the walk? Vines over the patio? A water feature in the back? What do you want to see when you look out the kitchen window? What do you want passersby to see from the curb?

Just to be clear, it's not our purpose here to teach landscape design; we'll leave that to the professionals. Do know, however, that a number of online sites provide sound advice for landscaping—the principles, the rules, and the absolute laws. The photos alone will inspire your creativity, triggering great ideas for landscaping, and we're here to translate the ideas into native.

Your yard and garden options are virtually limitless—well, maybe limited by your energy, time, and pocketbook—and way more options exist than we can even suggest. Creativity, kicked into full gear, will turn your efforts into spectacular rewards. Think about some of these:

Prairie Garden

If you have a super-sized yard, maybe even acreage, a prairie garden may be for you. Depending on its proximity to your house or to your neighbors'

Butterfly weed (*Asclepias tuberosa*) makes a showy front for a prairie garden.

abodes, the garden may incorporate paths, some boulders, or even statuary. Or you may go for a mini-imitation of the vast plains with only the heights of the plants to offer visual interest.

Within the confines of a mid-sized yard, however, you can still create a prairie corner, clustering plants like tall coreopsis (*Coreopsis tripteris*) or cutleaf coneflower (*Rudbeckia laciniata*) in the back and stepping down to blue giant hyssop (*Agastache foeniculum*) mixed with purple coneflower (*Echinacea purpurea*) in the middle, edged by butterfly weed (*Asclepias tuberosa*) in the front. Tuck in some prairie dropseed grass clumps (*Sporobolus heterolepis*) for texture.

Woodland Garden

If you live in the woods, you already know that very few songbird species spend full time in the forest. Even woodpeckers forage away from dense trees, and the high-canopy migrants that nest in forests still forage for bugs across a wide variety of habitats. In fact, most forest-dwelling songbirds forage and nest along woodland edges. If your plot of land is dense with trees, you likely need no further shelter for birds and are hoping, instead, to add low understory, perhaps some color, and visual interest close to your house, or maybe add foundation plantings that attract birds within window view.

Here's an idea: Consider a part-shade-part-sun spot that, over the course of the day, offers enough sun to promote blossoms. Add a foundation planting of shrubs, like holly shrubs, possibly inkberry (*Ilex glabra*) or winterberry (*Ilex verticillata*), both of which can be pruned if you prefer. Then tuck in some ostrich ferns (*Matteuccia struthiopteris*) to soften the edges, and add color with patches of bird-friendly red columbine (*Aquilegia canadensis*) and one of the *Agastache* species, accented with sweet-scented joe-pye weed (*Eupatorium purpureum*). For more visual interest and to add an invitation for a walk in the woods, add an upright garden feature, like a trellis, arbor, or arch, described in the section Vertical Garden, beginning on page 65 below.

Rock Garden

Pebbles, beach rock, river rock, even boulders and slabs from I-can-carry size to need-a-crane size—everything is an option to add interest, depth, height, or surprise to a yard. While there's nothing inherent about rock that attracts birds to the yard, under every rock is almost always something edible, including, for birds, numerous arthropods. And birds have a way of finding bugs, eggs, and larvae around the edges of rocks. I've watched Carolina Wrens glean, over the course of numerous consecutive days, around the edge of a dry-stacked stonewall, obviously rewarded by finding enough morsels to make the effort worthwhile—and repeatable.

Nothing is more natural among rocks—especially rocks in partial shade—than eastern red columbine (*Aquilegia canadensis*). It self-seeds among the cracks and crannies and puts on a month-long show every spring.

Since eastern red columbine (*Aquilegia canadensis*) grows naturally among shaded rocky terrain, it's a perfect fit for at-home partial-shade rock gardens.

If yours is a super-sized yard, a rock garden can break it up into hidden gems. Stones can set off a berm, help retain a steep slope, form a dry streambed, mark the boundary of a garden, add a focal point to a mass planting—or anything else inspired by your creativity. If yours is a mid-sized yard, a rock garden can become the central feature, perhaps at the front entrance, along the front curb, or in a back corner enhancing a water feature. If yours is a tiny yard or a pots-and-patio garden, a single large stone may set off a native flower bed or accent a clump of mini trees, like 'Gray Owl' juniper (*Juniperus virginiana*) or 'Fastigiata' hemlock (*Tsuga canadensis*). Or maybe a trio of boulders forms a contrast among grass clumps, like switchgrass (*Panicum virgatum*), Indian grass (*Sorghastrum nutans*), or bottlebrush grass (*Elymus hystrix*).

The range of natives that fits well in rock gardens is almost limitless, unless, of course, soil or moisture conditions put restrictions on the effort.

Cottage Garden

Given the delightful array of native shrubs, both deciduous and evergreen, and given the height variations available among native small trees and their cultivars, and given the almost limitless array

Wild blue indigo (*Baptisia australis*) and its white species (*B. alba*) make beautiful bush-like perennials for cottage gardens—or for almost anywhere else!

blossoms and striking foliage of a cluster of tall coreopsis (*Coreopsis tripteris*) in the center, surrounded by masses of purple-to-lavender New England asters (*Symphyotrichum novae-angliae*), orange coneflower (*Rudbeckia fulgida*), yellow sweet coneflower (*Rudbeckia subtomentosa*), and purple giant hyssop (*Agastache scrophulariifolia*). Maybe several wild white indigos (*Baptisia alba*) accent a simple fountain, and tucked along the stone path to the front door are washes of color from scarlet monarda (*Monarda didyma*), white-blooming foxglove beardtongue (*Penstemon digitalis*), and great blue lobelia (*Lobelia siphilitica*). How I wish I had a cottage!

Vertical Garden—and Vertical Garden Features

Any yard or garden can benefit from a trellis, arch, or even a more substantial arbor or pergola. Tiny yards and pots-and-patio gardens can double or even triple the surface habitat by adding a vertical garden. Verticals add visual interest to mid-sized and super-sized yards, and add height to cottage and rock gardens. They frame entryways, mark paths and sidewalks, and suggest a friendly invitation to wander through. Of course, bird habitat increases exponentially with the increased surface habitat that the vertical gardens and vertical features provide.

In urban areas or suburban areas where houses sit closely together, the space between can become a charming vertical garden with a "skinny" tree like a 'Little Volunteer' tulip tree (*Liriodendron tulipifera*), accompanied by two or three New Jersey teas (*Ceanothus americanus*) or common ninebarks (*Physocarpus opulifolius*), and underplanted with ferns like Christmas fern (*Polystichum acrostichoides*) or ostrich ferns (*Matteuccia struthiopteris*). Voila! You've turned an otherwise dead space into a green canopy of shelter for birds and improved the oxygen levels in the neighborhood.

of height and color of native perennials, a cottage garden likely offers more possibilities for plantings than does any other approach. Even if the garden is limited to curbside between sidewalk and property fence or to some abbreviated portion of the front yard, the landscaping options can make quite a statement—and attract birds during all four seasons.

Visualize four or five lavender-blooming native American wisterias (*Wisteria frutescens*) climbing a two-dimensional trellis near the cottage wall with a clump of wax myrtles (*Myrica cerifera*) to the side and fronted by mapleleaf viburnum (*Viburnum acerifolium*). Add to them an array of blue, yellow, pink, and orange blossoms. Visualize the yellow

To fill in and add texture, consider ostrich ferns (*Matteuccia struthiopteris*), a native that will thrive even in sun, although they do suffer in full sun if combined with high temperatures.

Verticals are typically synonymous with vines, and we recommend a good selection of native vines in a later chapter. But verticals can come in other forms as well. Vertical pocket gardens, made with a series of containers attached to the side of a building, wall, fence, or self-purposed structure, permit plants to grow either upward or draping. The typical small size of the pockets, however, severely restricts plant choices. Assuming the pockets you've chosen are adequate, consider tickseed coreopsis (*Coreopsis palmata*), bushy aster (*Symphyotrichum dumosus*), black-eyed Susan (*Rudbeckia hirta*), or blue sage (*Salvia azurea*)—all producing blossoms that attract pollinators and seeds that attract birds. Maybe a series of containers, each filled with Virginia strawberry (*Fragaria virginiana*), would turn the trick for you—especially if you can resist the sweet wild strawberries long enough for the berry-loving birds to find them!

Formal, Urban Chic, or Rustic Gardens
The overall atmosphere of your native garden is readily accomplished with features like paths (stone, wood chip, boardwalk, tinted concrete, or whatever materials you prefer); fences (picket, split rail, stone, or wrought iron); statuary (large or small, formal or whimsical, featured or tucked under foliage as a hidden gem); benches (modern chic, rustic stone, formal white, natural plank, cushioned or not); pots (metal, plastic, ceramic, wood, clay, or repurposed items like buckets, sprinkling cans, teapots, or antique containers or other artifacts); and water features (ponds small to large, bubbling rocks, fountains simple to elegant, birdbaths, streams, and waterfalls). Natives planted in formal symmetry may suit your fancy. Most native gardens I've enjoyed, however, seem to stay in keeping with their heritage: a natural look with a variety of heights, color washes, and textures. But it's your yard, your garden, your image. Do what you love best—just do it with natives!

Pots-and-Patio Gardens
We've mentioned a variety of possible approaches to planting natives in tiny spaces: using tall, skinny trees and shrubs (listed separately in the following chapters); going vertical with trellises and arbors; and terracing layers of pots both large and small. Other options include window boxes, raised planter boxes, and stair-step pots.

Yards and gardens are highly personal. Maybe these few ideas will trigger a vision of your own yard and garden preferences and how they might come to fruition. Dream the dream. Plan to make your personal space your own, and invite the birds to join you.

Making the Plan
Assuming you now have a vision of what you'd like your birdscape to look like, you're ready to get organized. Yard map in hand, let's make those

put-it-on-paper decisions and organize your plan forward. Decide about the following three key questions:

1. Which yard spaces are for people? Think about seating areas, pathways, recreational uses. Check actual dimensions. Pace off the spaces in your yard, take measurements, and transfer the space to your yard map. The last thing you want to do is add plants and then find them in the way of your personal space. Sketch those personal spaces onto your map.

2. Given the space remaining, where can you add vegetation? Can you increase the density in already-planted areas? Can you expand or add to already-planted areas? How much lawn are you willing to give up? Mark the areas where you can accommodate new plants—singles, small clusters, or groves.

3. Are there unique needs that you hope to meet? Do you need a living privacy fence? Will a strategically placed shrub or tree help block a view or hide an eyesore? Do you want a patio border or a screen beneath an elevated deck? Add such notations to a sticky note and post it on your map as a reminder.

The best deciduous tree for supporting bugs for birds is oak, this one in bloom attracting a foraging Tufted Titmouse.

Planning for a Tree or Two or More

Once you have identified space for new plants, think about what kinds of plants can go where— trees, shrubs, vines, and perennials. Because of their size, let's start with trees. Don't be concerned yet about what kind of trees. Think only about where you have space for and prefer to locate a tree, or trees. So:

> Where can you add a tree?
>
> How large a tree can the space accommodate?
>
> Can you add more than one tree?
>
> How many can you add?
>
> Are there size limits on additional trees?
>
> What birdscaping assets should trees add to your yard—missing food, shelter, nesting?

Consider: Trees anchor landscapes. Their height lets them serve as a backdrop for everything else. They draw the eye and establish sight lines for your property.

Consider: Where do you want the anchor? Several trees alongside or planted diagonally toward the house enhance a curbside view. Trees nearer the curb set up a backdrop for the view from inside your home, perhaps adding a note of privacy. Generally avoid the middle-of-the-front-yard tree, as that positioning limits what else you can do aesthetically with your landscaping.

Consider: Not every tree is a towering giant. Smaller trees can add to the biodiversity without going out of bounds. Later, we'll offer suggestions for trees of many sizes. So if space allows for only one maxi tree, perhaps plan for two or three or more mid-sized or even mini trees. Even dwarf trees in a rock garden add to the biodiversity.

Consider: How will the tree(s) look from your windows? Since you're planting to host birds, you'll want to be able to see those birds from the comfort of your indoor space, especially the space from which you'll most likely enjoy sitting and watching.

Consider: What limits do you have on tree placement? Some rules apply:

> Don't plant trees under utility lines or where their mature limbs will reach into utility lines.

> Don't plant trees so close to a building that mature tree limbs overarch the structure, perhaps damaging the roof.

> Don't plant trees directly on property lines, thus intruding into your neighbor's space and giving rise to potential arguments over pruning.

Revise your yard-map plan accordingly, marking the location for a tree or for multiple trees. Make a note about any necessary size limits.

Planning for Shrubs

Next, consider how many shrubs you can add to your available space:

> Where can you add some shrubs, preferably at least four?

> Can you add more than four?

> Are there size limits on any of the shrubs—either height or spread?

> How much space can you devote to additional shrubs?

> What birdscaping assets do you hope to add with shrubs—food, shelter, nesting?

While trees provide the landscape anchor, shrubs and tall understory plants flesh it out. They're the background fillers. Or in a pots-and-patio garden

Among the many birds that love flowering dogwood berries (*Cornus florida*), this male Northern Cardinal visits the tree daily for its lipid-rich fruits. Flowering dogwood stays small enough to grace a mini yard.

or mini yard, shrubs, rather than trees, may be your anchors. Later, we'll offer suggestions for shrubs that are actually dwarf cultivars of native trees. They carry some of the same benefits for birds as do their larger standards. You'll be feeding birds nearly as effectively as your friends with super-sized yards—you'll just do it on a smaller scale. Think of it this way: If you could somehow arrange the surface of a shrub on flat ground, it would take up considerable space. The more shrubs, the more space. All of that space offers habitat—and feeding opportunities for birds. See what I mean?

Given shrubs' relatively small size, and given the many kinds of shrubs available, they can serve a surprising number of purposes in your yard and landscape. Here are a few ideas that may trigger yet more ideas for ways in which shrubs can add pizzazz to the yard while drawing birds into your habitat:

Shrubs in corners: Corners are usually abundant across landscaping, and shrubs can soften both inside and outside corners and enhance architectural design. House footprints often have one or more inside corners. Or where sidewalk meets driveway, where sidewalk meets house, where driveway meets house, where sidewalk meets street, or where patio joins house. Or property-border corners, of which most of us have at least four. You get the idea. Shrubs tend to fit nicely into these niches.

Shrubs for privacy: Evergreen or semievergreen shrubs especially work well strategically placed along property lines to establish privacy, such as aligned with windows or doors that give passersby or neighbors a direct eye's view into your personal space. Shrubs around the pool or patio can also serve to block outsiders' views.

Shrubs for hedges: Depending on their height, hedges can act as low living fences or tall privacy screens. Most native shrubs can be pruned, but consider the shrubs' typical growth patterns if pruning is your intent.

Shrubs for borders: To edge an area within the yard, to accent an architectural feature, or to border a sidewalk, driveway, or property line, shrubs—pruned or not—add to the aesthetics of the landscape.

Shrubs in cottage gardens: Since most cottage gardens would be monotonous with nothing more than same-height perennials, shrubs add the texture, bulk, and height. Whether the cottage-style garden fronts the house, establishes curb appeal, marks the property boundary, hugs the side yard, or edges the backyard, shrubs accent the space. Accents may serve as garden bookends, as a central attention-getter, as asymmetrical focal points, as dense background, or, given a mini-sized shrub, as a garden's front border.

Shrubs as formal symmetry: Although most native shrubs listed here don't take kindly to meticulously pruned box or meatball shapes, they can take on a formality in their natural shape, serving as borders along sidewalks, around patches of perennials, or along boundaries.

Shrubs as foundation gardens: Clusters of shrubs arrayed along house foundations not only cover any unattractive bare foundation structure, but also soften the lines where house meets ground. Shrubs can accent doorways, emphasize window structures, parallel upright features like outside chimney structures, or surround porches or patios. In such cases, the shrubs themselves and by themselves become the garden, rather than accenting a garden of perennials.

Shrubs for concealment: Sometimes an annoying but permanent yard feature needs a cover-up. Trash bins, a neighbor's unsightly shed, or a utility structure may need to disappear from your dining-room view. Shrubs to the rescue!

Shrubs as feature specimens: Many native shrubs stand alone for their lovely flowers against striking foliage followed by abundant berries. Planting in clusters dramatizes their features, adding interest to the yard.

Shrubs for interest: Shrubs often serve to add height to a series of perennial plantings or to vary the topography of an otherwise flat surface.

Okay, we've suggested 10 categorical uses for shrubs in your landscape, and most likely these suggestions triggered additional ideas for your specific situation. Consider these many options for shrub purpose and placement. It's unlikely birds will care where you plant those berry-producing shrubs or tuck in those sheltering nest sites, so let the shrubs serve you as well as the birds. Mark your yard map now to identify places where you want to plant shrubs—preferably four of them, one for each season.

Planning for Vines
A vine is actually a unique shrub, a multi-stemmed woody plant that has really, really, really long stems. A vine adds a note of height to virtually any yard, so consider:

Do you have space suitable for a vine's support structure?

Do you have space for more than one such structure, perhaps of a different shape or size?

What birdscaping assets should the vine(s) add to your yard—food, shelter, nesting?

Across my yard, I've trained vines to climb fences, wind around free-standing trellises and posts, drape across a pergola, or hang on decaying tree snags. They're all bird magnets!

Vines also add drama to the smallest spaces, including pots-and-patio gardens, adding significant bird-friendly habitat to limited space

The orange-blossomed crossvine (*Bignonia capreolata*), twining up its trellis, makes a perfect nest site for a variety of songbirds, including a Northern Cardinal with three eggs in her nest. Note in the background the trellis's sturdy 4-inch-square support post.

and adding vertical pizzazz to otherwise flapjack flat. One of my friends often speaks about the hummingbirds that visit his trumpet vine (*Campsis radicans*), twining on a trellis alongside his tiny patio—in downtown Atlanta. His experience proves once again that vines offer a great means for expanding surface habitat, including especially nectar, nesting, and shelter. Of course, adding height to any space dramatically increases habitat square footage.

Still, some considerations are in order:

Consider: On what structure will the vine twine its way up? Planting a vine requires some sort of sturdy, long-lasting support. When planting time comes, we'll talk about how to choose a support.

Consider: What size structure will your space allow? While vines can be regularly and readily pruned to keep them small, the idea of a bird-friendly vine is one that is dense and bushy and sports abundant vegetation.

Consider: Where in your landscape does a vine best fit? A vine can become a landscape feature, perhaps overarching a sidewalk, as part of your curb appeal, at a doorway, or over a pergola, or even be a focal point in the yard or garden, perhaps adjoining a patio, bookending a deck, climbing across a balcony rail, or framing a water feature.

Consider: Sometimes vines serve well as ground covers, climbing over rocks or perhaps covering an eyesore.

On your yard map, sketch in the footprint of a vine and its support structure.

Planning for Perennials

To add color and provide birds with seeds and nectar, perennials fill the bill. They work well tucked in among other kinds of vegetation or in stand-alone beds, perhaps as yard features, borders, or accents. Consult your yard map to answer the following:

> How much space do you want to fill with perennials?
>
> Do you have space for washes of plants rather than sets of twos and threes?
>
> Will you add perennials in pots?
>
> Will you have space for clumps of ornamental perennial grass?
>
> What birdscaping assets do you hope to add using perennials—seed, nectar, shelter?

On your map, designate where you plan to add perennials.

Planning for Water

Water. It's that fourth mandatory element of good habitat, the elements that also include food, shelter, and places to raise young. Just as you and I don't sit down to a meal without something to drink, so birds need something to drink to accompany the buffet you'll be offering in your yard's ultimate bird feeder. If you live on a waterfront lot, or your neighbor has a lake or pond, or a stream meanders through your neighborhood,

or some other natural water source exists nearby, you're home free. You have a great asset. Thus, providing water in your own space is not essential.

On the other hand, if there is no nearby natural water source—or if you'd just like to provide water for the enjoyment of luring birds in to drink and bathe—now's the time to plan.

Whether you choose to mount your birdbath on a pedestal, hang it from a hook, or situate it on the ground, consider the birds' safety as they drink and bathe. As a general rule of thumb, birds should find safe shelter no more than 20 feet from a bath. I've noticed that when given a choice, birds will alight on a closer shelter. However, shrubs too close, grass clumps too tall, or perennial clusters too dense can all give predators a place to hide and make a sneak attack on an unsuspecting bird at the bath. So here are suggestions:

> Place a birdbath or other water feature where you can enjoy watching from your favorite window. Not only does that placement enhance your pleasure, but you'll also tune in to potential problems: soiled water, low water, overarching vegetation, or any other dangers birds might face while enjoying a sip and a splash.
>
> Place a birdbath near vegetation, allowing bathing birds to quickly and readily flee danger and dash to a safe place to preen.
>
> Remove dense, adjoining ground-level vegetation that might hide marauding predators.

While it's relatively simple to situate a small birdbath amid the landscape, if you're thinking something bigger—a water feature complete with a recirculating pump or a four-season bubbling rock, for instance—add the dimensional

Amid deep snow, six Mourning Doves enjoy a drink at a heated bubbling rock, a benefit that saves birds significant energy during trying times.

footprint sketch of that feature to your yard map. By locating it now, you'll know to plan around the water feature if you choose to landscape before you have the time, money, or energy to actually install it.

In Chapter 8 we'll provide more details about recommended water features and suggest plants suitable for landscaping both waterfronts and water features.

THE NEXT STEPS

Wow! Your plan is complete. Now all you have to do is plant, right?

Well, in part. But what exactly do you plant? Even dedicated folks, having decided to "go native," often throw up their hands in dismay at the overwhelming number of native-plant choices. Every source, either in print or online, lists a vast array of native plants, all reportedly fine choices, all touted as "bird magnets"—and mostly only perennials. But just what do these sources mean by "bird magnet"? Will any "bird magnet" draw birds in during four seasons? Will the magnet serve up seeds? Nectar? Berries? Does it host bugs? Provide winter shelter? Nest sites? Amid all the confusion, how does a responsible landowner pick from the array so that his or her yard offers the best possible balance of bird habitat—from berries to bugs, from nectar to nesting, from shelter to seeds, from spring through summer into fall and winter?

Every successful birdscape begins with a plan. You have that. But two key words direct the implementation of the plan: baby steps. So while

Anything—tree, shrub, perennial, or vine—that blooms and attracts bees will likely attract Summer Tanagers in search of their favorite food. This female, bee in beak, smashed the stinger before swallowing her prize.

you now have an inventory and analysis of your yard as well as a plan to fill in what's missing, you'll do well to begin by choosing only one portion of your yard to initiate your native-plant effort. If, for instance, you fear making mistakes that will be detrimental to your home's curb appeal, start with the back or side yard. Everyone learns by doing. Planting in only one area helps you focus on a single set of soil and light conditions. The south side, for instance, unless already shaded by vegetation or structures, will get direct sun and likely exhibit arid conditions. What you plant in full sun on the south side of your house will be different, for instance, from what you plant in full shade on the north side. Don't make life complicated; begin with a single set of conditions, tackling only one part at a time.

Comfort yourself with this thought: Yards and gardens are almost always works in progress. We add and subtract. We substitute with new ideas and improved plans. Just because you put in a set of native plantings on one side of your house doesn't mean it's a permanent set and forever unchangeable. I have a friend who always jokes about adding any new plant to her yard. She says, "Well, it doesn't really matter where I plant it because I'll move it again anyway." It's okay to make changes if your first effort isn't your best. We've all done it. Trust me on that one.

Comfort yourself too with this thought: The same individual plants need not serve you forever. Think of plants as crops: Some of them grow and mature and then fade. Some plants, like people, simply have a shorter life than others. Some perennials may lose their luster after four or five years. Some shrubs may max out in 20 years, their attractiveness spent. It's okay to replace the crop, even if you replant with the same species, one showing more vigor and vibrancy in its youth.

The Five-Step Plan

With that in mind, you're ready to get going with this simple Five-Step Plan. It lets you add an array of natives, a few at a time, in appropriate proportions, and helps you choose what's right where you live. Most of all, the plan helps you get the birdscape done, from start to finish. Here's our plan for implementing your plan—and we devote a full chapter to completing each step.

> **Step 1:** Choose a tree. Or two. Or three. We'll tell you which ones are best. And why.
>
> **Step 2:** Choose a shrub (including, perhaps, a vine) for each season. We'll show you how to choose, season by season.
>
> **Step 3:** Choose perennials (including, perhaps, ornamental grasses and ferns)— three each of six flowering species. We'll guide you through the maze of options.
>
> **Step 4:** Add water. We'll recommend successful water features as well as native plants that like wet feet, growing along or in the water.
>
> **Step 5:** Put the plan in action. We'll smooth the way to getting the deed done, from buying to planting to adding finishing touches.

With your yard map in hand, your analysis complete, you're ready to go. Step 1 begins now.

Prior to 1492, the eastern US was heavily forested, supporting all forms of wildlife. Now, with much habitat disrupted and lost, birds suffer, some dramatically so.

"Forests precede civilizations; deserts follow."

—UNKNOWN

"The best time to plant a tree is 20 years ago. The second best time is now."

—DAMBISA MOYO, Zambian economist

Chapter 5
CHOOSING NATIVE TREES

Like people, not all birds like the same foods or prefer the same restaurants. You know the score: A wide range of restaurants attracts a wide range of diners. If folks find they enjoy the area for other reasons—good housing, good schools, suitable shops, adequate services—they may move in.

Likewise, a wide range of vegetation attracts a wide range of birds. If birds find they enjoy the area for other reasons—good shelter, good nest

sites, suitable nesting materials, adequate water—they may move in. Trees help provide that wide range of food, not only for the insects trees support or the seeds and berries they produce, but by their height. As crazy as it may sound, some birds simply prefer to hang out, forage, and nest in high canopy. They just like it up there, safe from ground-level predators and away from ground-feeding species. Perhaps reduced competition at the high-rise buffet makes more pleasant—and maybe more nutritious—avian dining. But we mere humans have to crane our necks something fierce to see them up there.

Here's another way to think about how trees affect your birdscape. Try to imagine the surface of a tree spread flat across the ground. For instance, a tree 50 feet tall and 20 feet in diameter, spread across the ground, would cover almost 3,800 square feet! That means, in essence, that if you have a quarter-acre lot (10,890 square feet), that tree increases surface habitat by about one-third! Of course, birds forage all through the tree, not just on the surface; but still, that's one-third additional surface area for birds to forage, find insects, nest, and find shelter. What a terrific—and inexpensive—way to increase your space, by going up, not out. No further land purchase, no legal fees, no insurance premium increase, and no additional taxes!

LIFE CYCLE

The natural cycle of a tree reaching old growth to death and its ultimate decay also dramatically impacts birds. To put it simply, trees introduce and continue to host a variety of micro biomasses. The older a tree gets, the more it changes, resulting in more birds, more bird droppings, more insect masses, more cover, more nesting. Then as the tree ages, still more insects find homes in the trunk and the tree becomes its own ecosystem. What a wonderful addition to your bird habitat!

Even when trees suffer damage or ultimately die, they continue to serve Mother Nature's plan, becoming her nursery and grocery store—a nursery for bug babies and a grocery store for birds that eat the bugs in all their forms. A sketchy description of how it all works goes something like this:

Insects such as long-horned beetles and round-headed, metallic, and other borers tuck their eggs in amid the crevices of the now-decaying bark. As the larvae develop, they chew tunnels under the bark and drill holes into the heartwood. Woodpeckers, keenly equipped to hear the larvae munching their way through the tree, zero in on the activity, and with their exceedingly long tongues, enjoy a larvae lunch. Of course, many larvae—well, probably most larvae—escape the woodpeckers' attack, and they continue with their tunneling activities. As they bore, they pack tunnels with frass, otherwise known as caterpillar poop. (There's a winning word for your next Scrabble game!) Because caterpillars do nothing other than eat and poop, the frass is ultimately pushed out of the tunnels, sometimes "raining"

A Red-headed Woodpecker forages on a decaying tree trunk, the frass visible in the wrinkles of the bark.

down from dead tree branches. What doesn't rain down often accumulates on bark, appearing as a sawdust-like "filler" in the wrinkles of the bark's surface.

But wait! Don't wrinkle your nose. It's a good thing! The frass provides massive nutrients to the ground below, enriching the soil for seedlings that may sprout from the now-dead tree—or, for that matter, seedlings from anything else. From the dead and dying, new vegetation is fertilized to provide for the next generation. Isn't that another amazing natural cycle!

And still the cycle goes on. Beetles, which are not only the most numerous species of insects, but also the most widespread among deadwood inhabitants, can now deposit their eggs in the crumbling deadwood, availing themselves of the ready passageways. Simultaneously, wild bees, wasps, and various fly and midge maggots dine on the fungi and bacteria that are "eating" on the deadwood. In turn, the beetles, wasps, and maggots create additional tasty meals for yet more and bigger bugs—all of them, large and small, prime targets for foraging birds. The onetime vital shade tree, now dead and decaying. becomes one-stop shopping for insect-hunting woodpeckers, nuthatches, creepers, and the like.

Incidentally, many beetles are tree-specific scavengers, so what joins the avian menu for decaying oaks, for instance, will be different from those on the menu for decaying pines or birches.

Once the beetles move in, the ants aren't far behind, surely to the delight of Northern Flickers that consider ants the equivalent of filet mignon. Meanwhile, wood-boring caterpillars, the immature stages of several kinds of moths (although the moths are rarely seen), may show up as well. Ah, talk about top-of-the-line baby food for all those nestlings!

As decay advances, woodpeckers will have hammered out cavities, nested, and left the single-use nurseries up for grabs by other creatures, including other cavity-loving birds that can't chisel out their own—like chickadees, titmice, bluebirds, Wood Ducks, Screech Owls, and Great-crested Flycatchers. Other critters may also move in to abandoned woodpecker sites, including squirrels and perhaps even bats. Eventually, when the trunk collapses (or when you leave a log lying in some out-of-the-way place), it deteriorates to become the home for newts, salamanders, toads, lizards, and others using it for cover and hibernation. Still more diversity for the yard!

Sadly, chain-saw-happy folks tend to disrupt Mother Nature's clever cycle and remove such trees, even when they pose no danger to anyone or anything. Instead, should you face such a situation, consider cutting the tree to a snag, leaving the trunk and perhaps a few limbs to incorporate the nursery and grocery store into your own yard. That's what we did at our house, and what a delight the old snag has become! All seven of our area woodpeckers as well as White-breasted Nuthatches and Brown Creepers make routine visits to the snag, many of them daily.

When a decaying 50-year-old tulip tree (*Liriodendron*) threatened the house, the tree guys cut only the parts that caused risk and girdled the trunk to prevent sprouting. In less than a year, the snag attracted woodpeckers and nuthatches daily, proving the tree's value as Mother Nature's nursery and grocery store.

Advantages of Trees

Trees serve multiple advantages for people, too. Their leafy canopies provide shade, reduce air-conditioning bills, filter harsh sunlight streaming in windows, clean pollutants from the air, turn carbon dioxide into oxygen, and slow runoff, as leaves hold rainwater long after raindrops cease to fall. Their roots stabilize topsoil. A reasonably well-placed tree increases property value, enhances neighborhood biodiversity, and aids privacy. Oh, and did I mention? Trees serve as magnificent bird feeders.

So as you situate native trees to serve your birds, locate them to also benefit you and your home. Evergreens anywhere shelter birds, but those arrayed on the north and west sides of your home cut your heating and cooling bills, standing as windbreaks from prevailing northerly and westerly winter winds, and offering shade against summer's heat. Likewise, deciduous trees anywhere feed and shelter birds in summer; but situated on the east and south sides of your home, they bestow summer shade, cutting air-conditioning bills, yet still allow weak winter sun shining through bare limbs to reduce maybe at least by a smidgen the winter heating bills.

So with that little bit of tree biology, let's get started with Step 1 of the Five-Step Plan.

Step 1: Choose a tree. Or two. Or more.

Unless trees are already a part of your landscape, your most important decision will be choosing a tree or two or more. Even if your landscape already includes a tree or more, if an oak is not among them, you may want to consider an addition.

That being said, begin developing your planting plan by choosing a tree from among the lists in this chapter. Trees add more habitat in a single specimen than anything else you can plant. A tree will also be the largest landscape piece in your yard, so it should be selected with care. Unless

Leaf litter, especially oak, holds the key to winter survival for many birds, including White-throated Sparrows.

yours is a pots-and-patio garden, choose at least one tree for your site. For the best bird-friendly habitat, *if you can plant only one tree, make that single choice some kind of oak*. If yours is a mini yard, consider the small oaks on the list. There's good reason for my making such a strong assertion. We'll explain shortly. Now, though, let's think about some issues you should consider in choosing the tree or trees right for your yard.

CHOOSING THE RIGHT TREE(S)

As anchors for most landscaping, tree choices merit considerable attention. Trees aren't something you plant on a whim. Most trees are big, so only a few—maybe only one—can grow successfully in a small yard. Trees are also generally slow-growing, relatively long-lived, and, once mature, not easily removed. So choosing the right tree for the right location in the right soil under the right growing conditions that will also feed the birds—well, it requires making a commitment. And it takes a bit of homework.

We've done much of the homework for you, so your choices will be more easily made—whether yours is a pots-and-patio garden, a mini yard, a mid-sized yard, or a super-sized yard.

Consider your situation.

If you've recently moved into a new home and are starting with a blank landscape canvas, trees are the initial plantings. Or instead, you may live where at least some landscaping is already deeply rooted, maybe even fully established, but may now be looking to add or substitute native plants in order to build a better birdscape. Should one of the changes be the addition of a native tree?

One of my favorite mantras bears repeating: If you're still mowing lawn, you have room to plant. That may well include planting one or more additional trees in an already landscaped plot. Some trees, for instance, because of their slow growth or compact size, could almost pass as shrubs. They're not 100-foot giants that shade the entire backyard. In fact, they may be understory trees like dogwoods or redbuds that prefer to grow under those giants—a clever way to expand your yard's biodiversity. In that case, we may have options for you that will serve both you and the birds—and serve well!

Review Your Neighborhood Survey

Let's say you have the necessary space to add a tree or two or three either to a blank-canvas yard or to improve the diversity of vegetation in your already partially planted space. Begin the decision-making process by referring to your completed yard map, looking especially at what's around the neighborhood. If the folks two doors down have red maples, give serious thought to something different, whether it be deciduous or evergreen. If the folks across the road have several American holly trees, consider an alternate berry-producing choice. Birds know no human-recognized boundaries, so again, diversity applies to the neighborhood as well as to your yard. You know the score: The more diverse the

Neighborhood with Poor Tree Diversity

12 houses, 12 trees
3 species of trees
1 species native

Neighborhood with Rich Tree Diversity

12 houses, 30 trees
15 species of trees
12 species native

neighborhood plantings, the more diverse the birds that live there. Compare the following two illustrations that represent some suburban neighborhoods and how the lack of diversity in such neighborhoods can be dramatically improved.

Obviously, however, house size relative to lot size typically puts constraints on landscape choices, especially when it comes to trees, and that may ultimately be the determining factor in your choice(s).

Even the most finicky among us, however, will find many choices among the following selections, each of which passes muster for all three of these requirements:

1. They must be natives, native varieties, or native cultivars.
2. They must provide at least one food source for birds.
3. They must be suitable for attractive landscaping.

Unless your neighborhood hosts a dramatically lopsided array of deciduous over evergreen trees or vice-versa, you'll do well to consider both

Oaks (*Quercus* spp.) support more *Lepidoptera* species than any other kind of tree; so resident and migrant birds alike, including this Northern Parula, often forage for bugs among the leaves.

Among Trees, What's the Difference between a VARIETY and a CULTIVAR?

*I*n Chapter 3 we differentiated between standard plants and those called "varieties" and "cultivated varieties," or "cultivars," and we ranked them for their attractiveness to birds. Those definitions—and rankings of poor, good, better, best—apply equally to trees.

Maybe the differences sound a bit nitpicky, but the pickiness helps clarify why varieties and cultivars often make perfectly good sense in a native birdscape. Horticulturalists and biologists explain that a cultivated change in characteristics like shape or autumn leaf color, for instance, does not alter the genotype for insect hosting. Since a cultivar carries the same chemical composition as the standard species, insects find cultivars as suitable as host plants as they do the standard. From a bird lover's perspective, then, feel comfortable choosing a standard (best choice), a variety (better choice), or a cultivar (good choice) that best suits your landscaping needs.

Berry production, however, might be a different story. Some native trees (and shrubs, for that matter) cultivated for more compact size, for example, may also produce far fewer berries than do the standard. It's worth checking before you buy.

Hybrids are definitely a different story, though, and rank poor for providing insect food for birds. Probably better to skip them if you're going native. Having said that, I would be remiss if I did not point out that hybrid trees do often occur naturally. More on that later.

deciduous and evergreen trees for your birdscape. But again, if you have space or the budget for only one, choose a deciduous tree and make it an oak.

If your space is mid-sized or super-sized, and if budget permits, choose two trees. Choose one deciduous tree, preferably some kind of oak, and then make the other choice evergreen.

If your space is large and sparsely planted—or if you're starting with a blank landscape canvas—if budget permits, choose three trees. Select a towering oak, pick an evergreen, and then add another deciduous species, one other than oak.

A Dark-eyed Junco finds shelter—a bit of warmth from a weak sun and protection from the wind—amid snow-covered branches of a hemlock tree (*Tsuga canadensis*).

Finally, given space, choose several small trees, perhaps planted in a cluster, for added benefits to your birdscape.

Making the Choice(s)

Here's how to choose, no matter the size of your yard or garden:

Consider: With your yard map in hand, which tree—or which kinds of trees—are absent from your yard and neighborhood? Is there an absence of oak? Are there no evergreens? Is there a dearth of native trees? The species you add will further the entire area's biodiversity; and the more diverse the vegetation, the more diverse the bird populations. But you know that.

Consider: What is your planting zone? Choose a tree that will thrive in your zone. To find your zone, check online at http://planthardiness.ars.usda.gov.

Consider: What are your soil conditions? Sandy? Clayey? Acidic? Wet? Arid? Not all trees native to your state will grow well in your bioregion or specific location. Check before you buy. If you have questions, consult your local arborist or county extension agent.

Consider: What is the likely mature size of the tree, both height and spread? A 5-foot sapling in a 3-gallon pot can expand into an incredible 80-foot tree shading a 50-foot spread at maturity. Allow for growing needs. Check your yard map to be sure your choice fits your space.

Consider: What size limits do you have for trees in your yard? If yours is a pots-and-patio garden, you'll of course look to container-growing dwarfs. For either the pots-and-patio garden or a mini yard, search the special lists for micro species found on pages 86, 95–97, and 104–6. And if yours is a super-sized yard, for sure choose at least one oak. It's the super-sized-quality bird feeder. Then, given acreage, fill in with a mix of

More than 25 species of birds and wildlife feed on the seeds of sweetgum (*Liquidambar styraciflua*), a tree with lovely autumn foliage and dramatic "gumballs."

bird-friendly deciduous and coniferous/other evergreen trees.

Consider: What do you most enjoy about trees? If you love autumn color, choose a deciduous tree recognized for its foliage. If you object to falling leaves, focus on evergreen trees.

To make your final choices, consult this chapter's lists of oaks, other deciduous, and evergreen trees. And remember that for mini yards, peruse the list of micro choices.

With these generalities in mind, to help you make your final choices, let's zero in on deciduous trees. Then we'll turn our attention to coniferous and other evergreen trees.

DECIDUOUS TREES

Deciduous trees are those that lose their leaves in winter. Come spring, when they again leaf out, deciduous trees also bloom. The blossoms may be showy or so inconspicuous that you miss them entirely. Resulting seeds may also be plentiful or nearly unnoticeable. Both features, flowers and seeds, have a certain effect on a deciduous tree's value to birds. Mostly, though, the value of trees in birdscaping is all about bugs.

Aside from birdscaping, from a homeowner/landscaper perspective, deciduous tree choice is typically based on the tree's growth pattern, shape, and size; leaf shape and size; blossoms, fruits, or cones; and/or fall foliage. Or folks may nix certain trees for some of the same reasons—too slow-growing, too susceptible to wind damage, too irregularly shaped, leaves too large, too few showy blossoms, too many cones, too little autumn splendor.

Oak: King of Deciduous

For attracting birds, oak trees rank so high—far and above any other tree species, deciduous or evergreen—that they merit their own section here among deciduous trees. And there's good reason: Virtually all kinds of oaks—ones native to your area—host a higher number of insect species than any other native tree.

About 25 years ago, I remember posting a query to a listserv to which hundreds of birders subscribed. My question was simple and straightforward: In what kind of tree or shrub do you typically find the most birds? The overwhelming response was unwavering: oak. Not

Acorn at the ready, a male Red-bellied Woodpecker prepares to cache his treasure, bracing for leaner times. Many bird species depend on oak mast for winter nutrition.

Red Oak OR White Oak?

The *Quercus* family includes two groups of oaks, designated as red oaks and white oaks. To compound the confusion, the red oak group is sometimes referred to as the black oak group. Go figure. But the real concern for birdscaping is obvious: Does it matter which you plant? In terms of their respective support for bugs in all forms, probably not. But here are some general comparisons of the two:

Red oak leaves are pointed. Typically red oaks produce smaller, lighter acorns than do white oaks, but production occurs only every other year. In terms of nourishment, however, red oak acorns contain more protein, fat, and calories than white oak acorns. On the flip side, red oak acorns are also higher in fiber and tannins, and that makes them harder to digest. As a result, red oak acorns are generally less desirable to animals.

White oak leaves are rounded. Typically, white oaks produce fairly large, heavy acorns and do so every year. Although white oak acorns contain less protein, fat, and calories than do red oak acorns, because the white oak acorns are easier to digest, they tend to be consumed more regularly by wildlife than red oak acorns.

About the Lists

*T*he tree lists in this chapter represent limited selections. Since the purpose of this book is to help readers narrow the hundreds of choices to the most suitable ones, the trees in this chapter's lists are restricted by the following four criteria:

1. The selected trees are, according to the United States Department of Agriculture Plant Database (online at www.plants.usda.gov), native to states listed. Note, however, that while a plant may be native in your state, it may not be native to every part of your state and certainly not to every eco-region. The USDA Plant Database maps provide county-by-county details.
2. The selected trees are attractive to birds for multiple reasons, meeting their needs for food, shelter, and/or nesting.
3. The selected trees are easily grown, well behaved, and suitable for landscaping in various settings, as described.
4. The selected trees are more readily available than other, perhaps similar, natives.
5. The selected trees grow most successfully when planted in their respective designated hardiness zones. To find your zone, check online at http://planthardiness.ars.usda.gov/.

When making your choices, consider soil texture, moisture, slope, and exposure to light. Your planting zone and eco-region combined will determine suitable growing conditions in your yard.

Always plant according to mature plant size relative to available space. Estimated height and spread sizes shown here are for mature trees, meaning, of course, that full size could be 30 years or more down the road. For advice specific to your locale, consult your local arborist.

only did the majority of responders name oak as their first target site for seeing birds, but second-place targets were so scattered that responders had no clear second choice. At the time, I don't think any of us understood exactly why, and there was no published data to explain.

We just knew birds foraged in oaks. Often. And regularly.

Our observations were recently confirmed by research published by Douglas Tallamy, which shows that a mature oak may host as many as 530 or so *Lepidoptera* insect species while, by comparison, an introduced Asian ginkgo tree (*Ginkgo biloba*) may host only three. If to feed the birds we must first feed the bugs, it's fairly obvious why oaks carry such importance in developing superior birdscaping in your yard.

Almost all birds find something attractive about oaks, from Northern Cardinals to the 40-something wood warblers, from every woodpecker species to nuthatches. Blue Jays and Red-bellied Woodpeckers carry off and cache the acorns; Cedar Waxwings and orioles eat the buds; migrating warblers feast on insects attracted by oaks' early blossoms; and virtually every songbird turns to oaks for the bugs to feed their babies. Once oaks have reached maturity, hawks find them suitable for nesting; and in the right location, Bald Eagles may raise their families in the extended, spreading arms of a massive old oak—although not likely in your yard!

Oaks for Yards of All Sizes

About 70 species of oak are native to the US. Mostly, oaks are big trees—tall, wide, sturdy, and handsome. If you have a mid-sized or super-sized yard, you'll find one or more oaks a dramatic addition to your landscape. Their spreading branches build a shady parklike yard and, located in the right spot, cast shade on your house. We've chosen 10 of the most landscape-friendly for your consideration.

On the other hand, if yours is a mini yard, you'll most likely want to choose oak cultivars that are narrow, columnar, or even dwarf. We've listed those, too, in the second table.

If you find a native oak species at your local nursery that tickles your fancy but isn't listed here, do the homework before you make the purchase. Check the online USDA Plant Database to learn where the tree is native and what characteristics it has that may help you make an informed decision.

The following 10 native oak species, arranged alphabetically by scientific name, should be the springboard from which to begin your decision-making. Then update your yard map by penciling in the diameter(s) of your chosen tree(s) and identifying it/them by name.

Oaks for Mid-Sized to Super-Sized Yards

COMMON NAME	SCIENTIFIC NAME	COMMENTS	NATIVE, PLANTING ZONES
Oaks	*Quercus* spp.	As genus, most effective deciduous tree species for feeding birds	As specified by species below
Northern white oak	*Q. alba*	Often to 80' tall, up to 80' spread; most widespread species of white oak group; moist, well-drained soil; deep taproot; attractive; commonly cultivated	Eastern US Zones 3–9
Swamp white oak (see also *Q. bicolor* micro cultivar, below)	*Q. bicolor*	To 70' tall, 60' spread; tolerates wet, dry; needs acidic soil; easily transplanted since lacks taproot; commonly cultivated	Eastern US except GA and FL Zones 3–8

COMMON NAME	SCIENTIFIC NAME	COMMENTS	NATIVE, PLANTING ZONES
Southern red oak	Q. falcata	To 90' tall, 50' spread; common in dry to sandy uplands; not commonly cultivated	Eastern US except MN, WI, IA, MI, and east of NY Zones 6–9
Chinkapin oak (white oak group) (see also Q. muehlenbergii micro cultivar, below)	Q. muehlenbergii	40–50' tall, 50–70' spread; deep taproot; tolerant of various soils and settings	Eastern US except NH and ME Zones 5–7
Pin oak (red oak group) (see also Q. palustris micro cultivar, below)	Q. palustris	50–70' tall, 40–60' spread; low maintenance; very commonly cultivated; choose other species to positively impact diversity	Eastern US except MN, LA, AL, FL, SC, VT, and NH Zones 4–8
Willow oak (red oak group)	Q. phellos	40–75' tall, 25–50' spread; tough tree adapted to urban conditions; commonly cultivated in yards and towns	Eastern US except MN, WI, IA, IN, WV, and east of NY Zones 5–9
Northern red oak	Q. rubra	50–75' tall, 50–75' spread; common, widespread; fast-growing, stately; commonly cultivated	Eastern US except FL Zones 4–8
Shumard oak (red oak group)	Q. shumardii	40–60' tall, 30–40' spread; fast-growing, adaptable, drought resistant, withstands short-term flooding; uncommon in cultivation	Eastern half US except MN, WI, IA, and east of NY Zones 5–9
Black oak (red oak group)	Q. velutina	50–60' tall, 50–60' spread; common in well-drained, mesic to dry soils; uncommon in cultivation	Eastern US Zones 3–9
Live oak (white oak group)	Q. virginiana	40–80' tall; 60–100' spread; from upland open woods to low wetland edges, including salt-marsh edges; common in cultivation; can be evergreen in southernmost locations	Coastal states from NC through LA Zones 8–10

Mini-Yard Alternatives for Oaks

As noted earlier, oaks are so important for bird habitat that, if you can plant only one tree, it should be some kind of oak. For smaller yards—or even for large yards in which you want a variety of oak species near the house—consider one of the following "micro" cultivars. These trees may reach significant height, but their spread is small.

Oak Micro Cultivars for Mini Yards

COMMON NAME	SCIENTIFIC NAME	COMMENTS	NATIVE, PLANTING ZONES
Swamp white oak 'Bonnie and Mike' ('Beacon')	*Q. bicolor* 'Bonnie and Mike'	40' tall, 15' spread; tightly columnar; urban adaptable; dense green foliage, good fall yellow color	Cultivar Zones 3–8
Chinkapin oak 'Prairie Pioneer' (white oak group)	*Q. muehlenbergii* 'Prairie Pioneer'	Dwarf, 24–28' tall, 16–24' spread; oval shape; in spring, covered in small yellow drooping flower spikes; extremely cold tolerant; grows best in rich, well-drained soil in full sun	Dwarf cultivar Zones 5–7
Pin oak 'Green Pillar' (Pringreen) (red oak group)	*Q. palustris* 'Pringreen'	Over time can reach 50' tall, 12–15' spread; columnar tree with nearly vertical branches; ½" oval acorns; scarlet red foliage in fall	Variety Zones 4–8

Thus, they will fit readily into narrow spaces common among suburban lots.

More Deciduous Trees

If limited space or budget restricts you to a single tree, we've already suggested that you aim for oak. However, since no one wants a monoculture of oaks in the yard or neighborhood, let's take a look at other really good deciduous insect hosts. The two deciduous tree species hosting the highest number of insects beyond oaks are black cherry (*Prunus* spp.) and willows (*Salix* spp.). These and other excellent bird-friendly trees are described here.

Wild Black Cherry

A migrant bird magnet with a delightful double whammy, wild black cherry opens in spring with its sweet, very early blossoms serving flocks of insects that must look like a royal feast to birds. I've had as many as eight warbler species simultaneously foraging through our fragrant wild black cherry branches. That alone makes the tree a top contender for a blue ribbon in my yard; but then in midsummer, when the tiny cherries ripen, the second wave of birds flocks in. From the comfort of my lawn chair, I can watch six species of woodpeckers along with jays, cardinals, orioles, waxwings, and finches snacking on dangling berries. Heavily laden branches seem to quiver with activity.

While a wild black cherry tree may not have the graceful elegance for a front-yard specimen, consider it for the back or side yards. And once a wild black cherry produces fruit and birds

A female House Finch feasts on midsummer berries in wild black cherry (*Prunus serotina*).

indulge in the delicacy, you can expect seedlings to sprout where birds have eliminated the seeds. While seedlings tend to come up along fences (because birds were perched there when they pooped), they are easily transplanted during early stages. Share the extras with your friends! Or sell them at the next neighborhood native plant sale.

Willows

Willows are a virtual tie with black cherries when it comes to serving as an insect host. Unfortunately, while willows are fast-growing, they are also somewhat brittle, making them susceptible to splitting from ice or wind. Be warned too that willows most often found in landscapes are almost always nonnative—like weeping willow and white willow, both Asian. So the low blow is that the only truly native willow tree is black willow or the more rangy sand willow. But hooray! Other suitable native willow landscape choices come in the form of shrubs (see more about *Salix* shrubs in Chapter 6, page 129). These small-form willows work well as edging, especially in damp or wet areas.

So whether you choose a tree or a shrub, willows support so many insects that they're virtual meccas for migrating wood warblers—and the wood warblers are hands-down the loveliest eye

Willows (*Salix* spp.) support several *Lepidoptera* species, thus satisfying many birds, like this male Yellow Warbler, a few caterpillars in his bill.

candy for any springtime bird-watcher. Almost all migrants, however, are looking for insects; so beyond warblers, count on also seeing the likes of thrushes, grosbeaks, and vireos. Of course, year-round resident birds like cardinals, chickadees, titmice, and wrens will feast as well. And you'll thrill to the corollary: Because willows are highly attractive to bees, expect to find Summer Tanagers in the area, feasting on them!

And, yes—there's more: Since willows serve as host plants to numerous butterfly species, they support numerous caterpillars that, in turn, serve as top-notch protein sources for birds to feed their babies. That's not to mention the butterflies in your yard, including red-spotted purple, viceroy, eastern tiger swallowtail, and mourning cloak, to name a few. An all-around winner!

Use caution, however, when siting willows. Because of their far-reaching root system, they can crawl their way into drain lines and clog them—never a good situation.

Flowering Dogwood

A trademark of early spring, flowering dogwood blossoms attract insects which, in turn, attract numerous birds, especially migrants. But the real attraction—and action—comes with the dogwood's fall red berries. The lipid-rich berries ripen just in time for southbound migrants to fatten up on the calories.

One day in our yard, Rose-breasted Grosbeaks feeding on our flowering dogwood berries were joined in a breathtaking array by most of the thrush family: American Robin, Eastern Bluebird, Swainson's Thrush, Gray-cheeked Thrush, Hermit Thrush—but, alas, no Veery. Seemed like the thrush family reunion! Woodpeckers, however, more than made up for the missing Veery. Downy, Hairy, Red-bellied, even the Pileated Woodpecker also came to feed, the Pileated's weight pulling branches dangerously low. But

A female Pileated Woodpecker dangles at the end of flowering dogwood twigs (*Cornus florida*) to snatch the nutritiously rich berries.

I certainly didn't mind! Nothing like a Woody Woodpecker–like critter hanging out among the thrushes. It was a crazy day in the yard that I'll never forget—thanks to those flowering dogwood berries.

Boxelder

Among the many maple species, boxelder earns buggy attention from birds. I have no idea how

A male Black-throated Blue Warbler pops up, bug in beak, while foraging in boxelder (*Acer negundo*).

many species of warblers I've watched foraging among boxelder branches, but the short list includes Prothonotary, Black-throated Blue, and Yellow Warblers as well as American Redstarts, all of them gleaning little green caterpillars from among the leaves. When given a chance to join the fray, our Carolina Chickadees, Tufted Titmice, and Carolina Wrens take their more-than-fair share. I can't argue with the fun I've had, although I'd likely not plant the boxelder in my front yard. It tends to be a bit leaning, usually multi-trunked, and wants moist soils. It's most happy near water—stream, pond, or marshy spot—so it would work well if your yard abuts a retention pond or you enjoy the luxury of a waterfront lot.

Red Maple and Sugar Maple

Red maple and sugar maple rank high among homeowners for their lovely autumn foliage, but bugs and birds love them as well. In fact, because maples bloom very early, their blossoms are among the first to feed birds teetering on the edge of survival after winter food supplies have vanished. Since blossoms hold the plant embryo, they carry significant nutrition for starving birds. No sooner than the weather warms, however, maples burst with protein. According to Tallamy's research, maples host 285 species of *Lepidoptera* insects. That means not only do maples host a dandy supply of caterpillars, but the moth and butterfly eggs hidden in the bark feed woodpeckers, nuthatches, and creepers. For your mini yard or even mid-sized yard, look to small cultivars of these handsome trees.

Red Mulberry

Functioning mostly as understory, red mulberry trees prefer some shade, but that doesn't prevent birds from rushing to the early summer fruits. Our mulberry trees boast quite a list of fruit lovers: both Scarlet and Summer Tanagers, all of

With deciduous trees comes the issue of autumn's falling leaves. You're left with the decision: To rake or not to rake.

Here's the deal: In late summer, butterflies, skippers, and moths lay their eggs under leaves and in bark crevices. When leaves fall, Mother Nature intends them to stay on the ground, safely harboring next year's butterfly crop. Raking up all the leaves means disrupting the nursery, destroying eggs and babies. By extension, it's also destroying birds' wintertime protein, a key to their very survival.

In spring, many songbirds also rely on leaves for a portion of their nest construction. You wouldn't want them to come up short on the building materials list and be forced to build elsewhere, would you?

So in the fall, be nice. Leave some leaves. Rake them under the shrubs. Blow them against a back fence. Pile them in a corner. Do it for the butterflies. Do it for the birds.

I rarely manage to sneak more than a few sweet morsels for eating fresh. The birds take all!

Beware, however, there's sometimes confusion between native red mulberry and the Asian white mulberry, an invasive plant common in urban areas. The confusion arises because both plants have red berries—and the two plants often hybridize. But our native so-called red mulberries, when fully ripe and juicy, are dark purple, almost black. Unfortunately, at our house, the birds rarely give the red mulberries time to fully ripen. They're way too eager to lap 'em up!

Southern Bald Cypress

Probably my single favorite native yard tree is southern bald cypress. No, I don't live in a swamp; and it's always a surprise to unknowing folks that bald cypress trees will thrive almost anywhere. They form beautiful pyramidal silhouettes, lovely in the landscape. Birds scour the feather-like deciduous leafy branches for insects in spring, so I've tallied Black-throated Green Warblers, Yellow-throated Warblers, Northern Parulas, Chestnut-sided Warblers, Yellow Warblers,

the thrush family, all of the woodpeckers, Rose-breasted Grosbeaks, Blue Jays, Northern Cardinals, both Baltimore and Orchard Orioles, finches, Gray Catbirds, Northern Mockingbirds—what a list! They barely wait for the berries to ripen, so even though the fruits make great jams and jellies,

A bald cypress tree (*Taxodium distichum*) attracts a fall migrating Magnolia Warbler with its ample supply of bugs.

Tennessee Warblers, Nashville Warblers, White-eyed Vireos—so many spring migrants feeding there. And because cypress trees have "shreddy" fibrous bark, Northern Cardinals in my yard almost always include strips of cypress bark in the foundations of their nests. Oh—and one other tidbit: One tree in particular has become a favorite daytime roost for the neighborhood Barred Owl. Gotta love any tree for that!

American Basswood

American basswood, also called American linden, hosts 150 species of insects, including caterpillars; so with this tree, you can count on butterflies in your yard! Furthermore, linden flowers hum with bees in late spring. I'm told the honey from these trees is downright gourmet! Even so, just knowing how our tanagers love bees and how 96 percent of songbirds feed their babies bugs, it's hard to think of this tree as anything other than terrific. Nicely conically shaped, it's relatively slow-growing so can nestle comfortably for years in mid-sized and perhaps even mini yards.

Tulip Tree

Fast growers, tulip trees form to a lovely shape. Unfortunately, that rapid growth pattern also makes them somewhat brittle. By the time they're 50 years old, they're susceptible to wind damage. Still, after watching Baltimore Orioles bury their faces in the blossoms to find spring's first nectar, tracking Northern Cardinals and Blue Jays feasting on winter seed heads, and following Brown Creepers spiraling up the trunk, snacking on insect eggs—well, I still really love having tulip trees in the yard.

Sweetgum

A winter staple for supplying small nutritious seeds, especially to American Goldfinches, Purple Finches, House Finches, Pine Siskins, and Dark-eyed Juncos, sweetgum gets a bum rap because of the very seeds that feed the birds. The problem is that those tiny seeds are encased in a woody, spiky case, commonly called a gumball. Stepping on a freshly fallen gumball can be downright painful, and stepping on one along a slope can cause a slip, so it's not the ideal tree for close to the house or in mini yards. But because the seed-laden balls cling to the branches, dangling throughout the winter and falling only in spring, the tree provides significant sustenance to winter birds. Besides, it's fun to watch birds swinging from the fruits in order to feed!

Tulip trees (*Liriodendron tulipifera*) serve up a year-round buffet: nectar in their tulip-shaped flowers in spring, seeds in late fall and winter, and, because they're host trees for butterflies and moths, a ready supply of caterpillars during three seasons.

Yellow-billed Cuckoos arrive late on breeding territories because they wait for the caterpillars to emerge, this one snagging a snack amid the branches of a sweetgum tree.

I would be remiss not to mention that sweetgum also hosts caterpillars and other insects. And I would be further remiss not to mention that nothing loves moth caterpillars more than Yellow-billed Cuckoos. In my yard, sweetgum is the magnet tree for these secretive birds.

Blackgum

Despite its similar name, blackgum is unrelated to sweetgum. Sometimes called black tupelo, blackgum's claim to fame for birds is in its rich source of nectar and nutritious fruit. Bees love the nectar and—without intentionally sounding like a broken record—where there are bees, there are other insects, all of which feed the birds. The little berry-sized fruits are startlingly sour, thus providing yet another common name, sour gum, for the tree. Bet you can guess, though, what loves those little, fleshy, blue-black, oval-stoned fruits that hang usually three to a long, slender stem. American Robins likely top the list, as these late-autumn fruits are essential to their post-breeding diets.

River Birch

Seed-eating birds will flock to catkins hanging from river birch branches throughout the winter. Finches—American Goldfinches, Purple Finches, House Finches, and Pine Siskins—as well as Northern Cardinals and some of the winter sparrows, including Dark-eyed Juncos, will all dangle from the catkins, foraging readily on the abundant buffet. Only in spring will seeds finally drop. That's assuming, of course, the birds haven't devoured them all!

Sycamore

If you live where old American sycamore trees trace waterways, you'll have an abundance of potential nest sites among the tree cavities—a characteristic of mature sycamores. Against bright winter skies, the mottled white bark all but glistens, and that alone makes this tree special to me. The advantage for birds, though, (besides the cavities, of course) is that the tree serves up "sycamore balls," the seed/fruit providing winter food. It's a common wintertime sight to watch American Goldfinches clinging to the sycamore balls, feasting on what to us seems like an unappetizing mass of fuzz. Beyond seeds, however, sycamores provide additional tidbits. Year-round, I see woodpeckers scouring the sycamores regularly, pulling insects, eggs, and larvae from the bark. Nuthatches do their upside-down search for the same reason. And I've watched female Northern Cardinals pull strips of bark from small branches, most certainly to construct a nest's foundation. Sycamores, however, are best suited for super-sized yards.

The following final two suggestions are also best suited for super-sized yards. They have the distinct benefit of colonizing, providing landscape benefits for landowners and foraging benefits for birds.

Sassafras

Most often found growing along roadsides and fencerows and in sparse woods or old fields, sassafras typically falls off the radar of landscapers, who miss the value of this shrub/tree for naturalized planting or screens. Left alone, a sassafras will spread by root suckers, forming an ever-widening colony with trees ultimately growing to 60 feet tall in attractive dense pyramidal forms. The late-summer dark blue berries, however, provide the quick-draw for birds.

Black Locust

Far less thorny than honey locust, black locust doesn't really work well in a small residential landscape. Where there's space for it, however,

Black locust blossoms (*Robinia pseudoacaci*), with their abundant sweet nectar, attract insects and, therefore, feed the spring birds.

the nectar almost as much as insects do! At least where I live, since the blossoms coincide with the hummers' arrival, we enjoy the great birds-and-bugs combo. Young trees bloom readily, but the stately old trees also attract woodpeckers, grosbeaks, thrashers, thrushes, mockingbirds, catbirds, and orioles. In spring, when I tire of watching the cypress trees, I turn to the locusts. It's never dull! However, a word of caution: Black locust can multiple readily by root suckers.

the tree is a boon for bees and other insects that visit its profuse, pendulous, grape-like clusters of creamy-white blossoms. A plethora of insects love the nectar, so you can bet birds follow the bugs. But would you believe, hummingbirds love

Here, then, in addition to the first-choice oaks, are details about the 14 additional deciduous tree species that birds love. They're arranged loosely from best *Lepidoptera* bug hosts to lesser bug hosts—although all work exceedingly well in their respective native habitats. Plant as many species as you have room to plant! You'll build a little bit of bird heaven—not to mention a big bit of bird-watcher's heaven. Make your choice(s) and update your yard map accordingly.

Deciduous Trees for Mid-Sized and Super-Sized Yards

COMMON NAME	SCIENTIFIC NAME	COMMENTS	NATIVE, PLANTING ZONES
Wild black cherry	*Prunus serotina*	50–80' tall, 30–60' spread; well-drained soil; white blossoms in spring; berries in midsummer; commonly cultivated	Eastern US Zones 3–9
Black willow (see also *Salix* shrubs and micro cultivar, below)	*Salix nigra*	Largest native willow, 30–60' tall, 30–60' spread; fast-growing; only willow suitable for lumber; rarely cultivated but easily rooted from cuttings; numerous cultivars; highly beneficial to pollinators; butterfly host plant	Eastern US Zones 4–9

COMMON NAME	SCIENTIFIC NAME	COMMENTS	NATIVE, PLANTING ZONES
Dogwood	*Cornus* spp.	Attractive landscape trees; low-growing	As specified by species below
Flowering dogwood	C. florida	15–30′ tall, 15–30′ spread; showy flowers, red fall foliage, berries; common in understory; prefers at least partial shade; commonly cultivated, with many cultivars	Eastern US except MN, WI, and IA Zones 5–9
Alternate-leaf dogwood synonymous with pagoda dogwood	C. alternifolia	15–20′ tall, 20–30′ spread; lacks showy flowers; moist to dry soils; commonly cultivated	Eastern US except LA Zones 3–7
Maple (see also *Acer* micro cultivars, below)	*Acer* spp.	Popular specimen tree; also noted for fall color foliage	As specified by species below
Boxelder synonymous with ashleaf maple, three-leaf maple	A. negundo	30–50′ tall, 30–50′ spread; common, mainly in moist soils, along streams and pond margins; tolerates drought, clay soil, and air pollution; commonly cultivated and naturalized	Eastern US Zones 2–10
Red maple	A. rubrum	50–70′ tall, 50′ spread; tolerates wide range of soils but prefers moist, slightly acidic; full sun; very cold-hardy; shallow, flat root system that can raise sidewalks or driveways if planted too close	Eastern US Zones 3–9
Sugar maple	A. saccharum	40–80′ tall, 60′ spread; easily grown in average soil; best in fertile soil, full sun; avoid compacted soil; intolerant of road salt and urban pollution; beautiful specimen tree	Eastern US except SC and FL Zones 3–8

COMMON NAME	SCIENTIFIC NAME	COMMENTS	NATIVE, PLANTING ZONES
Red mulberry	*Morus rubra*	35–50' tall, 35–40' spread; attractive understory; fruits early; occasionally cultivated outside native range; avoid similar white (Asian) mulberry	Eastern US except NH and ME Zones 4–8
Southern bald cypress and variety **pond cypress** (see also *T. distichum* micro cultivars, below)	*Taxodium distichum* and *T. distichum* var. *impricarium*	50–75' tall, 20–45' spread; grows most anywhere; attractive shape, ferny foliage	Eastern US except MN, IA, WI, and east of NY Zones 4–9
American basswood synonymous with **American linden**	*Tilia americana*	50–80' tall, 30–50' spread; easily grown in average conditions, sun or part shade; showy, fragrant flowers attract bees; handsome ornamental but intolerant of city conditions	Eastern US Zones 2–8
Tulip tree synonymous with **yellow poplar** (see also *L. tulipifera* micro cultivars, below)	*Liriodendron tulipifera*	60–90' tall but very old trees up to 200' tall, 30–50' spread; host plant for numerous butterflies; flowers provide early nectar; seed lasts the winter; many cultivars	Eastern US except MN, NH, and ME Zones 4–9
Sweetgum (see also *L. styraciflua* micro cultivar, below)	*Liquidambar styraciflua*	60–80' tall, 40–60' spread; prefers deep, fertile soils; avoid alkaline soils; intolerant of shade; birds fond of seeds (fruits dangling, woody ball of pointed capsules); widely cultivated as street tree	Eastern US except ME, NH, VT, MI, WI, MN, and IA Zones 5–8
Blackgum synonymous with **sour gum** and **black tupelo** (see also *N. sylvatica* micro cultivar, below)	*Nyssa sylvatica*	30–50' tall, 20–30' spread; tolerates wide variety of conditions, including standing water; need male and female to set fruit (½" berries on 1–5" stems, usually 3 or more per stem); heavy nectar-producer attracting insects and birds; deep taproot precludes transplanting; excellent ornamental yard tree, best in super-sized yards; commonly cultivated	Eastern US except MN and IA Zones 3–9
River birch (see also *B. nigra* micro cultivar, below)	*Betula nigra*	30–50' tall but can reach 90' tall, 40–60' spread; often multi-trunked, rounded crown; moist soil not required; commonly cultivated	Eastern US except ME Zones 4–9

COMMON NAME	SCIENTIFIC NAME	COMMENTS	NATIVE, PLANTING ZONES
American sycamore	*Platanus occidentalis*	75–100' tall, 75–100' spread; most massive tree east of Rockies; mottled bark peels to white; ball-like fruit; best suited for super-sized yards	Eastern US except MN Zones 4–9
Sassafras	*Sassafras albidum*	30–60' tall, 25–40' spread; aromatic; dark blue fruits on female plants in late summer; can form thickets, thus best for super-sized yards	Eastern US except MN Zones 4–9
Black locust	*Robinia pseudoacacia*	30–60' tall, begin as shrubby; can be invasive; blossoms hang in grape-like clusters; can form thickets as small trees; best for super-sized yards	Throughout US Zones 3–8

Mini-Yard and Pots-and-Patio Garden Alternative Deciduous Trees

Since not everyone has ample square footage for standard-sized deciduous trees, and since not everyone wants to limit the landscape to a single deciduous tree, some options for smaller cultivars make viable alternatives. Even in super-sized yards with abundant space, sometimes a feature planting of a single micro cultivar or even a little grove of them might function well near the driveway or entryway or perhaps as a central focal point.

Here are nine bird-loving trees with 17 specific species, varieties, or cultivars, all well worth considering for multiple landscaping uses—especially, of course, providing the ultimate bird feeder. When you make your choices, update your yard map accordingly.

Deciduous Micro Cultivars for Mini Yards and Pots-and-Patio Gardens

COMMON NAME	SCIENTIFIC NAME	COMMENTS	NATIVE, PLANTING ZONES
Willow	*Salix* spp.	Generally prefer moist soils	As noted below
American pussy willow	*S. discolor*	Shrubby, 6–15' tall, 4–12' spread; average, medium to wet soil in full sun or part shade; tolerates drier soils than most willows; may be cut to ground every 3–5 years to maintain smaller size; good as hedge or in rain garden	Eastern US except TN, FL, SC, GA, AL, LA, and AR Zones 4–8
Pink pussy willow	*S. discolor* 'Rosea'	15–20' tall; 12–15' spread; average water needs; full sun to part shade; pink flowers mid-spring	Cultivar Zones 4–8

COMMON NAME	SCIENTIFIC NAME	COMMENTS	NATIVE, PLANTING ZONES
Purple willow	*S. purpurea* 'Nana'	3–5' tall; 3–5' spread; full sun, medium to wet soil; tolerates clay soil; showy gray-white flowers attract butterflies; deer resistant; winter interest	Cultivar Zones 4–8
Dogwood	*Cornus* spp.	As noted below	As noted below
Flowering dogwood	*C. florida*	15–30' tall, 15–30' spread; showy flowers, red fall foliage, berries; common in understory; prefers at least partial shade; commonly cultivated, with many cultivars	Eastern US except MN, WI, and IA Zones 5–9
'Red Pygmy'	*C. florida* 'Red Pygmy'	3–7' tall, 2–5' spread; easily grown in average, moist but well-drained soil; full sun to part shade; slow-growing; rose-red blossoms	Dwarf cultivar Zones 5–9
Red maple	*Acer rubrum*	Popular specimen tree; also noted for fall foliage	As noted below
'Bowhall'	*A. rubrum* 'Bowhall'	40–50' tall, 15–25' spread; columnar; narrowest of red maples; urban, clay-soil and wet-soil tolerant	Cultivar Zones 3–9
'Armstrong Gold'	*A. rubrum* 'Armstrong Gold'	40' tall, 12' spread; columnar, tightly upright branches; bright-gold fall foliage; perfect for narrow street planting	Cultivar Zones 3–9
Sugar maple 'Reba' ('Belle Tower')	*Acer saccharum* 'Reba'	45' tall, 18' spread; narrow oval shape; superior heat tolerance; yellow-orange fall foliage	Cultivar Zones 3–8
Bald cypress	*Taxodium distichum*	Attractive landscape tree; tolerates many soil conditions	Eastern US except MN, IA, WI, and east of NY Zones 4–9
'Lindsey's Skyward'	*T. distichum* 'Skyward'	Dwarf conifer, 25–30' tall, 5–10' spread, can be pruned to keep smaller; no roots or knees; highly resistant to ice-storm stress; copper fall foliage	Cultivar Zones 4–9
'Falling Waters'	*T. distichum* 'Falling Waters'	8–15' tall, 8–10' spread; weeping; full sun, cold tolerant; bronze to rust fall foliage; use as specimen, edging; can be espaliered against or draped over walls	Cultivar Zones 4–9

COMMON NAME	SCIENTIFIC NAME	COMMENTS	NATIVE, PLANTING ZONES
'Mickelson' usually sold under 'Shawnee Brave'	*T. distichum* 'Mickelson'	50–70' tall, 15–20' spread; narrow pyramid; denser foliage than other cypresses; performs well in concrete cut-outs	Cultivar Zones 4–9
Tulip poplar	*Liriodendron tulipifera*	As noted below	Eastern US except MN, NH, and ME
'Little Volunteer'	*L. tulipifera* 'Little Volunteer'	Only ⅓ size of original; 30–35' tall, 18–20' spread; compact pyramidal; prefers well-drained soil; moderate growth rate; all benefits of original, including tulip blossoms	Cultivar Zones 4–9
'Arnold' synonymous with 'Fastigiatum'	*L. tulipifera* 'Arnold'	50' tall, 15' spread; columnar shape; prefers well-drained soils; flowers, butter-yellow fall foliage; fast-growing	Cultivar Zones 4–9
'Ardis'	*L. tulipifera* 'Ardis'	Compact, ⅓ size of original; 15' tall, 15' spread; excellent for compact landscapes; small leaf; pollution tolerant; golden-yellow fall foliage	Dwarf cultivar Zones 4–9
Sweet gum 'Slender Silhouette'	*Liquidambar styraciflua* 'Slender Silhouette'	34–50' tall, 4' spread; highly praised; produces very small fruits that fall in very small space; fast-growing	Variety Zones 5–8
Blackgum 'Tupelo Tower'	*Nyssa sylvatica* 'Tupelo Tower'	30–40' tall, 10–15' spread; columnar; low maintenance, slow-growing; prefers moist soil; gold, amber, scarlet fall foliage	Cultivar Zones 3–9
River birch 'Little King' also sold as 'Fox River'	*Betula nigra* 'Little King'	8–10' tall, 9–12' spread; multi-stemmed, shrub-like; extremely disease resistant; orangish to brownish bark, exfoliates to lighter brownish inner bark; good in rain garden	Cultivar Zones 4–9

Flowering dogwood trees (*Cornus florida*) display lovely early-spring blossoms attractive to insects and, therefore, to birds.

CONIFERS AND OTHER EVERGREENS

As a group, conifers (cone-bearers) and other evergreens rank close to being "must-haves" for great bird habitat. They provide better shelter than does any other vegetation for two obvious reasons. First, as a whole, evergreens are generally fairly dense. Second, of course, they keep that dense quality year-round. So especially for folks who live in mid-states and north where other trees go bare half the year, evergreens offer that essential shelter against the elements—in some cases, maybe the only shelter. While oak is still the single most important species to plant for birds, some sort of sheltering evergreen, if at all possible, should garner a spot in your birdscape.

In spite of the traditional emphasis on feeders and feed, or even natural foods like seeds, berries, nectar, and buds and blossoms to create attractive bird habitat, a yard without shelter will be a yard with few birds. And those few birds will only dash in to grab a bite and then rush off to someplace safe. Birds equate "safe" with "shelter"—be it from weather or predators. In short, building safe havens in your yard will not only draw birds in, but also help keep them alive. Planting evergreens is key.

American Holly

Having said that, I should emphasize that some evergreens are better than others. Consider the quality use of space, for instance, if the evergreen you plant serves a dual purpose, providing not just shelter but also food. Many cone-bearing evergreens do that, but perhaps a more telling example is American holly.

In spring, tiny blossoms add sweetness to the air and draw insects. You know what happens then: Birds follow. While green berries form in early summer and seem to sit idle the remainder of the season and into fall, they finally turn red in early winter, adding a holiday air to the landscape. Only after a series of freeze-thaw cycles, however, do the berries soften enough for birds to flock in for dinner—often as late as early February. Birds that arrive to pluck the ripened red berries inevitably gulp them down whole, including American Robins, Northern Mockingbirds, Eastern

An Eastern Bluebird forages on holly berries (*Ilex opaca*) after several freeze-thaw cycles soften the winter fruit.

Bluebirds, Gray Catbirds, Cedar and Bohemian Waxwings, Blue Jays, and all the woodpeckers.

Probably the most dramatic winter scene in my two holly trees is the day our robin regulars figure out the berries are suddenly perfect for their dining pleasure. "Our" few robins apparently send word out on the airwaves that it's chow time. Within hours, up to 300 robins arrive to ravage the trees. In spite of the multitudes and their obvious gluttonous appetites, stripping the trees is a carefully systematic process. And it happens this way every year. They start at the top of the tree to the north and clear the tree of berries to about halfway down, then move to the second tree, again from the top down to the middle. Maybe berries near the top, collecting even the weakest of the winter sun's rays, ripen ahead of the rest; but given that the birds take only three or four days to finish the buffet, I hardly see how that's the case. A couple of cold winter days surely can't make much difference in berry ripening.

Whatever the reason for their systematic work, they finally work their way down to the bottoms of both trees. The feast is at its end—or so it seems to me. But on the final day, they move to the ground, flipping leaves, scratching in the loose ground cover, picking up every berry—whole or part—that fell during their haste to gobble berries from tree twigs. And then they're gone, surely sated, off to strip another tree in another yard on another day.

So hollies are wonderful evergreen choices for a bird-friendly habitat. When you consider holly choices, however, avoid the temptation to choose a cultivar that produces those bright little yellow berries—unless you're buying one tree for you and another for the birds. Because birds and yellow-berried hollies didn't evolve together, they apparently don't recognize yellow berries as food. Be in the know!

Eastern Red Cedar

Likely the second-best evergreen is eastern red cedar or one of its many cultivars, including some tidy shrub versions, dandy for small spaces or for masses in large areas. Red cedar is dense, slow-growing, tough, long-lived, nicely shaped, and carefree. A cluster creates the perfect windbreak. Then the final feature takes it over the top: It produces berries—actually tiny cones—that birds love. Watch Cedar and Bohemian Waxwings enjoy the "fruits" when winter puts the kibosh on other fruit. The berries also help Eastern Bluebirds survive the winter. Owls find the branches perfect for day roosts; numerous songbirds enjoy the nesting protection; everything gathers in cedar safe-ports in a storm. Tuck one or some into your habitat somewhere, even if only a couple of the smaller cultivars like 'Gray Owl' or 'Royo'. (We'll come back to eastern red cedar cultivars later, when we talk about shrubs.)

A Cedar Waxwing dines on namesake eastern red cedar cone-like berries (*Juniperus virginiana*) that serve as a favorite nutritious winter staple for many berry eaters.

Pine Trees

Given the vast array of choices for landscape conifers and evergreens, however, pine trees head the A-list in one very important aspect: They host an amazing array of *Lepidoptera* species. While according to Tallamy's research, oaks support 534 butterfly and moth species, pines support an equally impressive 203 species, the highest among evergreens. Translation: Pines host oodles and bunches of caterpillars! If you're a bird, that's a yum-yum buffet, especially when you're feeding a nest full of hungry babies. It's also no wonder, then, when I'm watching for spring and fall migrants in the yard, I see lots of flitting about among the pines. Those long-distance fliers are gobbling up protein to fuel the rest of their journey. Ah, those little green caterpillars!

Pines trees, however, have another claim to fame. Among the myriads of birds attracted to pines, some actually eat pine seeds, those little nuggets buried deep within the cone. Most notable, of course, are Red Crossbills and White-winged Crossbills, northern birds with namesake bills especially adapted (crossed) to split open cones to reach the precious seeds inside. Finches, especially Pine Siskins and Purple Finches, as well as Pine Grosbeaks also forage among cones. Nuthatches, including the cute little southern Brown-headed Nuthatch, manage to eke out seeds, and Red-bellied Woodpeckers and Yellow-bellied Sapsuckers love 'em as well!

Beyond the caterpillar and cone interests, however, pines offer a good many other benefits to birds. Our Eastern Bluebirds build their nests almost entirely of pine straw because, simply, it's readily at hand, and they're opportunistic nesters. Hummingbirds often rely on pine sap to seal their nests, using it to glue everything in place. And during a snow, I find more species sheltering in the protection of pines than in anything else—well, maybe except eastern red cedar. But

Top: A Pine Warbler forages for caterpillars in its namesake jack pine (*Pinus banksiana*), native in the bird's summer breeding range.
Bottom: On its northern breeding grounds, a Common Redpoll gleans seed from spruce cones (*Picea* spp.).

the pines grow on the east side of the garage, protected from winter's worst northwesterly winds. That probably gives the pines an edge-up in the shelter-popularity scale.

Still, all those little green caterpillars that I can't see but birds find in abundance—well, they feed a ton of babies in our neighborhood. Gotta love pines!

White Spruce

Tallamy's research supports the claim that spruce trees rank second among evergreens for hosting those little green caterpillars—156 species of them. Given the right location, white spruce serves well to attract Black-capped Chickadees, American Goldfinches, White-breasted and Red-breasted Nuthatches, Pine Siskins, Hoary and Common Redpolls, and both crossbills. Since lower branches stay strong as trees mature, these spruces also provide perfect protection for ground-loving feeders and roosters. Where else could secretive Fox Sparrows tuck in?

Atlantic White Cedar and Northern White Cedar

Because Atlantic white cedar is also a host plant for various insects, it's another magnet for birds.

Planted within the birds' normal ranges, the tree will likely attract Pine Siskins, Ruffed Grouse, Slate-colored Juncos, Tree Sparrows, and both redpolls. As with northern white cedar, older trees draw Pileated Woodpeckers looking for carpenter ants. Between them, these two cedars provide super nesting habitat for a half-dozen warbler species, Golden-crowned Kinglets, Yellow-bellied Flycatchers, Winter Wrens, White-throated Sparrows, Swainson's Thrushes, and, underneath in groves, Ovenbirds.

Sweetbay Magnolia

Depending on how far north you live, sweetbay magnolia may be evergreen. Up to the 38th parallel, it's at least semievergreen, but farther north it may lose its glossy leaves during the worst cold. I'm in love with these trees because

Berries on a sweetbay magnolia (*Magnolia virginiana*) attract an early-fall female Northern Cardinal, the rich lipids serving to brighten her new feathers.

they're beautiful in the landscape: Sweet white blossoms follow with luscious berries, set amid glossy green, elongated, oval leaves. But oh my! Wait till you see the warblers foraging among the leaves, cardinals plucking the berries, and White-throated Sparrows tucking in among the foliage during winter snows. Hard to imagine anything better—unless it's the flocks of Dark-eyed Juncos foraging under the low branches.

Hemlock

Hemlocks provide similar attributes. A few species find the tiny hemlock cones of interest, including Black-capped and Carolina Chickadees, Pine Siskins, American Goldfinches, Red Crossbills, and White-winged Crossbills. In the right habitat, Wild Turkeys and owls roost on mature hemlock branches. Black-throated Blue Warblers, Black-throated Green Warblers, Blackburnian Warblers, and Solitary Vireos nest in hemlocks growing in their northern breeding range. And Yellow-bellied Sapsuckers are famously attracted to hemlocks in northern ranges.

So, in order of preference, depending on your location, here are my lucky 13 recommendations for conifers and other evergreens. When you make your choice(s), update your yard map accordingly.

Evergreens for Mid-Sized and Super-Sized Yards

COMMON NAME	SCIENTIFIC NAME	COMMENTS	NATIVE, PLANTING ZONES
American holly (see also *Ilex* shrub cultivars, pages 125–26)	*Ilex opaca*	15–30′ tall, 10–20′ spread; upright, branches to ground; fairly dense; male and female required for berry production; dozens of cultivars, but birds may not like cultivars' berries	Eastern US except MN, WI, IA, MI, VT, NH, and ME Zones 5–9
Eastern red cedar (see also *Juniperus* micro and shrub cultivars, below and page 131)	*Juniperus virginiana*	30–60′ tall, 8–25′ spread; only native juniper commonly upright and columnar but many rounded and bushy; commonly cultivated, with many cultivars	All eastern US Zones 2–9
Pines	*Pinus* spp.	Year-round shelter, cones for some bird species, sap often used by hummingbirds to seal nests	As specified by species below
Virginia pine	*P. virginiana*	15–30′ tall, 10–20′ spread; easily grown; prefers clay or sandy loams and well-drained soil; spiny-scaled cones 3″ long; common in dry uplands; uncommonly cultivated mainly within native range	Eastern US except MN, WI, MI, IA, AR, LA, FL, and east of NY Zones 4–8

COMMON NAME	SCIENTIFIC NAME	COMMENTS	NATIVE, PLANTING ZONES
Jack pine synonymous with scrub pine	*P. banksiana*	30–50' tall, 20–30' spread, smaller in East; usually crooked, leaning, gaunt; very short needles, curved cones; commonly cultivated	North of Ohio River except IA; all of Northeast except NJ, DE, and CT Zones 2–6
Red pine	*P. resinosa*	50–80' tall, 20–25' spread; common in dry woodlands, sandy soil, boreal forests; very commonly cultivated and naturalized	Coastal states from SC through ME and central, including MO, IL, IN, MI, WI, and MN Zones 2–5
Pitch pine	*P. rigida*	40–60' tall, 20–30' spread; common, widespread in dry sandy or rocky soil; 2" cones; fairly commonly cultivated	Eastern US except FL, MS, AL, LA, AR, MO, IA, MI, and WI Zones 4–9
White pine (see also *P. strobus* micro cultivars, below)	*P. strobus*	50–80' tall, 20–40' spread; common, widespread in well-drained soils; very commonly cultivated, with many cultivars including dwarf and weeping forms; often in public parks	Eastern US except FL, MS, and LA Zones 3–8
White spruce (see also *Picea* micro cultivar, below)	*Picea glauca*	40–60' tall, 10–20' spread; smallest cones of spruces; common, widespread in muskegs, bogs; commonly cultivated, with several cultivars	MD, DE, NJ, and PA north through ME; also MI, WI, and MN Zones 2–6
Atlantic white cedar synonymous with **white cypress**	*Chamaecyparis thyoides*	30–50' tall, 30–40' spread; columnar, narrow, upright; dense crown; common in swamps, bogs, wet woodlands, along streams; rarely cultivated	All coastal states from ME through LA Zones 4–8
Northern white cedar synonymous with **American arborvitae** (see also *Thuja* micro and shrub cultivars, below and pages 130–31)	*Thuja occidentalis*	20–40' tall, 10–15' spread; native in swamps, along waterways; commonly cultivated as ornamental and hedge plant	Eastern US except FL, GA, AL, MS, LA, AR, and MO Zones 2–7

COMMON NAME	SCIENTIFIC NAME	COMMENTS	NATIVE, PLANTING ZONES
Sweetbay magnolia synonymous with **laurel magnolia**	*Magnolia virginiana*	10–35' tall, 10–35' spread; shrubby and deciduous north but treelike and evergreen south, 10-35' tall; aromatic; common in wet soils; commonly cultivated	Gulf and Atlantic coastal states except CT, RI, and ME Zones 5-10
Hemlocks	*Tsuga* spp.	Short, flat needles and tiny cones; untrimmed branches to ground	As specified by species below
Eastern hemlock synonymous with Canadian hemlock	*T. canadensis*	40–70' tall, 25–35' spread; common but local in rocky, wet swales; very commonly cultivated, including as compact shrubs, dwarfs, and large, graceful trees	Eastern US except FL, MS, LA, AR, IL, and IA Zones 3-7
Carolina hemlock	*T. caroliniana*	45–60' tall, 20–25' spread; uncommon and local on rocky slopes; commonly cultivated, with many cultivars available	OH, VA, NC, SC, GA, and TN Zones 6-7

Evergreen Alternatives for Mini Yards and Pots-and-Patio Gardens

A good many evergreen micro cultivars offer almost endless options for landscaping plans. From tall to creeping, from hefty to skinny, evergreen micros can even fill pots on patios or decks. Obviously the larger the tree, the more shelter it provides; but some is better than none.

If everyone offered a little something, imagine how much more habitat birds would have. It's a plan! And here are 10 micro cultivars to help you implement the plan—no matter the size of your yard or patio.

Remember to update your yard map, noting decisions about micros.

Evergreen Micro Cultivars for Mini Yards and Pots-and Patio Gardens

COMMON NAME	SCIENTIFIC NAME	COMMENTS	NATIVE, PLANTING ZONES
Eastern red cedar (see also *Juniperus* shrub cultivar, page 131)	*Juniperus virginiana*	Dense evergreen; birds love the berries (actually tiny cones) for winter survival	All eastern US Zones 2-9
'Taylor'	*J. virginiana* 'Taylor'	14–20' tall, 3–4' spread; upright columnar shape; tolerant of wide range of soils in full sun; excellent drought resistance	All eastern US Zones 2-9

COMMON NAME	SCIENTIFIC NAME	COMMENTS	NATIVE, PLANTING ZONES
'Burkii'	*J. virginiana* 'Burkii'	10–25' tall, 4–10' spread; can be pruned; tolerates wide range of soils in full sun; serves well as specimen or screen; best drought resistance of any conifer native to eastern US	All eastern US Zones 2–9
'Blue Arrow'	*J. virginiana* 'Blue Arrow'	12–15' tall, 2' spread; perfect for narrow spots; groupings form nice hedge; easy to grow; tolerates seashore and roadside salt conditions; fall berries	All eastern US Zones 2–9
White pine	*Pinus strobus* 'Fastigiata'	30–40' tall, 7–10' spread; columnar, branches ascend upward; easily grown; wide range of soil conditions; full sun; good as specimen, small grouping, or as screen	Eastern US except FL, MS, and LA Zones 3–8
White spruce 'Dwarf Alberta'	*Picea glauca* 'Conica'	10–13' tall, 7–10' spread; cone-shaped dwarf to semi-dwarf, shrub-like, very dense; grows slowly at 2–4" per year; rarely produces cones; often trimmed as topiary tree when grown in containers	MD, DE, NJ, and PA north through ME; also MI, WI, and MN Zones 2–6
Northern white cedar (see also *Thuja* shrub cultivars, pages 130–31)	*Thuja occidentalis*	Cultivars as described below	Eastern US except FL, GA, AL, MS, LA, AR, and MO Zones 2–7
'Nigra'	*T. occidentalis* 'Nigra'	20' tall, 5–10' spread; retains good color year-round; good as hedge; can be pruned	Eastern US except FL, GA, AL, MS, LA, AR, and MO Zones 2–7
'Lutea' synonymous with 'Peabody'	*T. occidentalis* 'Lutea'	25–30' tall, 12–15' spread; compact, grows about 1' per year; new growth bright cream-yellow, turns light gold, then green	Eastern US except FL, GA, AL, MS, LA, AR, and MO Zones 2–7
'Emerald' synonymous with 'Emerald Green'	*T. occidentalis* 'Smaragd'	7–14' tall, 3–4' spread; semi-dwarf, dense growth; becoming most popular white cedar variety; ½" urn-shaped cones; makes good hedge, its most common use	Eastern US except FL, GA, AL, MS, LA, AR, and MO Zones 2–7

COMMON NAME	SCIENTIFIC NAME	COMMENTS	NATIVE, PLANTING ZONES
'Mission' synonymous with 'Techny'	*T. occidentalis* 'Techny'	20–25′ tall, 6–10′ spread; compact, broad-based upright; long-standing traditional cultivar loved for year-round bright-green foliage	Eastern US except FL, GA, AL, MS, LA, AR, and MO Zones 2–7
Hemlock 'Fastigiata'	*Tsuga canadensis* 'Fastigiata'	5–6′ tall, 2′ spread over 10 years; multi-stemmed dwarf; likes more shade than sun; will not tolerate urban conditions or road salt; best in rural or suburban landscapes	Eastern US except FL, MS, LA, AR, IL, and IA Zones 3–7

So there you have it. Trees are more than decoration. They—like all landscape vegetation—serve a biological purpose (or should). Understanding that purpose not only helps landowners realize the importance of planting native trees, but also helps folks identify which of those native trees will best serve the biodiversity of any given yard and neighborhood, regardless of yard size. Here's to your yard's diversity!

That's Step 1. Now, updated yard map in hand, you're ready for Step 2.

Winterberry shrubs (*Ilex verticillata*) hold fruit well into winter, sustaining berry lovers like Northern Mockingbirds that will often guard a shrub as their private fruit stand.

"We abuse land because we regard it as a commodity belonging to us. When we see land as a community to which we belong, we may begin to use it with love and respect."

—ALDO LEOPOLD in Foreword, *A Sand County Almanac (1887-1948)*

Chapter 6
CHOOSING NATIVE SHRUBS (AND VINES)

Unlike a tree with its single, sometimes massive trunk, a shrub is usually multi-stemmed, hence the term "shrubby." What's the difference, then, between a bush and a shrub? Some sources try to distinguish between the two by suggesting bushes are found in the wild and have stems and leaves closer to the ground. Shrubs, on the other hand, have thicker foliage and are maintained and pruned. According to a Utah State University Extension bulletin, however, "A shrub by any other name is a bush." Most sources ultimately confess that "bush" is just another name for "shrub."

The difference between an understory tree and a shrub, however, sometimes blurs. An understory tree, like redbud (*Cercis canadensis*) for instance, may be multi-trunked but grows sometimes 30 feet tall. By habit, we call it a tree, and field guides typically name it a tree, not a shrub. It prefers and thrives under the partial shade of another, larger tree, thus redbud becomes commonly referred to as an "understory" tree. Some shrubs like bayberry (*Myrica* spp.), however, stay relatively short—maybe only upwards of 10 feet—but appear in field guides as a tree. Even the experts don't agree.

This whole business is confounded by the fact that a shrub can be pruned into a treelike form.

So here's my point: This isn't a scientific reference, so forgive me for my perhaps somewhat lax terminology. I'll be using the term "shrub" to refer to all woody plants that are relatively short and bush-like, and that grow no higher than, say, to the eaves of a one-story house. I'll use the term "understory tree" to refer to relatively short trees, some perhaps multi-stemmed, but especially those that thrive best in the shade of high-canopy trees.

In short, for our purposes: *If you can walk under it, it's a tree. If you have to walk around it, it's a shrub (or bush).*

Nitpicking aside then, let's get down to the business of Step 2, choosing shrubs that serve your plan and meet your birdscaping goals.

Step 2: Choose at least four shrubs—one for each season.

Keep in mind that "shrub" also includes tall understory "shrubby" trees. And since vines are merely woody shrubs that twine, they're possible choices, too. As well, we'll make mention of brambles, yet another woody shrub—not suitable everywhere but worthy of high praise from some ground-loving birds.

The tree or trees you chose in the last chapter may well be the biggest players in the landscape, rather like captains of the team, but generally shrubs make up the team. They become the foundation for the overall landscaping and function well in many landscaping capacities. And since

there are literally hundreds of kinds of shrubs for your planting pleasure, even keeping to the natives, the range of choices can boggle the mind.

There are three kinds of shrubs:

1. Deciduous shrubs, of course, lose their leaves in winter. They tend to offer showy blossoms and work well as feature plantings.
2. Broadleaf evergreen shrubs, those that stay green year-round but often have oval-shaped leaves, also work well as feature plantings. Typically adorned with showy blossoms, usually in spring, they maintain year-round interest, provide shelter for birds, and depending on where you plant them, add privacy to your home or yard.
3. Needled evergreen shrubs look more like typical evergreen trees. Likewise, they maintain year-round interest, provide winter shelter for birds, and can add privacy to your home or yard.

Fragrant white mid-spring smooth witherod viburnum blossoms (*Viburnum nudum*) strike a sharp contrast with the plant's shiny green leaves, attracting pollinators and later producing berries that ripen from pink to deep pink to blue to purplish black.

MAKING CHOICES BY SEASON

Because there are so many native shrubs from which to choose, we recommend making choices based on what you can plant to best serve up a year-round buffet. Of course, no single shrub serves as a four-season buffet. Take this approach:

1. Think about which specimens bloom in early spring. Those provide buds and blossoms for food and also attract bugs for protein.
2. Next pick a plant that produces summer blooms. They attract insects for nesting birds to feed their babies. Some are also sufficiently dense to serve as secure and nicely camouflaged nest sites.
3. Come fall, birds need the rich nutrition found in the lipids of berries. The fats fuel them in migration and prepare them for winter. So think berries. Lots of berries.

4. Finally, winter demands both food and shelter. Late-winter berries will help birds survive the elements, and evergreen shrubs create life-saving shelter from bitter-cold winds and storms.

Many shrubs serve well, but all serve for only a limited time. The aim here, of course, is to provide for birds in all four seasons—bugs, buds, and shelter in spring; bugs, nest sites, and nest materials in summer; bugs, fruit, nutritious berries, and shelter in autumn; and seeds, berries, and shelter in winter.

In order to serve up a year-round buffet, consider at least one shrub from each column in the table below. (Detailed descriptions of each shrub make up the remainder of this chapter.) Choose more if space and budget permit. A pots-and-patio garden will benefit from several potted shrubs, perhaps situated as a grouping.

Seasonal Choices for Shrubs and Tall Understory Plants

SPRING FOOD	SUMMER FOOD, NEST SITES AND MATERIALS	AUTUMN FOOD	WINTER FOOD AND SHELTER
Alder	Bayberry	Beautyberry, American	Bayberry
Bayberry	Beautyberry, American	Buttonbush	Beautyberry, American
Chokeberry	Blueberries	Chokeberry, Black	Buttonbush
Dogwood, Alternate-leaf	Buttonbush	Chokeberry, Red	Chokeberry, Red
Dogwood, Gray	Devil's Walking Stick	Dogwood, Alternate-leaf	Dogwood, Gray
Dogwood, Red Osier	Dogwood, Gray	Dogwood, Gray	Hawthorn, Green
Dogwood, Roughleaf	Dogwood, Roughleaf	Dogwood, Red Osier	Hawthorn, Washington
Dogwood, Silky	Dogwood, Silky	Dogwood, Roughleaf	Inkberry
Fringetree	Elderberry, Am. Black	Dogwood, Silky	Ninebark
Hawthorn, Green	Hawthorn, Green	Fringetree	Possum Haw (*Ilex*)
Hawthorn, Washington	Hawthorn, Washington	Hawthorn, Green	Sumac, Fragrant
Inkberry	New Jersey Tea	Hawthorn, Washington	Sumac, Smooth
Ninebark	Possum Haw (*Ilex*)	Inkberry	Sumac, Dwarf

SPRING FOOD	SUMMER FOOD, NEST SITES AND MATERIALS	AUTUMN FOOD	WINTER FOOD AND SHELTER
Redbud	Serviceberry, Allegheny	Ninebark	Viburnum, Nannyberry
Serviceberry, Allegheny	Serviceberry, Canadian	Spicebush	Winterberry
Serviceberry, Canadian	Viburnum, Blackhaw	Sumac, Dwarf	Witch Hazel, American
Spicebush	Viburnum, Mapleleaf	Sumac, Fragrant	
Sumac, Fragrant	Willows	Sumac, Smooth	
Sweetspire		Viburnum, Arrowwood	
Viburnum, Arrowwood		Viburnum, Mapleleaf	
Viburnum, Blackhaw		Viburnum, Nannyberry	
Viburnum, Mapleleaf		Viburnum, Sm. Witherod	
Viburnum, Nannyberry			
Viburnum, Sm. Witherod			
Willows			
Witch Hazel, Ozark			

Depending on which plant(s) you choose for container gardening, you may want to think of them as "garden crops," accepting that they won't grow forever in limiting pots. Still, given 10 years or more, you'll offer birds a dramatic addition to an otherwise barren landscape. Some is always better than none.

PLANT DESCRIPTIONS

With the seasonal guide above in mind, you'll find in the following pages all the necessary details about the shrubs and tall understory plants.

Speckled Alder

Most alders like wet feet, even boggy conditions, especially in northerly cool climates. Obviously, then, they're not happy in my southwestern Indiana area—not that I haven't tried to make them happy. It just didn't work. So, for those of you farther north with a wet patch somewhere in your yard or garden, give this one a try. Birds

Pine Siskins forage heavily on early-spring speckled alder (*Alnus incana* ssp. *rugosa*), a shrub of wet places in northern climes.

feed heavily on alders, especially in spring when the catkins hang heavy. As a shrub, it's big, but it can be pruned and, if you're not one to try for naturalized colonies, it can also be reined in by removing suckers. Given space, though, I'd go for it!

Bayberries: Northern and Southern

Depending on where you live, you'll look at either northern bayberry, sometimes called candleberry, or southern bayberry, sometimes called wax myrtle. Both offer attractive foliage, a glossy, waxy broadleaf semievergreen (depending on how far north you live) that makes lovely landscaping year-round. An added advantage is the pleasing bay scent from crushed leaves and berries. In fact, by boiling the berries, American colonists made clean-burning scented candles.

Because bayberry berries have a somewhat waxy skin, they have limited appeal to many birds. But that being said, Yellow-rumped Warblers tolerate the consistency so well that bayberry is their primary sustenance during winter months when they congregate in southern states. Many ornithologists believe that it is, in fact, the native natural abundance of southern bayberry that allows Yellow-rumped Warblers to overwinter in the southern states. We're certainly unlikely to see many other warbler species in the US in January!

American Beautyberry

American beautyberry, sometimes called American beauty bush, has become a fall migrant magnet in my own yard. In June, tiny blossoms wash the gracefully arching branches in pinkish

A delightful Blue-headed Vireo forages through American beautyberry bush (*Callicarpa americana*) in search of both berries and bugs.

lavender, a color just slightly more pink than the berries to come. What a lovely color, both! The blossoms' scent, however, is remarkably delightful, given the tiny size of the flowers. What they lack in size, though, they make up for in mass. Mini bees find the blossoms as delightful as I do, so if wind direction causes me to miss the fragrance, the hum of bees will bring me around. Ruby-throated Hummingbirds take interest in the blossoms, too, but I'm never sure whether the hummers explore the branches for the nectar or the bugs. I suspect both.

The real joy of having beautyberry, however, arrives on wings in August and September. The lovely lavender berries garner intense interest from many migrants, especially Rose-breasted Grosbeaks and all of the thrush family. Swainson's Thrushes slip in regularly to partake, while Hermit Thrushes stay shyly in the back. As crazy as it sounds, however, Nashville and Tennessee Warblers spend more time in the beautyberry than anything else. The berries are just the right tiny size for their consumption, and the bugs that find the occasional droplets of sap especially tantalizing add a great opportunity for a protein boost among migrants. Since one of our bubbling rocks adjoins the beautyberry, it's like one-stop shopping for migrants during September.

By late October and early November, most of the beautyberry berries—and all the migrants—are gone. But Northern Cardinals, Northern Mockingbirds, and American Robins forage until the final berry is gone.

Beautyberry plants also let birdscapers make the most of our investments. The shrubs can be propagated via cuttings. Buy one, get the rest free!

Blueberries

Most folks plant blueberries for the sheer anticipation of blueberry pancakes, blueberry muffins, blueberry pie, blueberries on ice cream, blueberries on cereal, and just plain blueberries, tossed in the mouth like popcorn kernels. I'll take 'em any way I can get 'em!

While blueberries have male and female flowers on the same plant, you do need two different plants to set fruit. Assuming you have the paired plants and have selected varieties suitable for your region, a likely abundance of blueberries will feed families—both human and avian. Most varieties produce significant crops of the luscious fruits—if the weather cooperates. While many blueberry varieties produce fruits too large for birds to swallow whole, Eastern Bluebirds, Blue Jays, American Robins, Northern Cardinals, Northern Mockingbirds, most of the woodpeckers, and some thrushes will be happy to partake of the berries in whatever form they can—whole, crushed, or pecked apart, directly from the bush or from the ground.

Buttonbush

Buttonbush, sometimes also called common buttonbush, button-willow, and honey-bells, has been long neglected for gardening purposes because folks have the wrong impression about this charming shrub's growing conditions. In the wild, we typically find it growing in or near water. But I'm here to tell you mine do just fine, thank you, in the middle of my well-drained garden.

The standard shrub is somewhat more loosely open than is the compact (I have both), but both bloom extremely well and both can be pruned—even severely if you wish. Above all, there's no other shrub—almost no other plant—in my garden that butterflies love more. The buttonbush seems all aflutter as butterflies—most spectacularly the tiger swallowtail—nectar there. The unusual ball-shaped flowers are worth the price of purchase, and when the blooms are spent, the ball shape becomes the seed head that serves birds well all winter.

Buttonbush blossoms (*Cephalanthus occidentalis*) create a buffet for a nectaring tiger swallowtail, a bumblebee, and at least two ailanthus webworm moths, creating, in turn, a buffet for birds.

Knowing that buttonbush blooms on new growth, early this spring I pruned the compact cultivar but left low growth so that branches touched the ground. The reward? Song Sparrows nested on the ground, under the security of the low growth. In winter, White-throated Sparrows, Dark-eyed Juncos, Mourning Doves, and Brown Thrashers forage in the leaf litter below, snatching up the tiny seeds.

Chokeberry

Both varieties of chokeberry, red and black, spread by suckers and can thus naturalize, growing slowly into a nice mass of shrubs birds love. Of course, if you prefer a single shrub, simply use a spade to cut roots that would ultimately form new plants. Depending on your preference,

however, you will likely choose one over the other. Red chokeberry is more aggressive, more likely to spread quickly, more often seen in wetland-type habitats, and best kept to super-sized yards or acreage. Black chokeberry, on the other hand, will naturalize, but it is much better behaved and considerably less aggressive—better for mid-sized or smaller yards.

Virtually every berry-eating bird loves the glossy red or black berries of the chokeberry shrub. While we humans find the berries quite bitter—and thus "choke" on them, accounting for the common name—birds seem not to mind. While chokeberry berries ripen in fall, the red chokeberry cultivar 'Brilliantissima' tends to hold berries into spring. Thus, it better serves over-wintering birds dependent upon winter berries for survival, like Eastern Bluebirds, Northern Mockingbirds, Cedar and Bohemian Waxwings, and woodpeckers, including Northern Flickers. The black chokeberry cultivar 'Iroquois Beauty' tends to be a good ornamental, better behaved and more compact than the standard.

Because of the similarity in names, let's note that chokecherry (*Prunus virginiana*) is more tree-like, while chokeberry (*Aronia* spp.) is a shrub rarely reaching more than 6 feet tall. Both species are attractive to birds and both are native in large parts of the eastern US, but space requirements differ.

Dogwood Shrubs: Gray, Roughleaf, Silky and Red Osier

Everyone is likely familiar with dogwood. The forest-edge flowering dogwood tree, flush with lovely early-spring white flowers—or maybe a pink cultivar—blooms before anything green steals the show. Dogwood shrubs, however, play a different role in the landscape. For one thing— the obvious thing—they are shrubs, meaning they're multi-stemmed and can, left alone, form thickets. In general, they rarely reach more than 12 to 15 feet tall. The dogwood name, then, takes on a different meaning in shrub form.

While the leaves of dogwood shrubs bear a similarity to the leaves of the flowering dogwood tree, other characteristics make the shrub and tree seem surely unrelated—but related they are.

Gray dogwood and roughleaf dogwood are sometimes difficult to distinguish. Both produce clusters of tiny white blooms in May, and both produce pea-sized white berries that sit in a cluster atop little red stems—and therein lies the joy for bird-watchers. Those white berries, ripening just as fall migrants move south, prove highly attractive to many birds, including warblers. What a dramatic sight, those confusing fall warblers flitting across the shrubs, hanging upside

down, stretching for the fattest berry, foraging at the speed of a gulp, hanging out just long enough for me to make the difficult ID. One fall, during a single morning, we watched American Redstarts and Bay-breasted, Chestnut-sided, and Blackpoll Warblers—more than 150 individuals, all moving through an old immense thicket of roughleaf dogwood. Not many species, but oh, what numbers!

Silky dogwood, sometimes called swamp dogwood because of its tolerance for wet feet, blooms somewhat later than the others, a flat-topped cluster of tiny white flowers that form white berries. When ripe, they turn porcelain blue.

Red osier dogwood, the name sometimes written as redosier and sometimes called red twig dogwood, also blossoms in clusters of tiny white flowers that form clusters of white berries, some of which may turn pale blue when ripe. Most who add red osier to their landscape do so because of the bright red twigs that almost glow against winter's gray—or snow white—landscape. Again, however, fall migrants devour the

Fall migrating birds, including this basic-plumaged Cape May Warbler, survive another leg of their southward journey with the aid of nutritious roughleaf dogwood shrub berries (*Cornus drummondii*).

berries, the birds' loveliness rewarding you for your berry-producing plantings.

American Black Elderberry

American black elderberry, or common elderberry, has been treasured for centuries for its tasty berries. Jams and jellies, pies and muffins, and, probably most famous of all, wine—especially the homemade variety—all claim fame with black elderberry berries. Grandpa knew the secret to good elderberry wine! Beware, however, that black elderberry seeds, stems, leaves, and roots are all toxic to humans. The plant parts contain cyanide-inducing glycosides, so if you ate enough, cyanide could build up to sufficient levels to make you sick. I can't imagine why you'd eat seeds, stems, leaves, or roots, but just so you know. The raw berries, however, also contain minimal toxicity—unless they're fully ripe. Boiling, baking, or drying eliminates the toxicity, though, and the result is a delightfully sweet treat. And again, just so you know, birds don't care!

Nowadays, in fact, I adore black elderberry for its almost dinner-plate-sized heads of tiny waxy-white flowers that turn into magnificent clusters of luscious purple-black berries hanging from scarlet red stems. Bees and other insects flock to the sweet blossoms and hummingbirds check them out, and then, in July when berries ripen, whoever gets there first dines well. Most birds don't wait until the berries are soft and fully ripe—I guess they are just too tempting to chance the wait. Perhaps the birds fear something else (like me!) will beat them to the fruity treats. Northern Cardinals, Northern Mockingbirds, Cedar and Bohemian Waxwings, even smaller birds like House Finches, Tufted Titmice, and Carolina Chickadees show savvy interest in ripening berries in our yard.

Some years ago, a volunteer black elderberry sprang up in our yard, the seed carried here no

Top: Dinner-plate-sized elderberry blossom clusters (*Sambucus canadensis*) brighten any part of the yard.
Bottom: Within a month, the elderberry blossoms are replaced with luscious berry clusters, magnets for birds and their fledglings.

doubt from the neighbor's yard by a tummy-filled, satisfied bird. But the seed sprouted in a spot too poor to thrive, too shady to be truly happy. Having seen the plant's minimal success there, however, I purchased another one from a native fruit producer and planted it in prime elderberry real estate. It has thrived. And sprouted babies. And the babies are now sprouting babies, as the oldest plants die off. In short, the black elderberry bush doesn't live a long time, but the roots send up new shoots as the older plants die off in three or four years. A single plant is a good investment—for both you and the birds!

Holly Shrubs: Inkberry, Possumhaw, and Winterberry

Most of us know and love holly trees, recognized for their holiday-time decorative red berries and sharply pointed, shiny evergreen leaves. But don't confuse the native American holly tree with the group of holly shrubs listed here as best-choice shrub selections. We've narrowed a long list of possibilities to three, including inkberry, possum haw (not to be confused with the *Viburnum* species by the same name), and winterberry. All three standards have quite suitable cultivars that, depending on your location, may serve you and your birds well.

As with virtually all *Ilex* species, in order for your holly shrubs to produce berries, you'll need both male and female plants. Typically, one male plant will pollinate about five females, especially if planted centrally among them. Your local nursery staff can verify your choices of male versus female and whether they will make happy couples.

So let's look at the three holly shrubs we've chosen.

Inkberry, also known as Appalachian tea (so named because Native Americans made tea from the plant's leaves), evergreen winterberry, and gallberry, is a clump-forming broadleaf evergreen. Unlike the tree member of this *Ilex* family, its berries are black (thus its common name) that hang in clusters. Several cultivars are less prone to suckering, so if you prefer a compact plant rather than one that will naturalize, consider one of the cultivars such as 'Shamrock' (a more shapely form than the standard), 'Densa' (more dense than the

standard and only 3 to 4 feet tall at maturity), or 'Compacta' (a more compact plant than the standard). Honey from inkberry is highly valued, so the plant's inconspicuous flowers are obvious attractants to bees and other pollinators. Birds come for both the bugs and the berries.

Possum haw, sometimes written as possumhaw, goes by a number of common names, including possumhaw holly, deciduous holly, meadow holly, swamp holly, prairie holly, welk holly, bearberry, and deciduous yaupon. Because of its height, possum haw is sometimes treelike. Setting it apart from inkberry in yet another way, it's deciduous, not evergreen. In winter, bright red berries are scattered along leafless gray stems, and, of course, that's the primary attraction to birds. But like other hollies, both trees and shrubs, the inconspicuous flowers attract bees and other insects—which, of course, also attract birds. Think of this shrub as an understory plant, preferring at least partial shade from its larger neighbors.

Winterberry originated in North America's wetlands, but its amazing adaptability allows us to enjoy it in a multitude of habitats. In my yard, four females and a male live happily together in the partial shade of two flowering dogwood trees (*Cornus florida*) and a redbud tree (*Cercis canadensis*). When the winterberries lose their leaves, the fabulous and abundant red berries along the length of the stem are exposed, both for my viewing pleasure and for the birds' dining pleasure. By late January, though, the berries are gone, thanks to repeat visits by Eastern Bluebirds, Northern Mockingbirds, migrating thrushes, and a flock of hungry American Robins. Occasionally a Northern Cardinal sneaks a few morsels or a group of Cedar Waxwings drops by. Larger shrubs with more-abundant berries may hold until the violets bloom.

Of the three holly shrubs, winterberry is my personal favorite, and a number of cultivars offer

While 'Winter Gold' winterberry shrubs (*Ilex verticillata*) look lovely against winter's drab landscape, birds seem unable to recognize yellow berries as food; so choose a yellow-berried variety for yourself if you wish, but choose a red-berried one for the birds.

choices that may work well in your yard. 'Red Sprite' is a small, nicely compact cultivar staying at about 3 to 5 feet tall. 'Winter Red' is likely the most popular overall (see photo at the opening of this chapter). If you're planting for birds, however, you'll probably skip the cultivar called 'Winter Gold'. Birds don't recognize the yellow berries as food. I watched during one severe winter when birds were starving, and not once did they approach 'Winter Gold'. In spring, the rotted berries fell to the ground. Plant it for yourself, if you wish, but know it won't serve the birds.

New Jersey Tea

New Jersey tea, a plant named for a popular tea made from its leaves during the Revolutionary War period, is quite similar to redroot and small-leaved redroot, although their native statuses differ. Small-leaved redroot is confined to southern sandy pine and oak woods. All three species, however, are quite small—max 3 feet tall—making them perfect for virtually every

space. In addition, all have extremely deep roots that allow them to recover from some of the most inhospitable conditions, including fire. Butterflies love the conspicuous flowers, and because it's a larval host for several small butterflies, birds find the plant attractive. The plant's seeds provide a certain amount of winter sustenance, but in terms of birdscaping, here's the most significant feature of all: Hummingbirds visit regularly for the tiny insects that pollinate the flowers. Can't not love a hummer's favorite protein source!

Common Ninebark

Only recently did I discover common ninebark. While I have several of the standard species, I also have a couple of the cultivars, one of which boasts wine-colored foliage. The odd name comes from the fact that the bark peels (properly speaking, it exfoliates) from mature stems in strips, somewhat like that of a paper birch. In winter, then, the various shades of reddish to light brown along the peeling stem create a nice contrast to the otherwise monotone winter world. For birds, however,

'Summer Wine' common ninebark (*Physocarpus opulifolius*) flowers beautifully in late spring before providing berries for birds in midsummer.

it's about blossoms and bugs in spring and drooping clusters of reddish berries in fall and winter. Because I made a mistake when I planted the first shrub, situating it in too small a space, I've learned that ninebark can be pruned significantly in winter and will still burst with growth the following spring.

Spicebush

A longtime standard in native plant gardens, spicebush is the larval host for the namesake spicebush swallowtail. In the laurel family, spicebush is one of the first shrubs to bloom in spring, even before leaves appear, and one of the first to produce berries in summer. But you'll need male and female plants if you want those bright red berries. The male flowers are showier—such as they are—but female plants bear the fruit. In short, spicebush is great for enhancing bird habitat because of its early blossoms and fruit, but butterflies and bees will thank you as well.

Sumacs: Fragrant, Smooth, and Dwarf

Sumacs add a wide range of interest to a native birdscape. Their twisted form, serrated leaves, brilliant fall foliage, and fuzzy red berries combine to create year-round visual treat.

Fragrant sumac is so named because when crushed, its leaves and stems smell heavenly. This sumac, however, is really closer to being a tall and relatively dense ground cover (mine stands about 18 inches) rather than a true shrub. It spreads slowly outward by root from its cluster center and blooms early, and the female plants form

The last berries still viable at winter's end are typically some form of sumac, perhaps *Rhus glabra*, often life-savers for non-seed-eating birds like American Robins (shown here) and Eastern Bluebirds.

fuzzy red berries that attract wildlife in general and butterflies and birds in particular.

Smooth sumac, very similar to staghorn sumac, often stands at winter's end as birds' last resort. While sumac berries lack the rich lipids of earlier-producing berries, Eastern Bluebirds in particular turn to it in hopes of survival. Because sumac lacks the richest nutrients, birds must eat more of it to satisfy their needs. It's a bittersweet experience, however, to watch bluebirds, robins, and mockingbirds picking at sumac heads in late March, knowing they are nearly starved but also knowing there's at least some sustenance at hand.

One winter some years ago, snows piled high late in the season and drew unusual birds to our backyard feeder area: bluebirds, robins, mock-ingbirds—birds that rarely eat seed and seem flummoxed by suet cakes, preferring bugs and berries. At winter's end, however, their favored foods were gone, and they faced hard times. Hard times call for hard choices, and these birds were attracted to other birds' feeding activity. Unfortu-nately, they found nothing to satisfy their hunger, so I feared for their survival. Remembering that sumac shrubs grew several miles from our house, I made my way there, cut several seed heads, brought them home, and tied one to a shepherd's hook, one to a platform feeder, and one to a fence post. Within minutes, all three species had visited the sumac seed heads, seeming—or so I hoped—to find some minimal nutrition. I trust they survived. Months later, when planting time was right, I added sumacs in the yard.

Dwarf sumac, also called winged sumac, flame-leaf sumac, and shining sumac, offers a viable alternative to suit smaller spaces. Despite the name "dwarf," the plant can, in optimum grow-ing conditions, reach as high as 15 feet tall, but pruning can keep it in check if that's your choice. As a result, it works well in containers and above-ground planters. As a shrub, it wants to be multi-stemmed, but again, it can be trained to grow single-trunked. While we usually think of sumac in terms of its long-holding seed heads, the dwarf sumac is especially good for its dense growth, thus providing superb shelter for birds.

Virginia Sweetspire

Three popular cultivars of Virginia sweetspire work similarly well, providing an abundance of showy flowers in early summer and then, planted in masses, a shrubby ground cover for the sum-mer, followed by its main attraction of long-lasting, showy foliage in fall. Check out 'Henry's Garnet', 'Little Henry', and 'Merlot'. Virginia sweetspire's scientific genus name, *Itea*, meaning "willow" in Greek, reflects the plant's leaf and

Virginia sweetspire (*Itea virginica* 'Henry's Garnet') invites pollinators of all sizes to visit its sweet nectar.

flower similarities to those of certain willows. In fact, the plant is also called Virginia willow. While the flowers—along with the insects and tiny bees they attract—and stunning fall foliage are the main attributes noted by landscapers, it's the low, dense cover for ground-loving birds that weighed heavily in my decision to plant a swath along a strip that tends to carry heavy runoff. Its root-suckering habit makes for excellent erosion control, and it's a perfect native for covering large banks, beds, and borders.

Viburnums: Arrowwood, Mapleleaf, and Smooth Witherod

Viburnums include more than 150 species of deciduous, evergreen, and semievergreen woody plants, many of which are native to North America. Some landscape designers claim there's a viburnum for every need, one to fill every trouble spot in any garden or yard! Well, that's quite a claim, but I can certainly vouch for a number of species. Most of the 150 tout an abundance of lovely spring blossoms, usually white, either flat-top clusters or snowball shape, followed by rich blue, black, red, or yellow berries popular with a wide variety of birds. Foliage on some turns brilliant red in fall. And it's worth noting, because of their size, that viburnums can all be pruned. Since pruning should be completed immediately after flowering, however, it will reduce fall berry production; pruning later would reduce next spring's blossoms. All in all, viburnums rank way up there among top choices for native plantings, both for birds and for dynamite landscaping.

It was with some hand-wringing then that I accepted the limiting factor of space and picked only three best-choice viburnums here (plus two in the "treelike shrub" category later in the chapter). My limitations, however, should not limit your consideration of other native viburnums or their cultivars. Check the USDA Plant Database online to determine their respective status in your region.

Let's look at the three:

Deciduous arrowwood viburnum gets its name from the Native Americans' supposed use of its straight stems for arrow shafts. While that attribution may or may not be accurate, the shrub certainly does grow straight and strong, perhaps too hefty for some locations. Good for backgrounds and hedges, its white spring blossoms on flat-topped clusters up to 4 inches in diameter turn into luscious blue or blue-black berries by late summer. Birds make quick work of the feast.

The smallest of the three best-choice deciduous viburnums listed here, mapleleaf viburnum, also called mapleleaf arrowwood, may fit well in your landscape. Its typical viburnum-type blossoms attract bugs and butterflies to nectar, and its handsome blue berries attract birds in fall. In this species, it's the relative compact size that matters.

Deciduous smooth witherod, sometimes called possumhaw, has somewhat glossier leaves than the other three viburnums we've selected here and is typically the most compact. The cluster of them in my yard adds a dark, rich green to an otherwise bare brick wall below high windows. Bugs, butterflies, and birds—the three Big Bs—take their seasonal pleasure among them. One probably needless warning: Don't let the name "possumhaw" confuse you with the *Ilex* species of the same name.

Willows: Silky and Meadow

We've already included willows in the tree section, and now we're adding them to the shrub section. Whether they're in tree form or shrub form, however, willows are among the top species supporting bugs—they're big-time butterfly hosts—and that makes them big-time targets for birds feeding on bugs. Willow shrubs are

Willows in all forms (*Salix* spp.) attract spring migrants like this White-eyed Vireo foraging for caterpillars among the branches.

A Northern Mockingbird, bug in beak, has found successful foraging amid Ozark witch hazel's (*Hamamelis vernalis*) very early blossoms.

clump-forming, but the silky willow stays to 6 feet, while the meadow willow, also called slender willow, can double that height. Plant what you have room for. I've just added two to my own yard, knowing full well the butterflies will find them first.

Witch Hazels: American and Ozark

One final pair of selections remain in this list: American witch hazel, sometimes called winter-bloom, and its spring counterpart, Ozark witch hazel.

There's good reason for American witch hazel to carry the moniker winterbloom: It blooms later than any other flowering shrub, often through December. Its other common name, snapping hazel, comes from the seed, the pod of which pops open with such a snap—or force—that the seed can rocket 30 feet from the plant. While American witch hazel can reach roof high, it can be pruned to suit your preference. Given its end-of-the-year blossoms, it's not only a boon for birds but a breath of spring-to-come even before winter encases the yard.

Ozark witch hazel, on the other hand, blooms early in the spring, before anything else—before dogwood, before violets, often before the calendar says winter is done. In fact, it often blooms while the previous season's fruit lingers, thus accounting for its genus name *Hamamelis*, meaning "together with fruit." Some sources suggest that the "witch" part of its name comes from folks using the twigs for divining rods. My grandpa used peach branches to water-witch, but nobody calls them "witch peaches." You be the judge. Aside from the charming folk-lore, Ozark witch hazel is a low-growing shrub worth considering. Given the very early blossoms when nectar is at a premium, the shrub attracts a wide variety of bugs and butterflies and, as a result, birds.

Here, then, in alphabetical order by common name, are my thirty native shrub selections, including a few cultivar choices. On the scale of poor-good-better-best, all rank as "better" or "best" choices for attracting birds to your yard, while cultivars rank as "good."

About the Lists

The shrubs and understory trees listed here are, according to the United States Department of Agriculture Plant Database (online at www.plants .usda.gov), native to states as indicated. Note that while a plant may be native in your state, it may not be native to every part of your state and certainly not to every eco-region. In the cases of cultivars, any native designation references the standard of the cultivar. As always, consider soil texture, moisture, slope, and sunlight required. Your planting zone and eco-region combined will determine suitable growing conditions in your locale. To find your planting zone, check online at http://planthardiness.ars.usda.gov/.

The plant lists in this reference are not, nor are they intended to be, all-inclusive. Rather, plants listed here are chosen because:

1. They are attractive to birds for multiple reasons, meeting birds' needs for food and shelter and, in the case of shrubs, are almost always attractive for nesting.
2. They are easily grown, well-behaved, and suitable for landscaping in various settings, as noted.

In addition, always plant according to size of mature plant relative to space available. Estimated height and spread sizes shown here are for mature shrubs and understory trees. Generally, however, shrubs can be readily pruned to maintain a preferred height and spread.

Thirty Shrubs for Super-Sized, Mid-Sized, and Mini Yards

COMMON NAME	SCIENTIFIC NAME	BENEFIT(S) I = INSECT HOST N = NECTAR B = BERRIES S = SUMMER F = FALL W = WINTER WS = WINTER SHELTER	COMMENTS	NATIVE, PLANTING ZONES
Alder, speckled	*Alnus incana* ssp. *rugosa*	I seed	15–20' tall, 15–25' spread; full shade to part sun; medium to wet, tolerates mucky soil; good to naturalize and in rain gardens; native to boggy grounds, cool climate; attracts birds	North of Ohio River Zones 2–6 (does not thrive south of zone 6)
Bayberry	*Morella* spp. synonymous with *Myrica* spp.	Bw (esp. for Yellow-rumped Warblers) WS	Broadleaf evergreen in south; semievergreen in north	As specified below
Bayberry, northern	*M. pensylvanica*	I N Bw WS	Semievergreen in southern part of range; 5–10' tall, 5–10' spread; dense branching; can be pruned; need male and female to produce berries (on female); full sun to part shade; best in groups or massed	East Coast and OH, PA, and NY, but not SC, GA, and FL Zones 3–7
Bayberry, southern synonymous with wax myrtle	*Morella cerifera* synonymous with *Myrica cerifera*	I N Bf, w WS	Broadleaf evergreen, semievergreen in northern habitats; 10–15' tall, 8–10' spread; grows in wide range of soils; full sun to part shade; fast-growing; tolerates salt spray; male and female required, waxy blue-gray fruits on female; versatile shrub; will colonize if allowed	Coastal states from NJ south plus WV and AR Zones 7–10
Beautyberry, American synonymous with **American beauty bush**	*Callicarpa americana*	N (pollinators) Bf, w	3–6' tall, 3–6' spread; insignificant flowers; clusters of lavender berries, esp. for fall migrants; fruits best in full sun; loose shrub, best in masses	Ohio River south Zones 6–10
Blueberries	*Vaccinium* spp.	I Bs	Numerous *Vaccinium* species produce delicious fruits for humans and birds	Depending on species

COMMON NAME	SCIENTIFIC NAME	BENEFIT(S) I = INSECT HOST N = NECTAR B = BERRIES S = SUMMER F = FALL W = WINTER WS = WINTER SHELTER	COMMENTS	NATIVE, PLANTING ZONES
Buttonbush	*Cephalanthus occidentalis*	N (pollinators) seed	5-12' tall, 4-8' spread; showy fragrant flowers esp. attractive to bees, butterflies; full sun to part shade; wet to medium soils; good in rain garden	Eastern US Zones 5-9
Chokeberry	*Aronia* spp.	Bf, w	Named for tart berries; easily grown and will readily sucker, given the opportunity	As specified below
Black chokeberry	*A. melanocarpa*, esp. 'Iroquois Beauty'; other cultivars suitable	Bf	3-6' tall; 3-6' spread; will sucker; showy May flowers, showy very tart fall fruit, attractive fall foliage; good for hedge, rain garden, or to naturalize; prune suckers to prevent naturalizing; cultivar 'Iroquois Beauty' more compact	Eastern US except FL and cultivars Zones 3-8
Red chokeberry	*A. arbutifolia*, esp. 'Brilliantissima'	N Bf, w ('Brilliantissima' holds berries until spring)	6-8' tall, 3-4' spread; can form colonies; glossy red fruit in clusters; red fall foliage; multi-season ornamental interest; plant in masses; best used only in super-sized yards	Eastern US except OH, IN, IL, MI, WI, MN, IA, and MO and cultivars Zones 4-9
Dogwoods	*Cornus* spp.	Varies by species	Dogwood trees differ from shrubs in that shrubs are multi-stemmed	As specified below
Gray dogwood	*C. racemosa*	N (esp. for butterflies) Bf, w (esp. beneficial for fall migrating birds)	10-15' tall, 10-15' spread; full sun to part shade; showy flowers leaving white berries on red stems; grows in poor soils; best if allowed to form thickets, so works well as border, screen, in rain gardens; magnet for fall migrants	Eastern US except FL, GA, AL, MS, LA, and TN Zones 4-8

COMMON NAME	SCIENTIFIC NAME	BENEFIT(S) I = INSECT HOST N = NECTAR B = BERRIES S = SUMMER F = FALL W = WINTER WS = WINTER SHELTER	COMMENTS	NATIVE, PLANTING ZONES
Red osier dogwood synonymous with red twig dogwood	*C. sericea,* formerly *C. stolonifera,* esp. 'Allemans'	N (esp. for butterflies) Bf	6–9′ tall, 8–12′ spread; best in fertile moist soils; red stems; suckers, trim with spade if thickets undesired; full to part shade; clusters of small, insignificant white blossoms, white fall berries; good as hedge, in rain gardens; cultivar 'Allemans' rarely taller than 5′, more compact	North of NC and TN except MO and cultivars Zones 3–8
Roughleaf dogwood	*C. drummondii*	N Bs, f (esp. beneficial for fall migrating birds)	6–15′ tall, 6–15′ spread; full sun to part shade; easily grown, tolerates poor soils; forms thickets, so good as informal hedge, property line screen, border, naturalized areas; white berries are bird magnets	Eastern US except MN, FL, SC, NC, WV, MD, and DE and east of NY Zones 5–8
Silky dogwood synonymous with swamp dogwood	*C. amomum*	N Bs, f	6–12′ tall, 6–12′ spread; likes moist, acidic soil in part shade; branches will root if touch ground; can form thickets if left alone; good in naturalized areas, stream banks, erosion control; dark blue berries	Eastern US except LA, AR, MN, and WI Zones 5–8
Elderberry, American black synonymous with **common elderberry**	*Sambucus canadensis*	N Bs	5–12′ tall, 5–12′ spread; can form thickets; full sun to part shade, well-drained soils; flat, rounded blossom; purple/blue fruit ripens Aug–Sept, preferred by bluebirds; good as shrub border, background, screen, in rain gardens	Eastern US Zones 3–9
Holly shrubs	*Ilex* spp.	Flowers insignificant; best noted for berry production	Mostly deciduous as shrubs; compare with broadleaf evergreen holly trees	As specified on the next page

COMMON NAME	SCIENTIFIC NAME	BENEFIT(S) I = INSECT HOST N = NECTAR B = BERRIES S = SUMMER F = FALL W = WINTER WS = WINTER SHELTER	COMMENTS	NATIVE, PLANTING ZONES
Inkberry 'Shamrock' (also other cultivars)	*I. glabra* 'Shamrock'	N Bf, w	Broadleaf evergreen, 5–8' tall, 5–8' spread; easily grown, slow growing; full sun to part shade; can spread by root suckers to colonize; cultivars have generally better form; excellent as border, foundation, low hedge; berries somewhat toxic to humans, esp. children	All eastern and southern coastal states and cultivars Zones 4–9
Possum haw synonymous with deciduous holly	*I. decidua*	N Bw	Deciduous, 7–15' tall, 5–12' spread; full sun to part shade, medium soil; small red berries in winter along leafless gray twigs; male and female required; good as specimen, group, or hedge; good winter color	Southeast to Ohio River but not WV; also IN, IL, and MO Zones 5–9
Winterberry (several good cultivars)	*I. verticillata*	Bw	Deciduous, 3–12' tall; 3–12' spread; need 1 male to 4 females; flowers insignificant, showy berries in fall and winter; original wetlands species; prefers acidic to medium soils, tolerates clay and wet soils and pollution; can be used as hedge	Eastern US and cultivars Zones 3–9
New Jersey tea similar to smaller **redroot** and **small-leaved redroot**	*Ceanothus americanus C. herbaceus C. microphyllus*	I N	3–4' tall, 3–5' spread; full sun to part shade; tolerates drought, rocky soil; easily grown; use as shrub border, ground cover; attractive to butterflies and hummingbirds	Eastern US Zones 4–8
Ninebark, common (also cultivars)	*Physocarpus opulifolius*	N Bf, w	5–8' tall; 6–8' spread; full sun to part shade; good as hedge, screen, erosion control; small flowers in clusters, followed by umbrella-like clusters of reddish berries that turn brown, persist through winter; grows in harsh conditions	Eastern US except MS and LA and cultivars Zones 2–8

COMMON NAME	SCIENTIFIC NAME	BENEFIT(S) I = INSECT HOST N = NECTAR B = BERRIES S = SUMMER F = FALL W = WINTER WS = WINTER SHELTER	COMMENTS	NATIVE, PLANTING ZONES
Spicebush	*Lindera benzoin*	I Bs	6–10' tall, 6–12' spread; full sun to part shade; tolerates clay soils; easy to grow; requires male and female plants; blooms very early, bright red drupes mature in fall	Eastern US except WI and MN Zones 4–9
Sumacs	*Rhus* spp.	B	Best for massing	As specified below
Fragrant sumac	*R. aromatica*	I N Bs, f, w	2–4' tall, 6-10' spread; easily grown in wide range of soils but needs good drainage; male and female plants; male catkins form late summer, bloom in spring; female blossoms form hairy red berry clusters in late summer persisting into winter; good for stabilizing banks, showy ground cover, informal hedge; spreads by root suckers	Eastern US Zones 3–9
Smooth sumac very similar to staghorn sumac	*R. glabra R. typhina*	Bf, w (persist until spring)	9–15' tall, 9–15' spread; full sun to part shade; tolerates wide variety of soils but needs well-drained; forms thickets; best massed to halt erosion or cover areas of poor soil; too weedy and aggressive for informal hedges; male and female plants; female forms pyramidal fruiting clusters that last well into winter as last resort for berry-eating birds; bright fall foliage	Entire US Zones 3–9

COMMON NAME	SCIENTIFIC NAME	BENEFIT(S) I = INSECT HOST N = NECTAR B = BERRIES S = SUMMER F = FALL W = WINTER WS = WINTER SHELTER	COMMENTS	NATIVE, PLANTING ZONES
Dwarf sumac synonymous with winged sumac, flameleaf sumac, and shining sumac	*R. copallina*	Bf, w (persist until spring)	7–15' tall, 10–20' spread; tolerates wide variety of soil but needs well-drained in full sun or part shade; best when allowed to colonize, form masses for erosion control, or cover poor soil areas; female plants form pyramidal berries, last resort for winter survival for birds; bright fall foliage	Eastern US except MN Zones 4–9
Sweetspire, Virginia, 'Henry's Garnet' (see dwarf cultivar in table below)	*Itea virginica* 'Henry's Garnet'	I N	3–4' tall, 4–6' spread; full sun to part shade; tolerates heavy shade, clay and wet soils; good as specimen, group, or mass; will naturalize; showy fragrant flowers in late spring	Cultivar Zones 5–9
Viburnums	*Viburnum* spp.	Berries especially attractive	All adapt to full sun or part shade; prefer well-drained soils; most have lovely fall foliage; easily grown; will sucker to naturalize but removing suckers controls growth	As specified below
Arrowwood viburnum	*V. dentatum*	I Bf	6–10' tall, 6–10' spread; prune as needed; showy white flowers early summer, blue-black drupes late summer and fall; very winter hardy	Eastern US except VT, NH, MI, WI, and MN Zones 2–8
Mapleleaf viburnum	*V. acerifolium*	I N Bs, f	3–6' tall, 2–4' spread; tiny white flowers in showy clusters, pea-sized bluish-black fruits late summer; prune immediately after flowering	Eastern US except MO, IA, and MN Zones 3–8
Smooth witherod synonymous with possumhaw	*V. nudum*	I N Bf	5–12' tall, 5–12' spread; showy, fragrant white flowers early spring, berries ripen to purplish black late summer; attractive purplish fall foliage	Eastern US except MO, IA, and MN Zones 5–9

COMMON NAME	SCIENTIFIC NAME	BENEFIT(S) I = INSECT HOST N = NECTAR B = BERRIES S = SUMMER F = FALL W = WINTER WS = WINTER SHELTER	COMMENTS	NATIVE, PLANTING ZONES
Willows	*Salix* spp.	Butterfly host plant	Most prefer wet soils	As specified below
Meadow willow synonymous with slender willow	S. petiolaris	I (butterfly host)	5–15' tall; multi-stemmed, forms clumps; wet, moist soils; esp. beneficial to pollinators	North of Ohio River to coast, plus MN and IA Zones 2–8
Silky willow	S. sericea	I (butterfly host)	6' tall; forms clumps; native to marshes, ditches, low woods	Eastern US except LA, MS, and FL Zones 2–8
Witch hazel	*Hamamelis* spp.	As noted below	As described below	As specified below
American witch hazel synonymous with winterbloom	H. virginiana	N I	15–20' tall, 15–20' spread; easily grown, prefers acidic moist soils but tolerates heavy clay; remove suckers unless want to naturalize; blooms Oct–Dec, so usually last native flowering plant; forms fruits through winter; good as hedge, shrub border	Eastern US Zones 3–8
Ozark witch hazel	H. vernalis	N I	6–10' tall, 8–15' spread; easily grown in average, medium moisture, well-drained soils; full sun to part shade; remove root suckers if colonizing not desired; first to bloom (Jan–Apr)	Southern, central US Zones 4–8

COMPACT SHRUBS FOR MINI YARDS AND POTS-AND-PATIO GARDENS

We've noted that some of the shrubs above could work in mini yards, especially if pruned. Of course, shrubs we're suggesting as great selections for mini yards will work as well in larger yards. In fact, planting masses in super-sized yards can prove to be a real show-stopper, for both birds and humans. The point here is that compact shrubs can have good uses in any-sized yard. Think rock gardens, accents near water features, sidewalk borders, front-row plants in a cottage garden, feature plants in accent gardens, year-round interest in seasonal perennial gardens—the list is limited only by your imagination.

So here goes with suggestions for seven compact shrubs—almost all evergreen. Take a look, no matter what size your space.

American Arborvitae

While we included American arborvitae (northern white cedar) among recommended trees in Chapter 5, these two small evergreen cultivars readily qualify as shrubs. 'Hetz Midget' and 'Rheingold' both grow slow and stay low, perfect for planting in tiny yards and rock gardens. Year-round, most any evergreen supplies highly desirable shelter for birds, and tiny yards often lack much shelter of any kind. So here's the opportunity to welcome birds year-round—but especially in winter—with a go-to safe place.

Hemlock

Likewise, the hemlock evergreen cultivar shrub 'Abbott's Pygmy', along with numerous other hemlock cultivar shrubs, provides good winter shelter. Since these small shrubs do well in containers, they're perfect even for pots-and-patio gardens.

Compact Shrubs for Mini Yards and Pots and Patio Gardens

COMMON NAME	SCIENTIFIC NAME	BENEFIT(S) I = INSECT HOST N = NECTAR B = BERRIES S = SUMMER F = FALL W = WINTER WS = WINTER SHELTER	COMMENTS	NATIVE, PLANTING ZONES
American arborvitaes synonymous with **northern white cedar**	*Thuja* spp.	Bw WS	Evergreen; supply significant winter shelter for birds	As noted below
'Hetz Midget'	T. occidentalis 'Hetz Midget'	Bw WS	Evergreen, 4–5' tall, 3–4' spread; slow-growing globed form; can be pruned, but no pruning needed to maintain form; tolerates clay soil; good for rock gardens, foundations	Cultivar Zones 2–7

COMMON NAME	SCIENTIFIC NAME	BENEFIT(S) I = INSECT HOST N = NECTAR B = BERRIES S = SUMMER F = FALL W = WINTER WS = WINTER SHELTER	COMMENTS	NATIVE, PLANTING ZONES
'Rheingold'	*T. occidentalis* 'Rheingold'	Bw WS	Evergreen, 3–5' tall, 3–5' spread; globed, slow-growing; unusual bright gold to copper-orange foliage year-round	Cultivar Zones 2–7
Hemlock 'Abbott's Pygmy' (many other small cultivars available)	*Tsuga canadensis* 'Abbott's Pygmy'	WS	Evergreen; tiny, matures at 18" tall, 1–1.5' spread; part to full shade; good in rock gardens, containers	Cultivar Zones 4–7
Junipers/ red cedars	*Juniperus virginiana*	Bw WS	Evergreen; many cultivars; berries (actually tiny cones) favorite winter food for many birds	Eastern US Zones 2–9
'Blue Mountain'	*J. virginiana* 'Blue Mountain'	Bw WS	Evergreen, 3–4' tall, 5-8' spread; blue-green foliage softer than most junipers; females produce berries; good foundation plant, border, or on slopes	Cultivar Zones 2–9
'Gray Owl'	*J. virginiana* 'Gray Owl'	Bw WS	Evergreen, 3–4' tall, 6–8' spread; silver-gray foliage attractive year-round; female produce berries	Cultivar, eastern US Zones 2–9
'Silver Spreader'	*J. virginiana* 'Silver Spreader'	Bw WS	Evergreen, 2–3' tall, 3–6' spread; sun, well-drained soil; deer resistant	Cultivar, eastern US Zones 3–9
Sweetspire, Virginia, 'Little Henry'	*Itea virginica* 'Little Henry'	I N	Dwarf deciduous, 1.5–2' tall, 2–2.5' spread; full sun to part shade; tolerates heavy shade, clay and wet soils; good as specimen, group, mass; will naturalize; superior flowers and brighter autumn leaves than standard	Cultivar Zones 5–9

Juniper/Red Cedar

Next, a trio of juniper cultivars takes the spotlight: 'Blue Mountain' juniper, 'Gray Owl' juniper, and 'Silver Spreader' juniper, all smaller than 3 feet tall. Some, however, do spread, so they're not really suitable for containers. Even in my super-sized yard, I've added a bed of Gray Owls that will, when they finally grow together, provide safety for roosting, nesting, and wintering birds. Simultaneously, the berry lovers, especially Cedar Waxwings, will enjoy the juniper's fall-through-winter berry-like cones. Because these are all *Juniperus virginiana* cultivars, not hybrids, they maintain the same characteristics as the standard red cedar. They're just smaller. Can't beat native red cedar for bird habitat!

Virginia Sweetspire

Finally, if you prefer a deciduous tiny shrub, consider the mini Virginia sweetspire 'Little Henry'. Not more than 2 feet tall, it looks exactly like the bigger 'Henry's Garnet'—just smaller. What's not to love?

TEN MORE HARD-TO-CATEGORIZE RECOMMENDATIONS

Finally, in this section, 10 of our recommendations fall into the hard-to-categorize realm. Are they tall shrubs? Are they short trees? Well, maybe both, depending on whom you ask. But in this reference, they're birdscape plants!

Alternate-Leaf Dogwood

We've already talked about a number of dogwood shrubs, but a 25-footer with a 30-foot spread seems more expansive than a shrub. Whatever its category, the alternate-leaf dogwood, sometimes called pagoda dogwood, brings typical dogwood attributes to the yard: berries that birds love. Indeed, the flowers also attract butterflies and other insects. And like other dogwood species, either trees or shrubs, alternate-leaf dogwoods prefer some shade, especially from hot afternoon sun. Still, it's adaptable enough to function well as a specimen shrub near patios and in bird gardens. Compare this larger species with the dogwood shrubs recommended earlier in this chapter.

Devil's Walking Stick

Devil's walking stick gets its name from its abundant thorns, so this is not the tree to plant next to a sidewalk or pool where you'll be brushing past. Given some space, put this tall shrub/tree along the wood's edge, out of the way, but where you can watch bird activity from your favorite window. You'll be rewarded! Despite its thorns, devil's walking stick serves as a bird magnet. Everything loves its flowers, especially bugs and butterflies. And you know what that means!

Fringetree

Fringetree can reach 20 feet tall, so the shrub is definitely treelike. And after all, "tree" is part of its name. An early bloomer, like dogwood, the flowers produce a spectacular show. Berries follow. You'll never be disappointed by this beauty.

Hawthorns: Washington and Green

Hawthorns produce fine crops of berries mid-fall holding into winter, so birds find winter food supplies among the branches. Handsome along streets in full sun, hawthorns can be pruned. The somewhat thorny Washington hawthorn and the largely thornless variety, green hawthorn 'Winter King', both work well in a wide variety of growing conditions. Unfortunately, our hawthorn succumbed to rust (most likely airborne from nearby cedar and apple trees) that, we're told, would render any thoughts of replanting misguided. I miss that tree—but probably not as much as the birds do.

Washington hawthorn blossoms (*Crataegus phaenopyrum*) turn into small red berries that hold well into winter, a feature highly attractive to many birds.

A House Wren, his throat puffed up in closed-beak song, defends his territory perched amid redbud blossoms (*Cercis canadensis*).

Redbud

Redbuds tend to come up voluntarily where we live, so we have numerous individuals. Because they bloom so early, we watched a number of bird species eat the buds, especially Cedar Waxwings, American Robins, Northern Cardinals, and even Tufted Titmice and Carolina Chickadees. The blossom is highly nutritious. Smart, aren't they, to find superfood among the flowers? What a treasure, then, these redbuds!

Serviceberry: Allegheny and Canadian

Whether you're in the region hosting Allegheny smooth serviceberry, sometimes considered the same species as downy or shadblow serviceberry, or more likely to find Canadian serviceberry in your area, you'll love the first blossoms of spring these understory trees bring. My dad used to come to supper grinning ear to ear to announce winter's end—the "sarviss berry," as he called it, was abloom, and his beehives were humming! We always felt a bit celebratory at the news. Little did I understand then, as a kid, the importance of that very early nectar to starving pollinators or the vital

nutrition in the berries that ripen within a month or so, serving up birds the rich lipids they need to prepare for nesting. Now my yard touts three.

Viburnums: Blackhaw and Nannyberry

Finally, we offer two more *Viburnum* species: blackhaw, named for its similarities to the unrelated hawthorn, and nannyberry, so named apparently because nanny goats, more than billy goats, like to feed on the ripe berries. Like the shorter *Viburnum* shrubs, the deciduous blackhaw and nannyberry blossom in late spring with flat-topped 4-inch-diameter blossoms followed by clusters of blue-black berries that birds adore. The primary difference between these viburnums and those in the shrub choices described earlier in the chapter is height.

Take another look at the four-season table on pages 109–10. Confirm your choices for four shrubs, more if you can, and add them to your yard map. Locate them, sketch in their mature sizes, and label them. Double check that soil and light conditions are appropriate for your chosen shrubs in your chosen locations.

Treelike Shrubs and Understory Trees

COMMON NAME	SCIENTIFIC NAME	BENEFIT(S) I = INSECT HOST N = NECTAR B = BERRIES S = SUMMER F = FALL W = WINTER WS = WINTER SHELTER	COMMENTS	NATIVE, PLANTING ZONES
Alternate-leaf dogwood synonymous with **pagoda dogwood**	*Cornus alternifolia*	N Bf	15–25′ tall, 20–32′ spread; "pagoda" suggests shape; full sun, part shade, well-drained acidic soils; showy flowers attract butterflies; fruits bluish-black drupes on red stems; good as specimen shrub, near patios, in lawns and bird gardens	Eastern US except LA Zones 3–7
Devil's walking stick	*Aralia spinosa*	N (pollinators) Bf	10–20′ tall, 6–10′ spread; umbrella shaped; thorny, so plant away from traffic areas; best naturalized; showy late flowers (July–Aug); tolerates drought, urban pollutants	Eastern US except VT, NH, MI, WI, and MN Zones 4–9
Fringetree	*Chionanthus virginicus*	N Bs, f	12–20′ tall, 12–20′ spread; treelike; tolerates air pollution, urban settings; grow in groups or as specimens, woodland borders; showy blooms, dark bluish-black berries support birds	Eastern US except MA, VT, NH, IN, IL, IA, MI, WI, and MN Zones 3–9
Hawthorns	*Crataegus* spp.	N Bf, w	Considered small landscape tree but can be pruned to shrub or hedge	As specified below
Washington hawthorn	*C. phaenopyrum*	N Bf, w	25–30′ tall, 25–30′ spread; small tree, thorny; full sun; showy fragrant fruit followed by red berries into winter; can prune as hedge; good street tree, flowering specimen	Eastern US except MA, VT, NH, WI, MN, and IA Zones 3–8
Green Hawthorn 'Winter King'	*C. viridis* 'Winter King'	N Bf, w	25–35′ tall, 25–35′ spread; small tree, can be pruned; showy flowers and fruit; largely thornless; tolerates drought, clay soil, pollution; disease-resistant cultivar; one of the best hawthorns for landscape, street, and urban settings	Cultivar Zones 4–7

COMMON NAME	SCIENTIFIC NAME	BENEFIT(S) I = INSECT HOST N = NECTAR B = BERRIES S = SUMMER F = FALL W = WINTER WS = WINTER SHELTER	COMMENTS	NATIVE, PLANTING ZONES
Redbud	*Cercis canadensis*	I N (esp. for butterflies)	20–30' tall, 25–35' spread; full sun to part shade; very early blossoms; good street tree, along patio, woodland margins; tolerates clay soil	Eastern US except MA, VT, NH, and MN Zones 4–8
Serviceberries	*Amelanchier* spp.	Very early blossoms with nectar for pollinators and fruit for birds	All *Amelanchier* species are popular with birds; only some listed here	As specified below
Allegheny serviceberry synonymous with smooth serviceberry; often considered same species as downy or shadblow serviceberry	*A. laevis* or *A. arborea*	N Bs	15–40' tall, 15–30' spread; full sun to part shade; tolerates air pollution; good street tree; attractive understory, woodland margins, informal hedge, screen; berries good for jams, jellies, pies; attractive fall foliage	Eastern US except FL, MS, LA, AR, and MO Zones 4–9
Canadian serviceberry	*A. canadensis*	N Bs	25–35' tall, 15–20' spread; full sun to part shade; tolerates wide range of soils; showy early-spring flowers yield green berries that turn red then purplish black late summer; best along woodland margins, stream banks, ponds	Eastern coastal US from ME to GA, including TN and WV Zones 4–8
Viburnums	*Viburnum* spp.	Berries especially attractive	Shrubs or trees, depending on pruning practices	As specified below
Blackhaw	*V. prunifolium*	I N Bf, w	12–15' tall, 6–12' spread; showy flowers late spring, showy edible fruit; tolerates drought, air pollution, clay soil; good as shrub border, tall hedge, screen; prune right after flowering	Eastern US except FL, MN, and east of NY Zones 3–9

COMMON NAME	SCIENTIFIC NAME	BENEFIT(S) I = INSECT HOST N = NECTAR B = BERRIES S = SUMMER F = FALL W = WINTER WS = WINTER SHELTER	COMMENTS	NATIVE, PLANTING ZONES
Nannyberry	*V. lentago*	I N Bf, w	14–16' tall, 6–12' spread; fast-growing, shade tolerant; showy white blossoms in spring; blue-black berry-like drupes can persist into winter; background planting, tall hedge, screen, shrub border; with pruning, can be single-trunked tree	Eastern US except TN, NC, SC, FL, MS, LA, and AR Zones 2–8

TWINING VINE BENEFITS

Vines, unique forms of shrubs, give your yard or garden a dramatic vertical-surface addition. Thus, it's likely no surprise that vines also add some big-time avian benefits. These generally vigorous, fast-growing plants have the amazing versatility to serve in not just one, but two almost opposite landscaping capacities—either twisting and twining up, along, and around some structure or reaching, winding, and trailing across ground features, acting as a tried-and-true ground cover.

As vertically growing plants, vines typically make dandy nest sites with easy in-and-out access for the likes of Northern Cardinals, Brown Thrashers, Northern Mockingbirds, Mourning Doves, and Gray Catbirds. All shrub-nesters readily accept a vine's dense cover for camouflage. Depending on the vine, its vegetation may also serve well as a four-season roost site, but nearly all of them serve birds extraordinarily well during at least three seasons.

As ground cover, vines create supportive habitat surface where perhaps there once was nothing. For instance, if the vine is covering something—like a rock pile, for example, or some eyesore otherwise without remedy—it can certainly add habitat. Think cover, insect support, nectar, and perhaps nesting in what would otherwise be a barren, wasted spot.

Although it likely goes without saying, the vines listed here also boast food value, mostly nectar and some berries.

American Bittersweet

The biggest danger of choosing American bittersweet to enhance your bird-friendly landscape is the risk of a purchase that, instead of being our native bittersweet (*Celastrus scandens*), turns out instead to be the Asian invasive, oriental bittersweet (*Celastrus orbiculatus*). The two look very much alike, so it's feasible that even without the intention to mislead, the invasives could end up on nursery racks. So be sure of your nursery's reliability. Ask questions. Double check the scientific name.

The native variety, however, will reward you for your efforts. Even though the red berries popping from their orange hulls offer nostalgic autumn home decor, who would want to rob the birds? Bittersweet berries are a favorite of berry lovers Eastern Towhees, Northern Mockingbirds, American Robins, and most other berry lovers. The vine is easily grown and will be happiest left alone in poor growing conditions along streamside or pond, trailing across bushes or twining on trees.

Crossvine

Crossvine makes a statement! Its early-spring burst of rich orange trumpet-shaped flowers sometimes occurs before Ruby-throated Hummingbirds arrive, but a few blossoms decorate the vine most of the summer. As if they're ever on the watch (and they most likely are), hummers

Early-blooming crossvine (*Bignonia capreolata*) attracts numerous insects and hummingbirds and serves well for nesting birds.

check out the nectar the minute flowers open. In my garden, Northern Cardinals set up housekeeping among the tangles. Mourning Doves like it, too, and a whole assortment of birds roost in the shelter from night to night, depending on who gets there first. The vine needs decent support, but compared to other native vines, it's relatively slow-growing and stays calm, cool, and collected, minding its manners in a tidy garden.

Dutchman's Pipe and Wooly Dutchman's Pipe

Funny name, Dutchman's pipe. The vine earns its moniker because its 2-inch-long, curved, somewhat trumpet-like flowers look a bit like Dutch smoking pipes. Even so, the flowers are rather inconspicuous, tucked among the leaves. The vines grow vigorously, although the wooly Dutchman's pipe is the far better behaved of the two. So I've listed both species (one is *not* a cultivar of the other) not only because of the behavior differences, but also because the wooly Dutchman's pipe is native farther north and west than the other. In addition, as the name suggests, the wooly species has a somewhat hairy texture to leaves and stems, while the other is smooth-leaved.

Both vines have heart-shaped leaves that hang overlapping, thus creating dense shade. In the wild, you'll find the vines along stream banks and in moist woods, climbing trees and shrubs. In your yard, on a trellis or other support, you can, if necessary, prune in late winter. Since the vines grow well from seed, they can be an economical addition to your landscape. Just keep in mind that these vines will not tolerate dry soils, so consider your planting spot before you choose.

The vines are recommended for butterflies, especially since they are larval hosts for the exquisite pipevine swallowtail butterfly. I'm always torn

Two similarly named vines, Dutchman's pipe (*Aristolochia macrophylla*) and the somewhat less vigorous wooly Dutchman's pipe (*A. tomentosa*), are host plants for the pipevine swallowtail, nectaring here on nonnative zinnia.

Wild grape vines (*Vitis riparia*) attract over 50 bird species, many of which, like this Chestnut-sided Warbler, come to forage for bugs.

about this vine. I love pipevine swallowtails, but the birds also love the caterpillars. Apparently, though, Mother Nature gets it all balanced out, because even when I see birds with caterpillars, I still see enough pipevine swallowtails to keep me happy.

Wild Grape

Probably no commercial nursery stocks wild grape vines, so I include it here as a reminder: If wild grape vines grow on your property, encourage their presence. More than 50 species of birds are known to dine on the berries, especially during fall migration. (Yes, wild grapes hang onto the vines much longer than those wine grapes cultivated for human consumption.) In fact, when I'm out and about watching for fall migrants, I look for grape vines and Virginia creeper vines (more on them later), knowing full well the buffet they offer will draw birds to the vines—lots of birds.

In spring, grape vines draw migrants by the score. I assume the hungry hordes are plucking bugs and caterpillars from the undersides of leaves and from hiding places in the stringy bark; but when I take a close look, I can never find anything buggy. Since the birds seem to readily find whatever is the main attraction, however, I'm willing to enjoy watching the treasure hunt.

Above and beyond berries and bugs, though, wild grapes may be the only source for the stringy bark that Baltimore and Orchard Orioles need for their swinging pendulous nests. Other birds use the bark for more traditional nest structures, too, including Northern Cardinals and Brown Thrashers.

Carolina Yellow Jasmine

Technically, in southwestern Indiana, I shouldn't be growing false jasmine, also called false jessamine, evening trumpet-flower, and Carolina yellow jasmine. I'm north of its native range. But given climate change and the northward-marching movement of vegetation, I've given it a try—primarily because I'm in love with its evergreen qualities. As crazy as it sounds, I've planted both crossvine and false jasmine on the same trellis. The combination means I get two sets of blooms, the bright yellow of jasmine and the rich orange of crossvine, but not at the same time! By significantly extending the blooming period—and nectar opportunities—the combo serves up nectar and bugs for double the time. And birds get double their money. Gives a whole new meaning to ordering a combo!

Trumpet Honeysuckle

Also called flame honeysuckle, my treasured trumpet honeysuckle came to my yard from my father's yard. It came to his yard from his mother's yard. And it came to his mother's yard from the yard of her mother who, in turn, grew up in her mother's house, the original 1853 homestead. It's an old plant. It's native. I've since bought three additional ones—and transplanted shoots from all of them for both friends and additional yard sites.

Trumpet honeysuckle, also known as flame honeysuckle (*Lonicera sempervirens*), is a favorite for its early hummingbird-magnet blossoms and dense vining habit, perfect for Brown Thrasher and Northern Cardinal nests.

Pruner's PAIN

Unknowingly, we sometimes cause nest failures by overzealous and untimely pruning. I'm guilty, and I'm not proud of it. You see, I once pruned a trumpet honeysuckle, unaware that Brown Thrashers were nesting within. Although I stopped the instant I understood, the nest was partly exposed, and my human scent was all over the vine. The following morning, the nest sat askew, the eggs gone, the adults nowhere to be seen. Pruning away protective branches or clearing tangled areas that serve as nest sites almost always invites predation, and evidence indicated my behavior gave a snake the clue it could find lunch. "Sorry" doesn't quite cut it in such a situation. I learned my lesson, and it was bitter. So, show your best manners by waiting until nesting concludes before whacking away at what seems to be overgrowth. Take it from one who—sadly—knows.

So you're guessing there's something about these plants that I really like? Indeed! It's the hummingbirds that visit these trumpet-shaped, apparently nectar-rich flowers. When I see Ruby-throated Hummingbirds with white heads, I know they've been nectaring on the honeysuckle and, in the process, dusted their heads with pollen. There's no question in my mind that hummers in my great-great-grandmother's yard did the same.

Trumpet Vine

Planting a trumpet vine demands effort. And space. It's not just about digging a hole and setting the plant. So give pause here for some details. Trumpet vine serves up a dandy supply of nectar to everything from bees to hummingbirds to Baltimore Orioles that, to feed, poke their beaks into the base of the flowers. The vigorous vine establishes really deep roots and will climb a utility pole in a matter of two years. So it needs ample sturdy support, lots and lots of space, and, in order to keep it somewhat contained, commitment to pruning annually. In reality, then, save this giant for a giant space where you can appreciate rather than fight its vigor, where it can climb and vine at abandon, well out of the way of the need for tidiness. The birds will love you.

Virginia Creeper

At plant-for-birds seminars, when I show photos of poison ivy vines next to Virginia creeper vines, someone almost always insists that the five-leaved Virginia creeper is, in fact, poison oak. Not so. In fact, poison oak, like poison ivy, has three leaves. It's a tough woody vine that sometimes grows into bush-like abundance, and it may grow where you live if you live south. But where I live, it's absent.

Virginia creeper, on the other hand, is a delicate vine that climbs trees (and buildings, if you let it) and produces clusters of deep-blue berries just in time for fall migrants to gorge on the rich lipids that energize their long flights south. Ironically, though, the vines are best identified in fall by their scarlet leaves—with the luscious berries almost hidden in the blaze.

Like wild grape, these vines are unlikely to be marketed at local nurseries. Just be aware of their presence if they pop up in your yard. Give them a home if and where you can. If I can't find grape vines in my search for fall warblers, I readily accept Virginia creeper vine watch-sites.

American Wisteria

Because there's Chinese wisteria (*Wisteria sinensis*) and Japanese wisteria (*Wisteria floribunda*), both of which closely resemble American wisteria (*Wisteria frutenscens*), make your native purchase from a trusted vendor. The highly invasive Asian varieties will climb everything in sight—and tear down sturdy trees along the way. The American wisteria, however, while fast-growing, is a gentle soul by comparison. Pruning may be

American wisteria (*Wisteria frutescens*), far better behaved than the commonly marketed invasive Asian wisterias (*W. sinensis* and *W. floribunda*), blooms beautifully and attracts birds with its repeat blossoms, seed pods, and stringy bark that female Baltimore Orioles love for their nests.

About the Lists

The vines listed here are, according to the United States Department of Agriculture Plant Database (online at www.plants.usda.gov), native to states as indicated. Note, however, that while a plant may be native in your state, it may not be native to every part of your state and certainly not to every eco-region. Before making final choices, consider soil texture, moisture, slope, and required sunlight. Your planting zone and eco-region combined will determine suitable growing conditions in your locale. To find your planting zone, check online at http://planthardiness.ars.usda.gov/.

The plant lists in this reference are not, nor are they intended to be, all-inclusive. Rather, the plants here were chosen because:

1. They are attractive to birds because, in some way, they meet birds' needs for food, shelter, and/or nesting.
2. They are easily grown, well behaved, and suitable for landscaping in various settings, as described.

Because vines typically take their size based on the their supporting structures and can be pruned to suit, no height or spread sizes are listed for them.

Vines for Any Sized Structure

COMMON NAME	SCIENTIFIC NAME	COMMENTS	NATIVE, PLANTING ZONES
Bittersweet, American	*Celastrus scandens*	Full sun to shade, lean soil; fall fruit, year-round cover, nesting, important winter food source; quick cover for fences and other structures; also used as ground cover	Eastern US except FL Zones 3–8
Crossvine	*Bignonia capreolata*	Full sun to part shade, average well-drained soil; grown mostly for early-spring trumpet-shaped flowers; vigorous grower; nectar, bugs; closely related to trumpet vine, *Campsis radicans*	Eastern US except ME, MA, VT, NH, PA, NY, NJ, RI, CT, MI, WI, MN, and IA Zones 5–9

COMMON NAME	SCIENTIFIC NAME	COMMENTS	NATIVE, PLANTING ZONES
Dutchman's pipe	*Aristolochia macrophylla*	Vigorous grower, forms dense shade, heart-shaped leaves; intolerant of dry soil; inconspicuous flowers May–June; prune in late winter to control growth; host to pipevine butterfly; good nesting protection; similar to *A. tomentosa*	East Coast and Southeast except FL but including KY, TN, and WV Zones 4–8
Wooly Dutchman's pipe	*Aristolochia tomentosa*	Similar to *A. macrophylla* but less vigorous, native farther north and west; forms dense shade, heart-shaped leaves; intolerant of dry soil; inconspicuous flowers May–June; host to pipevine butterfly; considered tried and trouble-free	Eastern US except MI, MN, IA, VA, WV, PA, and Northeast Zones 5–8
Grape, wild	*Vitis* spp.	Fruit eaten by more than 50 birds, excellent nesting and nest material (shreddy bark); nearly 70 cultivars available but wild best for birds; full sun best, tolerates wide range of soils but needs good drainage	Eastern US Zones 3–9
Jasmine, Carolina yellow synonymous with **evening trumpet-flower, false jessamine, false jasmine**	*Gelsemium sempervirens*	Evergreen vine; full sun, organically rich, well-drained, moist soil; showy, fragrant yellow flowers Feb–Apr; without support, grows as bushy ground cover; drapes in patio containers	AR, TN, VA, and south Zones 7–10
Trumpet honeysuckle synonymous with **flame honeysuckle**	*Lonicera sempervirens*	Full sun to part shade, average well-drained soil; nectar for pollinators, hummingbirds; good cover, nesting; can be pruned to ground in winter to refresh vine tangle	Eastern US except WI Zones 4–9
Trumpet vine synonymous with **trumpet creeper** and **cow itch vine**	*Campsis radicans*	Full sun; good in hot, dry spots; hummingbirds and orioles attracted to nectar; grows vigorously, forming weighty vines; prune to ground every few years to tame	Eastern US except MN and ME Zones 4–9
Virginia creeper	*Parthenocissus quinquefolia*	Tree-climbing vine; full sun, easily grown in medium well-drained soil; striking scarlet fall foliage; fall fruit magnet for migrating birds	Eastern US Zones 3–9

COMMON NAME	SCIENTIFIC NAME	COMMENTS	NATIVE, PLANTING ZONES
Wisteria, American	*Wisteria frutescens*	Full sun, slightly acidic, moderately fertile, well-drained soil; prune regularly to control shape and size and promote flowering; flowers hang in grape-like lilac-purple clusters; dislikes being transplanted	Eastern US except MN, WI, ME, VT, and NH Zones 5–9

necessary, depending on where your support structure stands and how much cover you want, but pruning also encourages blossoms. Again, birds and bees as well as other insects find the nectar enticing, and the vine offers adequate shelter for nesting. Female Baltimore and Orchard Orioles have visited my vines as well, stripping string-like bark shreds for their nests.

If at all possible, tuck in a vine somewhere on your property. Check your yard map, allow for the vertical space, and sketch in the footprint. Label the space with the vine you've chosen.

BRAMBLES

Finally, I would be remiss if I didn't mention brambles—only because the birds love, love, love

A Veery, like most of its thrush cousins, likes to stay in the thick of things—thick vegetation, that is, low to the ground—so brambles must surely be ideal for its secretive ways.

'em! Where we live, blackberry and dewberry brambles (*Rubus* spp.) grow wild and tend to pop up in unmowed areas. The native bramble patch on the hillside behind our house hosts nesting Eastern Towhees and Song Sparrows. It's also where Northern Cardinals and Carolina Wrens take their fledglings to keep them safe until better flight days. The berries feed most of the avian species in our yard, so I never get that blackberry pie I so love.

Though I'm not fond of thorns, I guess, in this case, thorns are okay. After all, thorns are the primary reason birds love brambles so much. Hawks won't usually crash headlong into thorny brambles chasing lunch, so birds feel safe among the canes.

So if yours is a super-sized yard, you may have room to create a bramble patch. If they don't come up naturally, plant a few berry stalks and let them multiply. The birds will love the shelter and berries—unless you manage a pie for yourself!

MARKING THE MAP

While you likely have many shrubs, tall understory plants, and vines on your "possible" list—all choices suitable for your location and your size yard—once again look first toward the species absent from your neighborhood. Consider, in light of your neighboring habitats, how you can best serve birds throughout the four seasons.

Then decide. If you haven't already, take time now to add the shrubs, tall understory plants, and vines to your yard list, updating your preferences.

I wish I could see your yard map now! I'm betting the excitement is growing. Onward to Step 3!

A rarely seen Mourning Warbler forages for bugs among the goldenrod leaves and blossoms (*Solidago* spp.), a habitat that perfectly suits this skulking warbler.

"If we could see the miracle of a single flower clearly, our whole life would change."

—BUDDHA, sixth century BC

Chapter 7

CHOOSING NATIVE PERENNIALS—FLOWERS AND GRASSES

After selecting trees and shrubs suited to your space and budget, it's time to add perennials for color, variety, depth, and texture—and to provide happy places for birds as well as bees and butterflies.

Among the plants we loosely call "flowers," there are two kinds: annuals and perennials. Annuals live one year and die. Perennials die to the ground every winter but come back. In other words, they're hardy. And the term for hardy plants that die back annually is "herbaceous." So this chapter addresses recommended native herbaceous perennials—both the ones we traditionally call "flowers" and the ones we traditionally call "grasses," which, of course, also bloom.

But don't confuse "hardy" with "native." Just because a plant returns year after year doesn't mean it's native. Vast numbers of introduced species remain hardy on foreign soil. In fact, some natives are not hardy. They don't return by root. Instead, they reseed themselves. So a perennial is any plant—native or not—that survives the off-season and greens up (or grows up) when the new growing season begins.

But there's more. Perennials are perennials only in their own eco-regions. Similar eco-regions, however, exist across the world. So a plant—native or not—that is hardy in Florida is probably not hardy in Minnesota; but it could be hardy in Morocco or India. Planted in the far north, a Florida perennial would likely freeze to death by mid-December and not green out the following spring. On the other hand, a perennial—native or not—growing in Minnesota will come up again next spring—in Minnesota. That same Minnesota perennial transplanted in Florida, however, will likely die of heat and exhaustion. Well, okay, maybe not exhaustion. In short, though, a perennial is not a perennial everywhere. It's perennial in its native eco-region, no matter in what parts of the world that eco-region occurs. That's why nonnative plants can get a foothold in our foreign soil and truly thrive.

Perennials typically hang on year after year because they also regenerate, albeit perhaps slowly. Perennials come up from root each spring, but they also reproduce in some manner. Some multiply themselves by seed; other spread by root, by suckering, or by rhizome. Unless something goes wrong, you shouldn't have to replace perennials for a long time—maybe never. Of course, everything eventually dies; but with perennials, typically new plants will have come up to replace the old ones before the aged reach their lifetime's end.

So, given that bit of background, you're ready for Step 3.

Step 3: Choose native perennials—six each of three different species.

While trees are the anchor and shrubs the fill, herbaceous perennials add the color—and still more biodiversity. Generally perennials stay low, hang out in tight beds, and draw birds to their nectar and seeds as well as to the bugs they support. Choosing and planting a dozen and a half perennials may seem daunting, but we think you'll find success with the easy-to-grow native perennials on our top-choice lists—native perennials that invite birds to your yard.

Maybe you're an experienced, sophisticated gardener who has for years cultivated a lovely wash of color, with masses of, say, pinks, lavenders, and purples drifting across the yard or garden. On the other hand, maybe gardening isn't your thing at all, but you'd like something snazzy in your yard—only you're thinking snazzy birds. You can relax. No matter your level of gardening or landscaping expertise, we've got you covered.

NATIVE PERENNIALS BY THE SEASON

Many native perennials fall into the category folks generally term "wildflowers." Wildflower field guides, some more comprehensive than others, categorize literally hundreds of native plants. Translation: You have literally hundreds of native plants from which to choose to enhance your bird-friendly habitat. But some wildflowers are fairly unruly, maybe even exceptionally aggressive, sometimes rangy and ragged, and occasionally just plain noxious. Not all wildflowers are created equal, and certainly not all wildflowers are lovely in the yard—or attractive to birds.

On the other hand, a range of native perennials, carefully chosen, can provide blooms three seasons of the year. Your garden can host bright color in spring, summer, and fall. In my own garden, early spring begins with violets, red columbine, Indian pinks, golden Alexander, and crossvine blossoms. Ostrich ferns unfurl, trumpet honeysuckle blooms, and water iris sprout purple.

A Blue-gray Gnatcatcher forages in joe-pye weed (*Eupatorium purpureum*), a perennial favorite butterfly plant among native gardeners.

Within a month, wild blue indigo, penstemon, wild petunias, butterfly weed, and aquatic milkweed feed bees and butterflies. By midsummer, liatris, monardas, coneflowers, coreopsis varieties, queen-of-the-prairie, agastache, rattlesnake master, mountain mints, lobelias, phloxes, and milkweeds make the garden crazy busy. In late summer into early fall, joe-pye weeds, washes of asters, goldenrod cultivars, late rudbeckias, and boneset host butterflies and migrating warblers. Each perennial has its bloom time, and planted in combination, you and your birds enjoy a nonstop array of color.

In winter, having left all the frost-killed perennials for seed and shelter, I watch from my window as winter sparrows, Mourning Doves, Dark-eyed Juncos, House Finches, American Goldfinches, Northern Cardinals, Carolina Chickadees, Tufted Titmice, and Carolina Wrens forage among the now-dead stalks, the seeds offering tasty treats for birds. What a reward for hosting all those native perennials in the four-season garden!

At the heart of the matter for you, of course, is how to find the right native perennials among the hundreds. That's what this chapter is all about. The following 21 native selections, suitable for mid-sized and super-sized yards and gardens, offer a range of heights, colors, and habitat demands. Some perennials we've reserved for super-sized yards only, and we have recommendations for the mini yards and pots-and-patio gardens as well.

But first, here's help in making sound choices for native herbaceous perennials for your yard or garden. We trust they'll be snazzy!

Consider: Think in masses of perennials, not single plants. Setting out only one or two plants of a given perennial species creates a lost-in-the-crowd kind of habitat for birds. To be drawn to potential nectar and seed sources, for instance, birds zoom in to forage among ample quantities. In the extreme, think about how difficult it would be for a hummingbird to find a single flower hidden in the greenery. But give that hummer a wash of 15 plants, all abloom with dozens of nectar-bearing flowers, and you'll see a regular busy visitor.

Consider: To reduce the risk of making big mistakes, let's start small, only a half dozen each of three native perennial species. Later, when you and your birds have found joy in your chosen perennials, add to the array of blossoms as your space, budget, and time permit.

Consider: Which perennials grow in your planting zone? Given climate change, you may get by planting something that typically grows to your south, but the opposite is unlikely.

Consider: Which perennials need full sun, part shade, or full shade? Where in your yard will plants get the right light? Some perennials will never bloom—or at best will bloom only poorly—without adequate sun. Other perennials need full shade in order to survive. Check before you choose—both for what the plants want and where they'll find it in your space.

Consider: Which plants will grow well in your soil? Even plants native to your state and situated in a compatible planting zone may not find the right kind of soil, temperature range, or moisture content to be happy in your setting. Consult local nursery staff, horticulturalists, or your county extension agent if you're unsure.

Consider: Will your perennial choices spread—either through rhizomes, self-seeding, or expanding clumps? Allow room for growth. You'll get more birds with more plants.

AN ARRAY OF NATIVE PERENNIALS

The perennials recommended here are well-behaved plants that will grow happily in your yard or garden without causing you grief. Meanwhile, the birds, bees, and butterflies will reward you for your efforts. While some of the following are more for pollinators and insects than specifically for birds, you know the drill: To feed the birds, first feed the bugs. In a few cases, we've recommended a cultivar or two.

Finally, although some of the following would certainly work in very small yards, they need space for light and air. We've pulled out a list beginning on page 173 that makes specific recommendations for small spaces.

So here we go, with great choices for native perennials:

Fall-blooming New England asters (*Symphyotrichum novae-angliae*) attract insects by the dozens, creating a popular buffet for birds.

Asters

How I love asters! The fall garden is awash in shades of pink, purple, and lavender, all from the varied flowers of aromatic and New England asters. Over the years, they've multiplied, New England asters more readily than the aromatic asters. In our rich garden soil, the New England asters stand stately, sometimes up to my waist, always aflutter with a myriad of butterflies and tiny nectar-loving insects. More constrained, aromatic asters tend to stay in a neat, upright clump, spreading slowly outward. Given asters' bloom time, the fall migrant birds are lively among them, too—not because of the nectar, but because of the bugs. It's just a delightfully busy place!

Bushy aster, also called rice button aster, is shorter and, as the name says, more bushy than the other two listed here. They work well in smaller yards and more compact gardens.

Wild Columbine

Hardy plants that self-seed, wild columbines, also called red columbines, are to my eye actually more salmon-colored. Found in the wild, they'll

Self-seeding wild columbine (*Aquilegia canadensis*), unlike its hybrids, produces nectar nearly irresistible to hummingbirds.

Black-eyed Susans (*Rudbeckia hirta*) attract insects to their nectar, but seeds are their biggest contribution to birds. American Goldfinches, however, often pluck the flower petals before seed heads fully mature.

be tucked among the ledges of a rocky hillside, so they thrive on neglect. But hummingbirds certainly don't neglect them! Because columbines bloom really early, they garner attention from both the birds and me. After a drab winter, gotta love that bright spot of warm color! The hybrids in the nurseries—the purple, yellow, and multicolored varieties—hang neglected in my yard. I've watched hummingbirds zip by and maybe check them out, but the birds never linger and never return. I have to assume the hybrids are sterile. Go native if you want to feed the hummers.

Coneflowers: Rudbeckia and Echinacea

Two genera of plants take on the common name "coneflower." Be sure to read the labels before you hand over your cash.

Probably the most common and most easily grown of all the *Rudbeckia* coneflowers is black-eyed Susan. It self-seeds and multiplies by root, stretching out each season to expand the mass. Because they multiply readily, you may find someone who has extras to share, saving you another purchase. To put it simply, I'd never want to be without black-eyed Susans. American Goldfinches absolutely swarm the plants. In fact, they don't even wait for the petals to fall—they eat petals, seed, and all! If anything remains, a few Carolina Chickadees and Tufted Titmice slip in for snacks, and Song Sparrows, House Finches, and Northern Cardinals will forage underneath for anything scattered or dropped. After the blooms are spent, black-eyed Susans' little button seed heads add a note of texture to the garden, and I leave them until early spring when I clear debris for the new sprouts.

As an aside, brown-eyed Susan (*Rudbeckia falgida*) is very similar to black-eyed Susan and functions equally well providing seeds to birds.

Cutleaf coneflower, also called tall or gray-headed coneflower, stands tall—head-high! This *Rudbeckia* is named for its distinctive leaves. The flowers have a bird-magnet seed head; and finches, chickadees, and titmice cling to the heads lunching, swaying in the breeze. In rich soil, this coneflower may need support to prevent blow-down in strong winds.

The *Rudbeckia* orange coneflowers are widely cultivated, and cultivars are more readily available than the standard. Depending on the cultivar, however, the color may vary from pale yellow to deep orange. While I love the colors, in my garden at least, the plants are not as reliably hardy as other *Rudbeckia* and *Echinacea* coneflowers. And if I misread a label or choose one not accurately or completely labeled and end up with a hybrid,

Popular among gardeners everywhere, coneflowers boast many varieties, cultivars, and hybrids; but for birds, the most suitable is the standard eastern purple coneflower (*Echinacea purpurea*).

it's often sterile. I've wasted my money, then, on a plant that won't feed either the birds or the bees.

Another reliable *Rudbeckia*, sweet coneflower is the tallest among those listed here and is the only yellow one among the trio.

Among *Echinacea* species, eastern purple coneflower has become an all-time favorite among gardeners, both native and nonnative. And therein lies a problem. Because the plant is extraordinarily popular, numerous cultivars and hybrids have hit the nursery racks. Some are lovely; others are stunning. But be careful. Cultivars contain all the chemistry of the standard, but hybrids do not. Purchasing a hybrid will very likely put a plant in your garden that offers neither nectar nor seeds—probably your only reasons for purchasing coneflower. I know—one cluster is blooming in my garden right now. It's a deep rose-purple. No bees stop to nectar. No butterflies stop to sip. No goldfinches stop to feed. Pretty but useless.

No matter the coneflower you choose, however, none of them tolerate wet feet and will rot in heavy clay soils.

Coreopsis

The *Coreopsis* genus offers quite a nice range of natives. They bloom yellow—bright yellow! Most are 2 or 3 feet tall, although lanceleaf coreopsis may hover at only a foot tall, and tickseed coreopsis—synonymous with prairie tickseed, prairie coreopsis, and stiff coreopsis—can be just a few inches taller. By contrast, however, tall coreopsis, sometimes called tall tickseed, can tower to 8 feet. Many, like threadleaf coreopsis, or whorled coreopsis, have delicate, namesake threadlike leaves, adding an airy touch to wherever they grow. Greater tickseed gets its moniker from its 2-inch-diameter flowers, the largest of the coreopsis blooms.

Whether you want background or foreground plants, some species of coreopsis can likely fill the bill. If allowed, most will naturalize. All are attractive to birds and bugs, and birds find the seeds alluring. Since common names vary and even overlap, you will do well to verify choices by checking scientific names.

In addition to these "best-choice" coreopsis listings, your local nurseries may also carry "better choice" varieties as well as "good-choice" cultivars that will also serve you well. Again, however, you probably should verify that you're not choosing a hybrid.

Goldenrods

Be careful with goldenrods. Some are exceedingly aggressive and ill-behaved, their rhizomes spreading quickly and smothering everything in their paths. Some native species, however, are well behaved and merit a patch or two in the garden, ultimately offering a wash of gold across the autumn landscape. Because I have about an acre suitable for planting, I have both the aggressive kind—on the hillside behind the house—and two well-behaved varieties in my front garden. And, oh, what a joy it is to have goldenrods! The blossoms are absolutely covered with bugs in late August and through September, even into October.

One autumn day during migration, I counted 17 species of migrants, mostly warblers, feeding in the goldenrod. They weren't eating flowers, nectar, or seed; they were gorging on bugs. A Mourning Warbler turned out to be a county record. How exciting, that patch of goldenrod! A month later, the goldenrod having gone to seed, the winter sparrows arrived: White-throated and White-crowned Sparrows, Vesper Sparrows, and Dark-eyed Juncos, as well as Savannah and Lincoln's Sparrows, the latter two only passing through. Joining the sparrows, a few early Purple Finches and Pine Siskins fed among the foraging flocks. Isn't it a thing of joy to be able to speak of those birds in terms of "flocks"!

Among the late blossoms and already developed seed heads of goldenrod (*Solidago* spp.), a Ruby-crowned Kinglet, having arrived to spend the winter, forages for bugs.

In the garden, consider showy goldenrod; wreath goldenrod, synonymous with blue stem goldenrod; or wrinkleleaf goldenrod 'Fireworks'. More later about the aggressive species.

Hyssops

Just as my favorite bird is whichever one I'm watching at the moment, my favorite native perennial is whichever one the birds are feeding on at the moment. Hyssops fall into that category. They host bees top to bottom on their long, tall, flowering spikes. Then, when seeds form, they host birds. Cardinals look famously majestic in winter, clinging to the spike, plucking seed after seed. It's win-win with these handsome plants.

Purple giant hyssop can reach 6 feet but, like all hyssops, the plant forms only a single spike. For instance, 10 of them could fit in 5 square feet—not that you'd necessarily plant them that way. Anise hyssop, staying closer to 4 feet tall, forms tidy upright clumps. Frequently, though, hyssops will retain their stature best if staked, especially if planted where winds and storms can push them down.

Close to the house, I have a growing cluster of short and sweet lavender-blooming anise hyssop. Paired with a patch of pink garden phlox, they make a delicate little flower bed only 6 by 5 feet, anchored in spring with wild columbine and in fall with aromatic asters.

Indian Pink

Indian pink, also called woodland pinkroot, is a truly lovely plant and extraordinarily well

Indian pinks (*Spigelia marilandica*) attract hummingbirds—and gardeners—with their lovely, long-lasting early-spring blossoms.

On a frosty early-December morning, a male Northern Cardinal finds breakfast among the giant hyssop seed heads (*Agastache scrophulariifolia*)—a clear illustration of the value of leaving frost-killed plants in the garden for winter forage and shelter.

behaved, with deep green leaves on straight stalks topped with long-blooming tubular flowers that are red on the outside and yellow inside. Everyone who visits my yard wants to know what it is. Hummingbirds don't have to ask; they just swarm it. If it's suitable in your area, get it—sooner than later.

Indigos

Indigos die back to the root every year, so it's a bit of a surprise that the blue false indigo looks more like a shrub than a perennial. The flowers are pea-like but on spikes, and the seed pods, when ripened, pop open to reveal almost pea-sized seeds. The morsels attract Blue Jays, Northern

Cardinals, Mourning Doves, and other seedeaters large enough to gulp seeds down. The pods cling well into winter. Wild white indigo, at least in my yard, blooms slightly later than the blue and is a more delicate-looking plant, its leaves more gray-green than those of blue false indigo. Deep roots on both white and blue make the plant highly drought-tolerant—but also nearly impossible to move. So plant it where you want it from the get-go. Bees visit both. At least six kinds of butterflies accept indigos as a host plant, and all delight in the nectar.

Joe-Pye Weeds

Both spotted and sweet-scented joe-pye weeds, as well as some others that are native here, attract butterflies and other pollinators to their flat-head clusters of pinkish flowers (see photo at beginning of this chapter). Even though they die back to the ground, they grow to sometimes 7 feet tall, so they need room to reach out. I've planted mine too close to the path, so they overarch, and I have to duck or push the stems aside.

Aside from medicinal qualities, joe-pye weeds bring glamour to the garden and feed the bugs and butterflies. I've watched the Eastern Wood-pewee take up an observation perch near joe-pye weed, darting after bugs on the wing, feeding for 20 to 30 minutes at a time. On alternate days, the Eastern Phoebe takes up the same perch. Flycatchers know the drill!

Liatrises

The *Liatris* genus of plants likes it hot and dry. They're prairie plants. Talk about a carefree garden plant! Just let 'em alone. All reach 4 feet tall or more, so in the open, they may need support. I stake mine, so the support is really unobtrusive.

Dense blazing star—synonymous with marsh blazing star, dense gayfeather, and just plain blazing star—stays shortest of the trio we've chosen here and also has the shortest spike of flowers. An even more compact and shorter cultivar is 'Kobold' blazing star, suitable for truly small spaces. Prairie blazing star and devil's bite, also called just plain blazing star, offer a little color variation, the prairie being somewhat more rosy

Like many other pollinators, this black female tiger swallowtail favors blazing star's (*Liatris pycnostachya*) striking flower spike.

than purple. The blossoms of all three attract butterflies, other pollinators and insects, as well as hummingbirds. Sparrows and finches and other small seedeaters find the spikes great seed sources.

Since common names among these species are similar—even interchangeable in some cases—you'll be wise to verify your choices using the scientific names.

Lobelias

Lobelias like it wet. Really wet. From an old, leaky, preformed fish pond filled with equal parts sand, peat, and rich loam, I've created a bog in my garden. While it requires my refilling the water about once a week, it hosts plants that otherwise would never grow here—including cardinal flower and great blue lobelia. Those aren't the only two species in the bog, but they bloom simultaneously and make a lovely red-and-blue contrast together. Hummingbirds visit both, usually first the cardinal flower and then discovering the blue. That wet spot in your yard or garden that has left you bumfuzzled? Here's your answer.

Milkweeds

The compassion people have for the dramatically declining monarch butterfly populations has recently put milkweeds front and center on nursery stock shelves. Sometimes, though, folks turn sour on the campaign after a year or two of struggling with common milkweed. It comes up everywhere, spreading both by root and by seed. And then it becomes an annoyance. Three other choices, however, may let you plant milkweed without suffering from the too-big-and-too-much syndrome.

Butterfly weed is my first choice. It's low-growing, does not spread, prefers hot and dry, and boasts lovely long-blooming bright-orange blossoms. What's not to like? Well, okay, if you are really trying to attract monarchs, and if the monarchs really do find your butterfly weed, and if

Swamp milkweed (*Asclepias incarnata*), more bush-like, smaller-leaved, and less aggressive than common milkweed (*Asclepias syriaca*), makes a well-behaved garden plant to host monarch butterflies.

Any of the mountain mints will attract insects and pollinators, but to my mind, short-toothed mountain mint (*Pycnanthemum muticum*) is the mother of all pollinator plants. I count 10 insects in this little section. You?

A variety of wild bergamot (*Monarda fistuloso*), also called bee balm, is true to its name, attracting pollinators that are so happy to gorge on the nectar that they seem oblivious to everything else.

A female Ruby-throated Hummingbird nectars on scarlet monarda (*Monarda didyma*).

they lay their eggs on it and if the eggs hatch into caterpillars before the birds eat them, the caterpillars will eat every part of the butterfly weed except the stalks. But that's why we're planting it, right? Just plant lots of it! This year I added 18 more of them. And as a note of assurance, even when caterpillars eat butterfly weed to bare stalks, the plants will survive, returning next year to feed more caterpillars.

Swamp milkweed is more bush-like and considerably better behaved than common milkweed. At least in my yard, it spreads only slowly and will actually die out if not protected from the spread of goldenrod.

Whorled milkweed is as short as butterfly weed, blooms white rather than pink or mauve, and attracts a wide array of butterflies. Its small stature makes it suitable for tidy borders.

People sometimes forget that milkweed, in addition to being the single host plant for monarchs, is a super nectar plant for all kinds of butterflies as well as other pollinators and bugs.

Monardas

Called bee balm, bergamot, or monarda, these natives will score high in your garden with bees and hummingbirds, but butterflies can't comfortably nectar on their heads-down blossoms. The name "bee balm" tells you how happy bees are to find a patch. Even with bunches of bees nectaring, I can work among the plants without them so much as noticing my presence. A balm, indeed!

My lavender-blossomed wild bergamot spreads slowly, so every year I edge the mass planting and give away the starts. They're shallow-rooted and pull easily. Scarlet bee balm seems to regenerate best by seed, so I sometimes have to move plants that come up too close to the path or someplace where it will disappear in the depths of some other vegetation. They transplant readily, though, again because they're shallow-rooted. Both monardas have been in my garden for at least 20 years without replacement. Got my money's worth out of those six plants!

Mountain Mints

In my garden, mountain mints are the unequivocal number-one attractor of pollinators. While I have three different species, I'm suggesting only two here. Some can spread like crazy, so blunt mountain mint, also called short-toothed mountain mint, and slender mountain mint are the ones most bird gardeners prefer. While mints attract pollinators, the blunt mountain mint is also an insect repellent. Put crushed leaves in your pocket to ward off gnats and rub leaves on your pant legs to ward off ticks and chiggers. Then sit back and try—just dare to try—counting the number of insects roving across these fabulous pollinators. Yep, first feed the bugs to feed the birds!

Penstemons

Among the many species and cultivars of penstemon, beardtongue (or beard tongue), also called foxglove beardtongue, is the taller of the two we've listed. The plant gets its weird name because, of the five stamen in its white flower, one is sterile—and has a tuft of small hairs. Gray beardtongue is not as highly recommended for bugs and butterflies as other penstemons.

Phloxes

Longtime garden staples, phloxes host bees, butterflies, and birds, offering nectar to all. The most tried and true is garden phlox, more resistant to powdery mildew than most. By adding meadow phlox, also called wild sweetwilliam or spotted phlox, and smooth phlox to the mix, you can vary colors from white to pink to purple to rose.

Rattlesnake Master

The name rattlesnake master, sometimes called button snake-root (see photos on pages 36 and 39), scares some folks, but it comes from the plant's former use as a treatment for snakebite. In spite of that unsettling history, it's one fabulous plant, unlike any other in your yard or garden. A bit prickly, somewhat reminiscent of yucca, it's big, showy, unusual, and a giant hit with pollinators, including butterflies and hummingbirds. The flycatchers perch and watch, not feeding on the plant but feeding on what's feeding on the plant.

Rattlesnake master, however, is a prairie plant. After all, it grows where rattlesnakes roam. It does not like wet feet, preferring hot and dry. In springs when we have heavy rain, this plant suffers, and sometimes its top rots out. So look for a well-drained spot, skip the moisture-holding mulch, and give it room.

Rosemallows

Rosemallows need space. Lots of space. And wet. I've tried on occasion to pamper them in my garden, but they need something wetter than I can offer. The height and spread of the two species suggested here make them incompatible in my garden, and I'm too selfish to plant them at the bottom of the hill in back of the house where I'll not see them daily. But given their almost treelike stature, they do work amazingly well in large containers. Since saucered containers can be kept continuously wet, the growing conditions are perfect. It's worth the try for this spectacular specimen and the butterflies it attracts!

Sage

I plant blue sage for hummingbirds. Period. Sometimes I have to grow it from seed if it's hard to find in the nurseries, but pitching the seed on the ground and stirring it about will serve the purpose. It's not finicky.

Vervain

While vervain is not readily available in most nurseries, it should be. In Costa Rica, where their native vervain looks very much like ours, I've watched more hummingbirds nectaring on it than on any other plant. We have our own native vervain that's equally attractive to our single species of hummingbird. It's worth the care necessary to keep it tidy just to watch the hummers.

Yarrow

Standard common yarrow blooms white, but I have cultivars in yellow and shades of rose. They're not the hottest item in the garden, but bugs do like them—especially tiny bugs—and they're lovely accents. But they're dry-weather plants and will root-rot if exposed to too much rain. Two years ago, after weeks of spring rains, I lost every one, some of which I'd had for 20 years or more. Bummer.

A hatch-year male Ruby-throated Hummingbird nectars on a September-blooming blue sage cultivar (*Salvia azurea*), fattening up for his journey south to winter in Costa Rica.

Common yarrow (*Achillea millefolium*) serves up nectar for a Delaware skipper and other insects.

About the Lists

The perennials listed here are, according to the United States Department of Agriculture Plant Database (online at www.plants.usda.gov), native to states as indicated. Note that while a perennial may be native in your state, it may not be native to every part of your state and certainly not to every eco-region. Consider soil texture, moisture, slope, and required sunlight. Your planting zone and eco-region combined will also help determine suitable growing conditions in your yard. Find your planting zone online at http://planthardiness.ars.usda.gov/.

The perennial plant lists in this chapter are not, nor are they intended to be, all-inclusive. Rather, the plants here were chosen because:

1. They are attractive to birds. Benefits noted in the table represent primary seasonal food sources for birds—insects, nectar, seed, and/or berries. Leaving frost-killed plants in the garden undisturbed until early spring offers winter forage and shelter, especially to ground-loving birds.
2. They are easily grown, well behaved, and suitable for landscaping in various settings, as described.

As has been the rule with earlier tables, we think of our recommended plants as falling along a sliding scale from "poor" to "good" to "better" to "best." All plants in the following table for mid-sized and super-sized yards rank mostly either "better" or "best" for attracting birds to the yard, while the few cultivars included, by definition, rank as "good." We do not include hybrids.

A final hint: Plant perennials according to the estimated height of mature plants, obviously placing taller plants toward the back of the garden or property, with shorter varieties tucked in toward the front.

An Array of Native Perennials

COMMON NAME	SCIENTIFIC NAME	COLOR AND BENEFIT(S) N = NECTAR I = INSECTS S = SEED B = BERRIES	COMMENTS	NATIVE, PLANTING ZONES
Asters	*Symphyotrichum* spp.	Varied N I S	Known for spectacular fall washes of lavender and purple; highly attractive to butterflies, birds	As specified below
Aromatic aster	*S. oblongifolius*	Blue, purple N I S	1–3′ tall, 1–3′ spread; blooms Aug–Sept; tolerates drought, poor soils; full sun; tends to stand upright; plant in masses	NY west and south except MI, SC, GA, FL, and LA Zones 3–8
Bushy American aster synonymous with rice button aster	*S. dumosum* synonymous with *A. dumosum*	Lavender N I S	1–3′ tall, can be sprawling; blooms Aug–Sept; tolerates variety of soils; full sun; most common on coastal plain; plant in masses	Coastal states and WV, TN, KY, IN, and IL Zones 4–8
New England aster	*S. novae-angliae*	Range from purple-rose to white N I S	Up to 4′ tall, 2–3′ spread; blooms late summer into fall; easily grown; full sun; beautiful in masses; attracts butterflies and birds	Eastern US except FL Zones 4–8
Columbine, red synonymous with **wild columbine**	*Aquilegia canadensis*	Salmon to red, yellow inside N I	Up to 2′ tall, 1–1.5′ spread; full sun to part shade; tolerates drought, dry soil; showy bell-shaped flowers attract hummingbirds; self-seeds, well behaved	Eastern US except LA Zones 3–8
Coneflowers	*Echinacea* spp. and *Rudbeckia* spp.	N I S	Attractive to butterflies; avoid deadheading to provide seed for many finches, winter sparrows	As specified below
Black-eyed Susan	*R. hirta*	Yellow N I S	2–3′ tall, 1–2′ spread; full sun; bright daisy-like flowers, 2–3″ across, June–Sept; deer resistant; seeds favored by finches, winter sparrows	Eastern US Zones 3–7

COMMON NAME	SCIENTIFIC NAME	COLOR AND BENEFIT(S) N = NECTAR I = INSECTS S = SEED B = BERRIES	COMMENTS	NATIVE, PLANTING ZONES
Cutleaf coneflower synonymous with tall coneflower or gray-headed coneflower	*R. laciniata*	Yellow N I S	2–9′ tall, usually 3–4′ tall in cultivation, 1.5–3′ spread; showy, drooping rays, green center; easily grown; full sun, well-drained soil; tolerant of heat, humidity, deer; naturalizes	Eastern US Zones 3–9
Orange coneflower esp. cultivars 'Goldsturm' and 'Viette's Little Suzy'	*R. fulgida*	Orange-yellow N I S	2–3′ tall, 2–2.5′ spread; full sun; spreads slowly; late summer blossoms; cultivars more readily available than standard	Eastern US except ME, VT, NH, LA, IA, and MN Zones 3–8
Purple coneflower, eastern	*E. purpurea*	Purple to pinkish purple N I S	2–4′ tall, 1.5–2′ spread; blooms through summer; tolerates drought, clay, rocky shallow soil; full sun; popular, easily grown; daisy-like heads form seeds favored by birds	Eastern US except ME, NH, VT, MA, and MN Zones 3–8
Sweet coneflower	*R. subtomentosa*	Yellow N I S	3–5′ tall, 1–2′ spread; showy, fragrant flowers July–Oct; full sun to part shade but may need support in shade; well-drained loamy soil; good for borders, cottage and native gardens	WI, MI, IA, MO, IL, IN, KY, TN, NC, AR, LA, AL, NY, MA, and CT Zones 4–8
Coreopsis	*Coreopsis*	Mostly delicate flowers with sometimes threadlike leaves	Generally easy to grow in variety of conditions	As specified below
Greater tickseed	*C. major*	Yellow N I S	2–3′ tall, 1–2′ spread; blooms June–July; easily grown, full sun; tolerates drought, dry soil; attracts butterflies; best naturalized	Eastern US east of Mississippi River except ME, VT, NH, MA, CT, RI, and NJ Zones 5—9

COMMON NAME	SCIENTIFIC NAME	COLOR AND BENEFIT(S) N = NECTAR I = INSECTS S = SEED B = BERRIES	COMMENTS	NATIVE, PLANTING ZONES
Lanceleaf coreopsis	*C. lanceolata*	Yellow N I S	1–2′ tall, 1–1.5′ spread; erect stems; single daisy-like blooms spring to early summer; tolerates drought, dry rocky soil; best naturalized	Eastern US Zones 4–9
Tall coreopsis synonymous with tall tickseed	*C. tripteris*	Yellow N I S	2–8′ tall, 2–8′ spread; blooms July–Sept; showy flowers, brown centers; full sun; thrives in poor soil with good drainage; good in rear borders; naturalizes	Eastern US except MN, ME, VT, NH, and NJ Zones 3–8
Threadleaf coreopsis synonymous with whorled coreopsis	*C. verticillata*	Yellow N I S	2.5–3′ tall, 1.5–2′ spread; flowers 2″ across, June–Sept; shearing plants midsummer promotes fall bloom; can spread by rhizomes, also self-seeds; good for poor, dry soils	AR and east of Mississippi River except IN, PA, VT, NH, and ME Zones 3–9
Tickseed coreopsis synonymous with prairie tickseed, prairie coreopsis, and stiff coreopsis	*C. palmata*	Yellow N I S	1.5–2.5′ tall, 1–1.5′ spread; full sun; tolerates poor, dry soil; daisy-like 2″ flowers, May–July; will naturalize; can be used in borders but must be kept in check to prevent spreading	Central US including MN, WI, MI, IN, IL, IA, MO, AR, LA, and MS Zones 3–8
Goldenrods (possible choices listed here from among dozens)	*Solidago* spp.	Superior for birds seeking fall bugs; seeds for winter birds	Goldenrods wrongly blamed for hay fever, which is actually caused by plants like ragweed	Native species almost everywhere; consider size and behavior for personal location

COMMON NAME	SCIENTIFIC NAME	COLOR AND BENEFIT(S) N = NECTAR I = INSECTS S = SEED B = BERRIES	COMMENTS	NATIVE, PLANTING ZONES
Showy goldenrod	*S. speciosa*	Yellow N I S	3' tall, 2–3' spread; red stems, erect; blooms July–Sept; most showy of all goldenrods; may need to divide every 2–3 years to control growth; not aggressive	Eastern US except ME and FL Zones 3–8
Wreath goldenrod synonymous with blue stem goldenrod	*S. caesia*	Yellow N I S	1–3' tall, 1.5–3' spread; purplish stems; blooms Aug–Sept; shade-tolerant, best in full sun; forms clumps, does not spread as fast as most other goldenrods; good for cottage and butterfly gardens	Eastern US except MN and IA Zones 4–8
Wrinkleleaf goldenrod 'Fireworks'	*S. rugosa* 'Fireworks'	Yellow N I S	Up to 3' tall, 2.5–3' spread; better behaved than most other goldenrods; lacy-flowered panicles resemble fireworks, Aug–Oct	Eastern US except IA and MN Zones 4–8
Hyssops	*Agastache* spp.	Shades of blue, purple	Tall but slender plants; attractive to butterflies and birds; seeds attract fall and winter birds	As specified below
Purple giant hyssop	*A. scrophulariifolia*	Purple N I S	3–6' tall, 2' spread; part shade, sun; flower spike up to 6" long, July–Aug	Eastern US except AR, LA, MS, AL, FL, and ME Zones 6–9
Anise hyssop	*A. foeniculum*	Pale to deep blue-violet N I S	2–4' tall, 1.5–3' spread; flower spike up to 6", June–Oct; sun to part shade, dry soil; grows in clumps; favored by pollinators; crushed leaves smell like anise	Limited to MN, IA, WI, MI, IL, KY, PA, NY, NJ, CT, and NH Zones 4–8
Indian Pink synonymous with **woodland pinkroot**	*Spigelia marilandica*	Red, yellow inside N	1–2' tall, 0.5–1.5' spread; clump-forming; part shade to full sun; easily grown in rich soil; good in front borders; esp. attractive to hummingbirds	South of and including MO, IL, IN, TN, WV, and MD Zones 5–9

COMMON NAME	SCIENTIFIC NAME	COLOR AND BENEFIT(S) N = NECTAR I = INSECTS S = SEED B = BERRIES	COMMENTS	NATIVE, PLANTING ZONES
Indigo	*Baptisia* spp.	Attracts butterflies	Grows deep roots so should not be moved after established; becomes shrub-like after blooming	As specified below
Blue false indigo	*B. australis*	Blue N I S	3–4' tall, 3–4' spread; best in full sun; blooms May–June on spikes to 12"; inflated seed pods attractive; good as specimen or in small groups	Eastern US except MN, LA, MS, and FL Zones 3–9
Wild white indigo	*B. alba*	White N I S	2–4' tall, 3–4' spread; best in full sun; blooms Apr–May on spikes up to 12"; inflated seed pods attractive; good in borders, cottage gardens, as specimens	Eastern US except north of VA and east of OH Zones 5–8
Joe-pye weeds	*Eupatorium* spp.	Pollinators heavily attracted to these plants	Fall bloomers	As specified below
Spotted joe-pye weed esp. cultivar 'Gateway'	*E. maculatum* 'Gateway'	Dusky rose-pink N I S (attractive, persist into winter)	4–5' tall, 1–2' spread; full sun, medium to wet soil; low maintenance; good in rain gardens, moist soils; blooms July–Sept; esp. attractive to butterflies; 'Gateway' more compact than standard	Eastern US except AR, LA, MS, AL, FL, and SC and cultivars Zones 4–8
Sweet-scented joe-pye weed	*E. purpureum*	Mauve pink N I S	4–7' tall, 2–4' spread; erect; full sun to part shade, moist soil; low maintenance; blooms July–Sept, seed heads persist into winter; spectacular in masses; good in rear borders, cottage gardens, along water	Eastern US Zones 4–9
Liatris	*Liatris* spp.	Purple N I S	Common names gayfeather because of feathery flower heads, blazing star because of fluffy flowers on spikes; all tolerate heat, humidity, drought; none tolerate wet winter soils; attracts butterflies, other insects, and birds, including hummingbirds	As specified on next page

COMMON NAME	SCIENTIFIC NAME	COLOR AND BENEFIT(S) N = NECTAR I = INSECTS S = SEED B = BERRIES	COMMENTS	NATIVE, PLANTING ZONES
Dense blazing star synonymous with marsh blazing star, dense gayfeather, and blazing star	*L. spicata*	Red-purple, occasionally white N I S	2–4' tall, 9"–1.5' spread; forms clumps; full sun; grasslike leaves with tall spike of flowers; blooms July–Aug on 6–12" spikes; good massed in borders	Eastern US except ME, VT, NH, and RI Zones 3–8
Blazing star 'Kobold'	*L. spicata* 'Kobold'	Deep purple N I S	1.5–2.5' tall; 6"–1' spread; small, compact cultivar of species above; remains upright; blooms July–Aug; attracts birds, hummingbirds, butterflies	Cultivar Zones 3–8
Prairie blazing star	*L. pycnostachya*	Deep rose-purple N I S	2–5' tall, 1–2' spread, tallest of species; easily grown in full sun, well-drained soils; forms clumps; blooms July–Aug top down on terminal spikes up to 20" long; may need support	Primarily west of Mississippi River and north of Ohio River Zones 3–9
Blazing star synonymous with devil's bite	*L. scariosa*	Reddish purple N I S	2–4' tall, 1–2' spread; blooms Aug–Oct on spikes up to 18"; prefers dry, sandy, or rocky soil, full sun; adds vertical accent to cottage gardens, good in borders	Eastern US except VT, TN, FL, and MS Zones 3–8
Lobelias	*Lobelia* spp.	Attract hummingbirds and butterflies	Moist soils, constant moisture, even standing water	As specified below
Cardinal flower	*L. cardinalis*	Red N I	2–4' tall, 1–2' spread, erect; short-lived; thrives in standing water or average soil; blooms July–Aug, showy red flowers on spikes; attractive to hummingbirds	Eastern US Zones 3–9

COMMON NAME	SCIENTIFIC NAME	COLOR AND BENEFIT(S) N = NECTAR I = INSECTS S = SEED B = BERRIES	COMMENTS	NATIVE, PLANTING ZONES
Great blue lobelia synonymous with blue cardinal flower	*L. siphilitica*	Blue N I	2–3' tall, 1–1.5' spread, erect; likes moist soil; tolerates full sun in north but likes part shade in heat; blooms July–Sept; good color for late perennial garden; effective along water	Eastern US except FL Zones 4–9
Rosemallows, (over 40 species; 2 suggestions here)	*Hibiscus* spp.	White, pink, or various shades of red	Moist, wet conditions produce most blooms; showy	As specified below
Crimsoneyed rosemallow	*H. moscheutos*	Deep burgundy red N I	3–7' tall, 2–3' spread; moist to wet soil, full sun; showy flowers July–Sept to 8" wide; can be grown in large containers	Eastern US except NH, VT, ME, and AR Zones 5–9
Rosemallow	*H. lasiocarpos*	White or rose with magenta I	3–7' tall, 2–3' spread; average medium to wet soil, full sun; tolerates heat and humidity but needs moisture; blooms July–Oct; attracts butterflies	Southern US Zones 5–9
Milkweeds	*Asclepias* spp.	Varied N I	All milkweeds serve as larval host plants for monarch butterflies	As specified below
Butterfly weed	*A. tuberosa*	Orange N I	2–3' tall clumps, 1–1.5' spread; full sun; low maintenance, drought tolerant; showy blooms June–Aug; attracts hummingbirds and butterflies; deeply rooted so best left in place once established	Eastern US Zones 3–9
Swamp milkweed	*A. incarnata*	White, pink to mauve N I	3–4' tall, 2–3' spread; full sun, best in moist soil; deep taproot; showy, fragrant flowers July–Aug; good in sunny borders, low spots, butterfly gardens	Eastern US except MS Zones 3–6

COMMON NAME	SCIENTIFIC NAME	COLOR AND BENEFIT(S) N = NECTAR I = INSECTS S = SEED B = BERRIES	COMMENTS	NATIVE, PLANTING ZONES
Whorled milkweed	A. verticillata	White N I	1–2.5′ tall, 1–2′ spread; easily grown full sun to part shade in well-drained soil; blooms June–Sept; attracts butterflies, other pollinators, hummingbirds; good in borders, butterfly gardens	Eastern US except ME and NH Zones 4–9
Mountain mints	Pycnanthemum spp.		Mountain mints esp. attractive to pollinators and, by extension, birds; in spite of name, not alpine; underlying silver bracts give impression of being dusted by snow	As specified below
Blunt mountain mint synonymous with short-toothed mountain mint	P. muticum	Pink N I	1–3′ tall, 1–3′ spread; easily grown, full sun to part shade; drought tolerant, vigorous grower; if naturalization undesirable, prune with spade; showy pink flowers July–Sept; good in borders, cottage and butterfly gardens	As specified below
Slender mountain mint	P. tenuifolium	White N I	2–3′ tall, 2–3′ spread; full sun to part shade, well-drained soil; sometimes aggressive grower; tolerates drought, clay soil, erosion; blooms July–Sept; good in herb gardens, naturalized areas, borders (if contained)	Eastern US except FL Zones 3–8
Monardas	Monarda spp.	Varied N I S	Esp. attractive to butterflies and hummingbirds, also finches and winter sparrows that enjoy seeds; susceptible to powdery mildew; M. didyma cultivars need more moisture than do M. fistulosa cultivars	As specified below
Scarlet bee balm	M. didyma	Red N I S	Up to 3′ tall, 2–3′ spread; full sun to part shade in moisture-retentive soil; showy red flowers July–Aug; good in border fronts, bird and butterfly gardens	Eastern US except FL, AL, MS, LA, and AR Zones 4–9

COMMON NAME	SCIENTIFIC NAME	COLOR AND BENEFIT(S) N = NECTAR I = INSECTS S = SEED B = BERRIES	COMMENTS	NATIVE, PLANTING ZONES
Wild bergamot	*M. fistulosa*	Lavender, pink, or white	2–4' tall, 2–3' spread; full sun to part shade, well-drained soil; tolerates drought, clay soil; showy fragrant flowers July–Sept; tends to self-seed; not as colorful as bee balms	US except FL and CA Zones 3–9
Penstemons (multiple species and cultivars available; 2 suggestions here)	*Penstemon* spp.	Varied	Most species and cultivars attract both butterflies and hummingbirds	As specified below
Beard tongue synonymous with foxglove beardtongue	*P. digitalis*	White N I	3–5' tall, 1.5–2' spread; full sun, well-drained soil; tolerates drought, clay soil; showy flowers Apr–June; mass in sunny borders, native plant and naturalized gardens	Eastern US except FL Zones 3–8
Gray beard tongue	*P. canescens*	Pale to dark violet N I	1–3' tall, 1–1.5' spread; full sun, well-drained soil; easily grown; showy flowers May–June; good for sunny areas, rock gardens	IL, IN, OH, PA, VT, MD, VA, WV, TN, KY, NC, SC, GA, and AL Zones 5–8
Phloxes (many species and cultivars; 3 suggestions here)	*Phlox* spp.	Varied	Most attract hummingbirds, butterflies, and other pollinators; some susceptible to powdery mildew	As specified below
Garden phlox esp. cultivar 'David'	*P. paniculata* 'David'	White N I	2–4' tall, 2–3' spread; staple of perennial borders; resists powdery mildew better than most; blooms July–Sept, longer bloom period that most phlox; other cultivars in alternate colors	Cultivar; eastern US except FL Zones 3–8

COMMON NAME	SCIENTIFIC NAME	COLOR AND BENEFIT(S) N = NECTAR I = INSECTS S = SEED B = BERRIES	COMMENTS	NATIVE, PLANTING ZONES
Meadow phlox synonymous with wild sweetwilliam and spotted phlox	*P. maculata*	Pinkish purple N I	2–3' tall, 1–2' spread; prefers organically rich, moist soil, full sun; blooms Aug–Oct; attracts butterflies and birds, including hummingbirds	Eastern US except WI, AR, LA, FL, NH, CT, and RI Zones 3–8
Smooth phlox	*P. glaberrima*	Reddish purple, pink, or white N I	2–4' tall, 2–2.5' spread; prefers moderately fertile, well-drained soil, full sun; blooms on panicles up to 12" tall, Apr–May, one of few tall phloxes to bloom early	Eastern US except MI and east of OH and north of VA Zones 3–8
Rattlesnake master synonymous with **button snake-root**	*Eryngium yuccifolium*	Greenish white N I S	4–5' tall, 2–3' spread; easily grown in full sun, well-drained soil; showy flowers June–Sept; attractive to pollinators; unusual-looking plant; good specimen, effective in broad borders, native gardens	Most of US Zones 3–8
Sage	*Salvia azurea*	Blue N I	3–4' tall, 2–4' spread; easily grown in variety of soils, full sun; drought tolerant, deer resistant; showy spikes of flowers July–Oct	Southeastern and south central US; but naturalized in most of the rest of eastern US, except east of OH and TN Zones 5–9
Vervain	*Verbena hastata*	Purplish blue N I	2–6' tall, 1–2.5' spread; full sun; forms colonies, slowly spreading by rhizomes and self-seeding; blooms July–Sept; attracts butterflies, hummingbirds	Eastern US Zones 3–8

COMMON NAME	SCIENTIFIC NAME	COLOR AND BENEFIT(S) N = NECTAR I = INSECTS S = SEED B = BERRIES	COMMENTS	NATIVE, PLANTING ZONES
Yarrow	*Achillea millefolium*	White N I	3' tall, 2–3' spread; feathery leaves; blooms in spring, seed heads remain through summer; forms colonies, best in wild areas; attractive to pollinators; cultivars in yellow and paprika, well-behaved for gardens	Eastern US Zones 3–9

Well, there you have it! Make your choices. If, however, you have a super-sized yard, we have more suggestions in the next table, eight more natives a bit too rambunctious for neat-and-tidy, but plants too good for bird habitat to ignore. Given space, then, include those eight among your possible choices as well.

NATIVE PERENNIALS BEST FOR ONLY SUPER-SIZED YARDS

Some native perennials have rambunctious habits. They're tall, or they spread aggressively, or they're rangy, or they flop over, or they're just plain untidy and ill-mannered. Still, some are so fabulous for bird habitat that, if you have a super-sized yard, they deserve a close look.

Boneset or Thoroughwort

In autumn, the sometimes chest-high white blossoms of boneset, very similar to thoroughwort, seem to host every pollinator and little bug on the planet. Surely an entomologist would find a little slice of heaven studying these visitors. I'm betting that's exactly the way all the warblers and flycatchers feel when they study the visitors, too. What a buffet the birds enjoy! Blended with the bright yellow of goldenrod, boneset brightens the path edges. I don't plant

it—it readily plants itself—but I also don't mow it down.

A fall migrating monarch nectars on boneset (*Eupatorium perfoliatum*), verifying the plant's worth to pollinators—and birds.

Goldenrods

We've already talked about some well-behaved goldenrod species that work in the garden, but the one listed here may be a bit too vigorous for a tidy yard or garden. Still, given a patch you would otherwise be mowing, let the goldenrods take over and feed the fall migrating birds. If you continue to mow the border, you'll readily contain the mass planting.

New York Ironweed

In spite of its name, New York ironweed has spread across more states than just its native. While crop farmers and cattle rangers fight to eliminate ironweed, the plant does serve butterflies well. Although I'm not recommending purchasing the plant (only limited well-behaved cultivars are on the horizon for purchase), if it does come up somewhere convenient, it's worth keeping.

Spotted Jewelweed

Again, I doubt you can purchase spotted jewelweed, also called touch-me-not, but learn to recognize the plant with its fairly specific growing conditions: wet shade, or at least moist shade. Since we quit mowing most areas, I've discovered spotted jewelweed in low spots at woods' edge. Since then, the plant has spread into a nice-sized patch, and fall migrating hummingbirds have taken up position there to guard small sectors, fattening up before moving on. During fall migration, Ruby-throated Hummingbirds throughout the eastern US depend almost exclusively on spotted jewelweed for nectar.

Common Milkweed

The trio of milkweed plants listed above may require a tiny bit of care for their hardiness, but common milkweed will grow anywhere any time and spread readily by root. Given the dramatic decline in monarch butterfly populations and given that milkweed are the only host plant monarchs will use to lay their eggs, if you have room, add common milkweed.

Mountain Mints

Because some mountain mints spread rapidly and because they're such fabulous pollinators,

consider cultivating a few in big spaces. The birds will take advantage of the bursting buffet.

American Pokeweed

Okay, American pokeweed is a weed. The name says so. I'm betting you've yanked out your fair share. So have I. As fabulous as they are for their abundant black-purple berries, they tend to come up where we don't want them. Given acreage, however, you may have a spot where you don't object to their annual return—and they do come up every year from very deep roots.

When fall migrants come through, like Rose-breasted Grosbeaks, Gray Catbirds, and Swainson's

To produce healthy, bright feather color, red-colored birds, like male Northern Cardinals, need an ample diet of lipids during molt, nutrition found in native berries like pokeweed (*Phytolacca americana*).

Thrushes and all their cousins, the berries will disappear like magic. And if any remain, leave it to the Northern Cardinals to finish them off. They rely on berries during molt to make their feathers red. Now who could turn down the opportunity to cultivate pokeweed knowing that?

Sunflowers

Oodles of native sunflowers dot the eastern US, but they're mostly not the ones found in big-box stores or area nurseries. Instead, look for native sunflowers while armed with the scientific names. That's your only chance of actually getting what you think you're getting. Know, however, that many—but not all—native sunflowers tend to reach to the sky and then flop over. Some spread rapidly. Some readily reseed. All, however, provide essential seed for birds' winter survival. That's a fact worth knowing.

Given space, then, here are additional native perennials for your consideration.

Eight Native Perennials Best Limited to Super-Sized Yards

COMMON NAME	SCIENTIFIC NAME	COLOR AND BENEFIT(S) N = NECTAR I = INSECTS S = SEED B = BERRIES	COMMENTS	NATIVE, PLANTING ZONES
Boneset very similar to **thoroughwort**	*Eupatorium perfoliatum E. serotinum*	White N I	3' tall, 3-4' spread; attracts pollinators; full sun to part shade; needs moisture; blooms in fall; all parts of plant toxic and bitter; best as border and in cottage and native gardens	Eastern US Zones 3-8
Goldenrod, Canadian	*Solidago canadensis*	Yellow N I S	4-5' tall, 4-5' spread; superior for birds seeking fall bugs; seeds for winter birds; blooms late summer; aggressive so best in wild areas, although not considered invasive; goldenrods wrongly blamed for hay fever, actually caused by plants like ragweed	Eastern US except FL, SC, GA, AL, and LA Zones 3-9
Ironweed, New York (cultivars available)	*Vernonia noveboracensis*	Purple N I	4-6' tall, 3-4' spread; prefers full sun and rich, moist, slightly acidic soils; beloved by butterflies and other insects; cultivars shorter	Eastern US except ME, NH, MS, LA, AR, MO, IA, MN, QI, MI, IL, and IN Zones 5-9

COMMON NAME	SCIENTIFIC NAME	COLOR AND BENEFIT(S) N = NECTAR I = INSECTS S = SEED B = BERRIES	COMMENTS	NATIVE, PLANTING ZONES
Jewelweed, spotted synonymous with **touch-me-not**	*Impatiens capensis*	Orange N	2–3' tall on weak stems, 1.5–2.5' spread; technically an annual but reliably self-seeds; prime nectar source for fall migrating hummingbirds; damp shade, lowlands, bogs	Eastern US Zones 2–11
Milkweed, common	*Asclepias syriaca*	Pink to mauve N I	Up to 4' tall on stout stems, 9"–1' spread; rough, weedy; blooms June–Aug; drought tolerant; best in wild areas	Eastern US except FL Zones 3–9
Mountain mints	*Pycnanthemum* spp.	Usually white	Esp. attractive to pollinators and thus birds; in spite of name, not alpine; underlying silver bracts give impression of being dusted by snow	As specified below
Hoary mountain mint	*P. incanum*	White, sometimes tinged in lavender N I	2–3' tall, 3–4' spread; best in full sun, well-drained soil; vigorous growth, so prune rhizomes with spade in spring if undesired; showy flowers July–Sept; good in borders (if contained), naturalized areas	Eastern US except ME, LA, AR, MO, IA, MN, and WI Zones 4–8
Virginia mountain mint	*P. virginianum*	White N I	2–3' tall, 1–1.5' spread; full sun, well-drained soil; blooms July–Sept; tried and trouble-free in naturalized areas, contained borders	Eastern US except LA, FL, and SC Zones 3–7
Pokeweed, American	*Phytolacca americana*	White (blue-black berries) B	4–10' tall, 2–3' spread; large-leafed, deep taproot; best in wild areas; all plant parts poisonous to humans; berries highly prized by fall migrants	Eastern US Zones 4–8
Sunflower, rough (many sunflower species, cultivars; *H. divaricatus* one of shortest)	*Helianthus divaricatus*	Yellow N I S	2–6' tall, 1–3' spread; showy blooms in part shade, July–Sept; divide every 2–3 years to control spread and maintain strong plants; tried and true, trouble-free	Cultivar Zones 3–8

NATIVE PERENNIALS SUITED TO POTS-AND-PATIO SPACES

Detailed in the preceding tables, the following native perennials are listed here to identify them as plants that work well in small spaces. Consider them for narrow borders next to a patio, in planter boxes or large containers, or as accents against small shrubs or evergreens. These selections are low maintenance, compact, and colorful. All attract butterflies, and what attracts butterflies will also attract birds. Several also produce seeds favored by finches and winter sparrows.

Native Perennials for Containers

Columbine, red, synonymous with **wild columbine**	*Aquilegia canadensis*
Coneflower: Black-eyed Susan	*Rudbeckia hirta*
Coreopsis: Threadleaf coreopsis	*Coreopsis verticillata,* esp. 'Zagreb'
Hyssop: Agastache 'Purple Haze'	*Agastache* 'Purple Haze'
Indian pink, synonymous with **woodland pinkroot**	*Spigelia marilandica*
Liatris: Dense blazing star	*Liatris spicata*
Hibiscus: Crimsoneyed rosemallow	*Hibiscus moscheutos*
Milkweed: Butterfly weed	*Asclepias tuberosa*
Monarda: Scarlet bee balm	*Monarda didyma*
Phlox: Garden phlox	*Phlox paniculata* 'David'
Salvia: Blue sage	*Salvia azurea*

Many of the compact coreopsis species and their cultivars work well in a pots-and-patio garden, like the 'Zagreb' cultivar of threadleaf coreopsis (*Coreopsis verticillata*) shown here.

PERENNIAL ORNAMENTAL GRASSES

Next, with trees, shrubs and tall understory plants, vines, and perennial "flowers" mapped out, look for landscape gaps or spots you envision needing some sort of accent. Perennial native ornamental grasses reach varying heights and form varying degrees of "droop." A few, in fact, are glamorously upright, charmingly tall, providing much-needed height amid modestly sized perennials. A few offer contrasting colors of yellow, bronze, or pink, especially for winter interest. Some arch slightly, adding grace against otherwise vertical perennials or permanent structures. With varying heights and behaviors, then, native grasses can transform a yard or garden from ordinary into extraordinary.

Benefits to Birds

What can native ornamental grasses add to a birdscape, you ask? The obvious benefit, of course, is seed—lots of tiny seeds for finches and winter sparrows, including migrants like Lincoln's Sparrows, Vesper Sparrows, and Savannah Sparrows—depending, of course, on the overall

Because of their small bill structure, Dark-eyed Juncos, among other winter finches and sparrows, prefer the tiny seeds of grasses.

surroundings. Sometimes Dark-eyed Juncos ride grass stems down, nearly to the ground, and stretch to reach the flimsy seed heads. Mostly, though, finches and winter sparrows forage on the ground below the arching stems, scratching up scattered seeds among the litter. Other birds, too, forage for fallen seed, including Northern Cardinals, Mourning Doves, Black-capped and Carolina Chickadees, and Tufted Titmice.

Grasses, however, add another resource for birds: nest sites. Ground nesters, especially during early spring attempts, will frequently nest under the arching grass stems, sometimes tucking nests into the edge of the clump, seeking the protection of the density there. Given that avian habit, if you plan to prune grasses annually, make certain to do so in late winter, well prior to any nesting attempts.

Because almost all songbirds use grasses in some part of their nests, many will check out any grass clump, break off suitably sized pieces, and weave them artfully into their abodes. Catching them in the act takes as much luck as winning the lottery, but if you do, you'll watch an amazing check-this, test-that, and finally bite-this-off process. You

have to wonder what thoughts go through their tiny brains as they check one grass blade after another. How do they make the choice of one over the other? We'll never know.

Decision Time

Here are some ideas you may want to think about when making your final choice(s) for native ornamental grasses.

Consider: Adding grass clumps expands biodiversity. Because native grasses host a number of insects, especially grasshoppers, avian diets benefit from those insects. Perhaps nothing else in your yard or garden—trees, shrubs, vines, or perennials—hosts the insects that grasses host.

Consider: Native grasses produce seeds favored by birds, especially little birds. While occasionally birds ride flexible grass stems to the ground (always an amusing exercise to watch) and then forage among the seed heads there, more often birds simply forage on the ground around the

Snow and ice crystals bend the blades of a sizable clump of switchgrass (*Panicum virgatum*), forming numerous sheltered "coves" for birds and other wildlife seeking protection against predators and winter's elements.

grass clumps, gathering fallen seeds. Allow room for their foraging.

Consider: Overarching grass clumps provide nest sites for early-spring ground-level nesters. When little else offers shelter in early spring, native grasses fill the bill. Planted in an already semi-protected place, grass clumps can serve as year-round shelter and/or spring and summer nest sites. Take protection into account as you consider planting spots.

Let's get going, then, with some possible native ornamental grasses to add assets to your birdscape.

Little Bluestem

A grass of the original tallgrass prairie, little bluestem serves a number of botanical purposes. Its deep roots make it drought tolerant and help control soil erosion. Masses of it, or at least a group of clumps, support prairie bugs and, therefore, feed yard birds like Song Sparrows, Northern Cardinals, and Eastern Bluebirds. While seed heads provide an important winter food source for finches and winter sparrows, choosing little bluestem as ornamental clumps throughout your cottage garden, along a walk, or as a border makes good ecological sense.

Bottlebrush Grass

My goodness, bottlebrush grass is pretty stuff! Who wouldn't love the 9- to 10-inch-long flower spikes edging a walk, bordering a garden, grouped in clumps as a backdrop for short perennials, or winding along the property line. Its specific epithet *hystrix* means "hedgehog," a nod to the seed head's seeming semblance to hedgehog quills. Well, okay, maybe some imagination there. Since the grass takes part shade and wants well-drained soil, this bunchgrass works well along woodland edges, delineating one part of the yard or garden from the other.

Grasses attract critters like katydids (shown here) and grasshoppers; and they, in turn, are favorite foods for many birds, including Eastern Bluebirds.

Indian Grass

Like other prairie grasses, deeply rooted Indian grass serves well on banks for erosion control. While it's slow to establish, you'll love its upright stance—although it may flop over in rich, moist soils. In its preferred poor, dry soils, however, it retains a different profile from many other "weeping" grasses and their arching stems. Put Indian grass in the background, or blend it with perennials in a prairie sweep. Seed heads, attractive as winter interest in landscaping, also provide winter interest to birds—as a nutritious lunch. Horticulturalists recommend cutting the plant to the ground in late winter, before any new sprouts appear.

Prairie Dropseed Grass

Perhaps the most popular of the native ornamentals, prairie dropseed grass gets its name from the tiny, round mature seeds that drop from their hulls in autumn. A finely textured, hairlike grass, it has showy, fragrant, pink- and brown-tinted cream-colored flowers that soar well above the grass blades themselves, sometimes topping at 3 feet tall. Probably the flower's most interesting feature, however, is its aroma, described variously but most often as having a hint of coriander leaf. Foliage turns golden orange in fall, fading to bronze in winter. Little birds, those seedeaters of the winter world, forage on the ground beneath, picking fallen seeds from the litter.

Sideoats Grama Grass

Funny name, that sideoats grama grass. But this interesting plant gets its name honestly—because its oat-like seed spikes hang from only one side of its flowering stems. The bluish-gray leaf blades form dense clumps, so planting in masses makes the best show. In autumn, grasses turn golden brown, sometimes with tinges of red or orange—most likely depending on moisture and soil conditions. It's one of the few ornamental grasses that also function satisfactorily as turf grass, mowed to 2 or 3 inches. Again, for birds, it's all about the seed and any bugs the plant might hide.

Switchgrass

Because it can reach up to 7 feet tall, switchgrass probably wouldn't work well in mini yards, but potted in a deep container, it could certainly add interest on a patio. While a single clump could add an accent to a small garden, I cultivate a ragged row (who wants marching soldiers in the landscape?) that sets off an unmowed area from the rest. Every fall, during migration, I watch the little seedeaters forage on both the flexible stems and the surrounding ground. But it's after the winter holidays, when I decorate a yard tree, that the real fun begins. By tying switchgrass seed heads to the tree branches, I can giggle at the Dark-eyed Juncos stretching to reach the farthest morsels. Carolina Chickadees, Carolina Wrens, and Tufted Titmice do their fair share of reaching, too.

Top: In winter, when bugs have disappeared, small birds with small bills turn to small seeds for sustenance; so Carolina Wrens are always on the hunt for fresh, viable grass seeds.
Bottom: Ornamental grasses drop seeds at their bases, providing great foraging for winter finches and sparrows, like this Song Sparrow, a switchgrass seed (*Panicum virgatum*) in its beak.

About the List

*T*he native grasses listed in this chapter are, according to the United States Department of Agriculture Plant Database (online at www.plants.usda.gov), native to states as indicated. Note, however, that while a plant may be native in your state, it may not be native to every part of your state and certainly not to every eco-region. Before making final choices, consider soil texture, moisture, slope, and required sunlight. Your planting zone and eco-region combined will determine suitable growing conditions in your locale. To find your planting zone, check online at http://planthardiness.ars.usda.gov/.

The plant lists in this reference are not, nor are they intended to be, all-inclusive. Rather, the plants here were chosen because:

1. They are attractive to birds because, in some way, they meet birds' needs for food, shelter, and/or nesting.
2. They are easily grown, well behaved, and suitable for landscaping in various settings, as described.

Estimated height and spread sizes are shown for mature ornamental grasses. Generally, though, ornamental grasses should be cut to within 6 to 8 inches of the ground each spring prior to their greening.

Here, then, is the table detailing six native ornamental grasses for your consideration.

Add grass clumps to your yard map now, locating them appropriately and labeling them.

Native Ornamental Grasses for Any-Sized Yard

COMMON NAME	SCIENTIFIC NAME	COMMENTS	NATIVE, PLANTING ZONES
Bluestem, little	*Schizachyrium scoparium*	2–4' tall, 1.5–2' spread; full sun, dry to medium well-drained soil; performs well in poor soil; purplish-bronze seed heads; winter interest; tolerates drought, air pollution; low maintenance in sun-baked areas; attractive to insects, esp. grasshoppers, a primary late-summer food source for birds	Most of US Zones 3–9
Bottlebrush grass	*Elymus hystrix*	2.5–3' tall, 1–1.5' spread; upright; full sun to part shade; tolerates drought, variety of soils; easily grown; showy flowers on 9–10" heads, Sept–Oct; good in clumps, masses, naturalized in light shade; will self-seed in optimum conditions; seeds attract birds	Eastern US except FL, MS, and LA Zones 5–9
Indian grass	*Sorghastrum nutans*	3–5' tall, 1–2' spread; noted for upright form; full sun, dry to medium soil; easily grown; tolerates drought and air pollution; blooms Sept–Feb; good in masses or vertical accents; seeds attract birds	Eastern US Zones 4–9
Prairie dropseed	*Sporobolus heterolepis*	2–3' tall, 2–3' spread; full sun, dry to medium soil; easily grown; tolerates drought and air pollution; showy, fragrant flowers Aug–Sept; good winter interest; good as ground cover, in rain gardens, naturalized; does not freely self-seed; attracts birds	Eastern US except NH, VT, ME, MA, WV, TN, AL, MS, LA, and FL Zones 3–9
Sideoats grama grass sometimes called just **sideoats**	*Bouteloua curtipendula*	1.5–2.5' tall, 1.5–2' spread; full sun, dry to medium soil; tolerates drought, shallow rocky soil, air pollution; showy purplish flowers July–Aug; cut clumps to ground in late winter; may self-seed in optimum conditions; best in masses, rock gardens, slopes; seeds attract birds	Eastern US Zones 4–9
Switchgrass	*Panicum virgatum*	5–7' tall, 2–3' spread; full sun to part shade, variety of soils; tolerates drought, wet, air pollution; important component of tallgrass prairie; spreads slowly by rhizome; airy blooms and seed heads, July–Feb; good as accent, group, mass, screen and in perennial borders, water gardens; seeds attract birds	Eastern US Zones 5–9

FERNS AND SEDUMS

Ferns and sedums are herbaceous perennials that are worth mentioning separately here—just in case you have the perfect spot begging for either or both of these plants. Ferns offer many of the same benefits as grass clumps—shelter and potential nest sites—but minus the seeds. Sedums, like ferns, form dandy hiding spots for all kinds of little ground-loving creatures—many of which make dandy meals for birds. Sedums also sport lovely little blossoms attractive to bugs. And guess what loves bugs! So maybe you have the perfect spot for a cluster of either or both of these plant species.

Ferns

While the eastern US boasts a good many native ferns, most are strictly woodland plants. So unless you live in a densely shaded forest or have rich loamy soil against the north side of your house, ferns may seem completely out of reach. Not so.

In fact, ostrich ferns (*Matteuccia struthiopteris*) will grow in nearly full sun—as long as the temps don't soar too high (preferably in Zones 3–7). In fact, in parts of the country, ostrich ferns are called "foundation ferns" due to their popularity as plants next to the house, concealing the structure's foundation. In part or full shade, these lovely ferns add grace and delicacy to the yard or garden, and birds find shelter among a dense stand.

While ostrich ferns can reach heights of 5 or 6 feet, most tend to stay at 2 to 3 feet. Rabbits won't bother them, and they tolerate clay soils. They do like moisture, but they don't want wet feet. In winter, they die back to the ground, only to unfurl in "fiddleheads" in the spring. (See photo in Chapter 4, page 66.) By late summer, they tend to look a bit ratty, so removing or pruning the unlovely fronds tidies their appearance.

On the other hand, one of the easiest-to-grow ferns is the woodland Christmas fern (*Polystichum acrostichoides*), so named because it's evergreen. Usually about 2 or 3 feet tall, it likes part shade and rich, well-drained but moist soil. Though Christmas fern tolerates less sunlight than does ostrich fern, it's happy in a broader range of planting zones, Zones 2–9. In short, Christmas fern works well if planted in appropriate spots in the landscape—like along a shady area next to a wall, in masses along a north-facing slope to help hold eroding soil, or in native woodland gardens.

Sedums

Like ferns, sedums in clusters provide cover for tiny critters that birds find tasty. While you'll find a good many sedum varieties on nursery shelves, not all are native. One native in particular has attracted my attention, commonly called three-leaved stonecrop (*Sedum turnatum*). Because it functions as a ground cover in full sun and part shade, it's a versatile, attractive, well-behaved addition to a trouble spot. Unlike ferns that do not bloom, this sedum produces a showy white starlike blossom in early spring.

Although, like most other native sedums, three-leaved stonecrop dies back in winter, it's hardy in

Native three-leaved stonecrop (*Sedum turnatum*) works well among stones and fossils.

Zones 4–8. Rabbits and deer don't like it, and it's drought and air pollution tolerant. In short, this is a perfect plant for many situations and locations, especially in rock gardens and in pots-and-patio gardens, tucked into nooks and crannies for a touch of green that requires no further attention on your part. Stems are easily broken off if it spreads beyond where you want it, and those same stems will readily take root tucked into loose soil. Many plants for the price of one—if you're not in a hurry.

ANOTHER UPDATE

With this rather wide-ranging list of herbaceous perennials suitable for yards large and small, you'll likely be limited only by time, space, and budget in offering a vast array of seeds, nectar, bugs, nest sites, and nest-building materials to lure birds to your habitat. While trees anchor and shrubs fill in, perennials add color—whether we're talking about blossom color, seed-head color, or vegetative color. At the same time, perennials add a variety of food sources across all season. And since perennials are small, even if your space is also small, you can include a nice selection. Of course, the wider the diversity of plants, the wider the diversity of birds!

Isn't the prospect exciting?

So update your map now, identifying and locating the perennials—flowers, grasses, and maybe ferns and sedums—that you plan to add.

PLANT-CHOICE WRAP-UP

That's it: the last of the many kinds of native plants we're recommending for landscaping. With anchor trees, filler shrubs and vines, an array of colorful perennial food sources, and a selection of grasses, you're armed with enough choices to make a delightful birdscape in virtually any location.

What's left? Water. On to Step 4. Your plan is almost finished!

A Swamp Sparrow, happy near water foraging among willows (*Salix* spp.), has snagged a caterpillar for its nestlings.

"If you are thinking one year ahead, sow seed. If you are thinking ten years ahead, plant a tree. If you are thinking 100 years ahead, educate the people."

—CHINESE PROVERB

"Ordinary people must think carefully about their own surroundings and how to preserve the biodiversity that occurs around them. The world that results will be a patchwork with bright spots, richer places and more beautiful areas. And that will happen because individuals took responsibility and acted."

—PETER H. RAVEN, President, Missouri Botanical Garden, St. Louis

Chapter 8
ADDING WATER

The purpose of this book, of course, is to speak to the matter of native plants that attract and support birds—more specifically, native plants that supply food, shelter, and nest sites and nesting materials. But we've consistently noted that satisfactory bird habitat also requires a fourth element: water.

So we really can't ignore the importance of water and making it available in your birdscape. In addition, certain native plants love wet feet and do well along water's edge. Others that thrive in water do well in submerged pots buried in customized water features. We've included lists of both in this chapter.

It's perhaps worth mentioning that in my own yard, we've tallied birds at our water features that we likely would have never seen otherwise. True, the birds are busy foraging around the yard and garden, but they're often hidden in the lush vegetation or up too high or down too low to reveal themselves. Everything needs water, however, so we catch sight of them when they're having a drink or a bath.

So, let's look at water sources, either natural or of your own making.

Step 4: Add water.
If we all enjoyed the ideal habitat, we would live on property boasting natural waters—a pond, lake, river, creek, wetland, or spring. In reality, however, most of us don't have natural waters on or even near our yards. That means we must figure out other means by which to provide water—the singularly important fourth element essential in bird habitat. We'll begin this chapter, however, talking about yards with natural waters and how to take advantage of this unique situation to add further biodiversity to the yard.

NATURAL WATERS

If you live where natural water is part of your habitat, your birds are happy. But maybe you can make them even happier. Assuming the water's banks are natural (as opposed to sterile riprap, retaining wall, or other inorganic barrier), birds find all the drinking and bathing resources necessary. They enjoy waterfront sites as much as we do. Think about what might happen, however, if you enhanced the water's edges with native plants, encouraging birds not just to make quick visits but to hang out, enjoying the protection as well as a quick lunch or even a lingeringly long, fine dinner.

Even though we've included most of these plants in earlier tables, they work especially well where they can enjoy wet feet. Additional species, specific to this list, are marked with an asterisk (★). Since these are abbreviated tables, see full details for each species in corresponding chapters for trees, shrubs, and perennials.

Great blue lobelia (*Lobelia siphilitica*), sometimes called blue cardinal flower, grows happily in wet places, even in standing water.

Adding to the List

So here's the deal: If you live on waterfront property, you'll want to give thought to plants that enhance the border where water meets land—shoreline, river bank, or creek bank. Having made those choices, based on the shoreline length, add them to your plant list and yard map. While you may choose to tackle the shoreline or river or creek bank as a separate project, you'll want the project to be part of the master plan. Update your yard map accordingly.

Plants for Water's Edge

COMMON NAME	SCIENTIFIC NAME	COMMENTS	NATIVE, PLANTING ZONES
TREES: DECIDUOUS			
Swamp white oak	*Quercus bicolor*	To 70' tall, 60' spread; tolerates wet; needs acidic soil; lacks taproot	Eastern US except GA and FL Zones 3-8
Black willow	*Salix nigra*	Largest native willow, 30-60' tall, 30-60' spread; fast-growing; easily rooted from cuttings	Eastern US Zones 4-9
Boxelder	*Acer negundo*	30-50' tall, 30-50' spread; mainly in moist soils, along streams and pond margins	Eastern US Zones 2-10
Southern bald cypress and variety **pond cypress**	*Taxodium distichum* and *T. distichum* var. *impricarium*	50-75' tall, 20-45' spread; a plant of wetlands but grows most anywhere; attractive shape, ferny foliage	Eastern US except MN, IA, WI, and east of NY Zones 4-9
TREES: EVERGREEN			
White spruce	*Picea glauca*	40-60' tall, 10-20' spread; smallest cones of spruces; common, widespread in muskegs and bogs	MD, DE, NJ, and PA north through ME; also MI, WI, and MN Zones 2-6
Atlantic white cedar	*Chamaecyparis thyoides*	Columnar, 30-50' tall, 30-40' spread; common in swamps and bogs, along streams	All coastal states from ME through LA Zones 4-8
Northern white cedar synonymous with **American arborvitae**	*Thuja occidentalis*	20-40' tall, 10-15' spread; native in swamps, along waterways; commonly cultivated	Eastern US except FL, GA, AL, MS, LA, AR, and MO Zones 2-7
Sweetbay magnolia synonymous with **laurel magnolia**	*Magnolia virginiana*	10-35' tall, 10-35' spread; shrubby and deciduous north but treelike and evergreen south; common in wet soils	Gulf and Atlantic coastal states except CT, RI, and ME Zones 5-10
SHRUBS			
Alder	*Alnus* spp.	15-20' tall, 15-25' spread; naturalizes; native to boggy grounds, cool climate	North of Ohio River Zones 2-6; does not thrive south of zone 6

COMMON NAME	SCIENTIFIC NAME	COMMENTS	NATIVE, PLANTING ZONES
American pussy willow	*Salix discolor*	6–15′ tall, 4–12′ spread; may be cut to ground every 3–5 years to maintain smaller size	Eastern US except TN, FL, SC, GA, AL, LA, and AR Zones 4–8
Silky willow	*Salix sericea*	6′ tall, forms clumps; native to marshes, ditches, low woods	Eastern US except LA, MS, and FL Zones 2–8
Silky dogwood synonymous with **swamp dogwood**	*Cornus amomum*	6–12′ tall; 6–12′ spread; likes acidic soil; can form thickets; naturalized areas, stream banks, erosion control	Eastern US except LA, AR, MN, and WI Zones 5–8
PERENNIALS (see also "Aquatic Plants for Submerged Pots" on page 189)			
*Arrowhead, broadleaf	*Sagittaria latfolia*	1–4′ tall, 1–3′ spread; grows in water up to 1′ deep or in mud at water's edge; full sun; white flower July–Sept; deadhead if don't want plant to self-seed; commonly used in pond restoration; seeds attractive to birds, tubers attractive to waterfowl	Most of US Zones 5–10
Cardinal flower	*Lobelia cardinalis*	2–4′ tall, 1–2′ spread; short-lived; thrives in standing water; blooms July–Aug	Eastern US Zones 3–9
Great blue lobelia synonymous with **blue cardinal flower**	*Lobelia siphilitica*	2–3′ tall, 1–1.5′ spread; blooms July–Sept; good color for late perennial garden, effective along water	Eastern US except FL Zones 4–9
*Milkweed, aquatic	*Asclepias perennis*	2–3′ tall, 1–1.5′ spread; full sun; white flowers May–Aug; value to bees, butterflies; grows in shallow water; considered poisonous if ingested	Southern coastal states plus AR, MO, TN, KY, IN, and IL Zones 6–9
Crimsoneyed rosemallow	*Hibiscus moscheutos*	3–7′ tall, 2–3′ spread; full sun; showy flowers July–Sept to 8″ diameter	Eastern US except NH, VT, ME, and AR Zones 5–9
Rose mallow	*Hibiscus lasiocarpos*	3–7′ tall, 2–3′ spread; tolerates heat and humidity but needs moisture; blooms July–Oct	Southern US Zones 5–9

ADDING WATER FEATURES

Of course, if you're fortunate enough to have a pond, lake, stream, spring, or other natural water source on your property or even nearby, adding water via some other feature probably isn't all that important. Still, I'm betting you may enjoy your avian visitors within your window view, arriving for a drink or a bath.

When you completed your yard map in Chapter 4, if you marked space for some sort of water source, you likely had in mind either a birdbath or more elaborate water feature. Before you take action, spending hard-earned dollars for water-source hardscape, consider the following guiding principles.

Simple Birdbaths

The simplest and most common approach for providing water, of course, is to place a birdbath strategically in your landscaping. Birdbaths can be elegant or rustic, elaborate or simple, useful or awkward, ground level or pedestal high, swinging or stationary, slippery or rough, easily cleaned or not, with or without a fountain. When it comes to birdbaths, it's never the price that speaks to the quality—at least not from the birds' point of view. They really don't mind bathing in a puddle in the street.

Everything comes with strings attached, however, and birdbaths are no exception. They come with two important obligations—to keep them clean and fresh and to maintain them year-round.

So here are some thoughts:

Consider: Birds are accustomed to finding and availing themselves of water at ground level. After all, have you ever seen a natural water source 4 feet off the ground? So consider a birdbath that

Ten American Robins enjoy a drink at an icy ground-level water feature. The shadow of an 11th bird suggests more on the way!

will sit solidly on the ground. Of course, even if your chosen birdbath comes paired with a pedestal, nothing says you must use the pedestal!

Consider: Birds need shallow water. Think about how small most songbirds really are. Their legs, for instance, generally measure no more than an inch long, so water 3 inches deep equates to a neck-deep bathtub—useless to little birds.

Consider: A birdbath with a combination of sloping sides and a rough surface lets birds step down securely to water's edge, check the level, and then drink or bathe in comfort.

Consider: Choose a birdbath that can be easily cleaned. A stiff wire brush works well, and I scrub mostly once a week but up that to every day in summer. It's the only safe way to keep birdbaths free of algae and other unhealthy yucky stuff. On the very rare occasion that birdbaths become severely soiled, consider using one part bleach to nine parts water to scrub. Be sure, however, to rinse, rinse, rinse to eliminate every minute particle of bleach. It's deadly to birds. I'd rather scrub with clear water and a little elbow grease—a combination guaranteed safe for birds.

Consider: Birds need water year-round, both for drinking and for bathing. Thus, you should take into consideration how you will keep your birdbath waters in liquid form all four seasons. In winter, it's true that they can eat snow, but warming snow to body temperature takes 12 times more energy than warming water to body temperature—a heavy toll in already severe conditions. So keeping birdbaths ice-free serves birds well. If you shop for a birdbath heater, look for one

> WARNING: Never, ever add antifreeze or salt to your water feature; you'll poison the birds.

appropriate for the volume of water. For safety's sake, always plug any outdoor electrical item into a ground fault circuit interrupter (GFCI) outlet.

Consider: During mosquito breeding season, scrubbing birdbaths every day is a must—without fail. If mosquitoes find a way to reproduce in your birdbath, you may promote more than just mosquitoes; you and yours may face West Nile virus, Zika, or perhaps other mosquito-borne illnesses . (And in some communities, you'll face a hefty fine.)

Moving Water

Moving water in a birdbath creates three distinct advantages—for you and the birds:

1. Moving water prevents mosquitoes from breeding. They breed only in still water. Electrical and solar-powered pumps do the trick.
2. Moving water deters, or at least delays, freeze-ups—depending on the size of your reservoir, size of the pump, and severity of the cold.
3. Whether it's dripping, bubbling, or running, your proffered moving water attracts even distant birds by its attention-getting sound.

> WARNING: Adding some sort of insecticidal mosquito control to your water feature is *not* an option, as you'd be offering toxic drinks and baths to your birds, making your water feature deadly.

So decide on some means by which to keep water in your birdbath moving—maybe a dripper, a mister, a bubbler, or a recirculating pump—all readily available online and where birdbaths are sold. For safety's sake, always plug any outdoor electrical item into a GFCI outlet.

Beyond Birdbaths

Water features have become popular with homeowners, but not all are designed to attract birds. They differ as much as homeowners themselves—some elaborate, sprawling, and dramatic; others simple, compact, and subtle. Some take up a large portion of the yard, while others nearly hide in the shrubbery.

If you choose to install a water feature, remember this requirement: Birds need shallow water. Think of "shallow" as a slope from zero to no more than 1 inch. I've enjoyed visiting dozens of water features that display quite a "wow" factor, but birds would find them unusable: There was no slope and no shallow water. So build a water feature to suit yourself, and enjoy the deep, plunging waterfalls and cavernous pools sufficient to house fish year-round. If, however, you want the water feature to also attract birds, make sure that within the drama there are abundant places where slope and shallow come together. Do it for the birds!

Algae Control

In summertime's typically oppressive heat, water draws a crowd. But nobody—especially not birds—likes yucky algae in a water feature. Three factors contribute to algae growth: sunlight, nutrients, and low oxygen.

> WARNING: Never use an algaecide in your birdbath. You'll expose birds to potential toxins.

In fact, it's a simple matter to naturally control algae growth. Once again, plants come to the rescue. Here's how:

Yellow marsh marigold (*Caltha paulstris*) works well as an aquatic plant in home water features.

Broadleaf arrowhead (*Sagittaria latfolia*), a wetland plant, attracts birds to the seed heads that form after the pure white blossoms drop.

Here's another opportunity to invite monarchs to the yard with this aquatic milkweed (*Asclepais perennis*) that grows in very moist soil, even standing water.

1. Use plants in and around the water to add shade, reducing algae's source of sunlight.
2. Add hardy water plants that zap significant nutrients from the water, thus starving out algae.
3. Add oxygen by adding plants that render the water too oxygen-rich for algae.

So, added plants will reduce algae and add a lovely, natural, graceful touch to a man-made water feature. Which plants work under these conditions? Consider natives like those in the table on page 189.

Bubbling Rocks

Our yard includes two standard birdbaths, each less than an inch deep, one placed directly on the ground. We also maintain a little water feature with a mini waterfall and small pool, planted with native cover adored by lots of happy little fish. Within the three distinct parts of the water feature, one riffles along as a mini "creek," offering ample shallow slopes and shallow water for drinking and bathing birds. But our homemade bubbling rock sees the real action, primarily, we think, because of its welcoming sound. We never know which birds will show up next. Already we've documented more than 80 species drinking and/or bathing there.

A male Scarlet Tanager takes a quick bath in water less than an inch deep, flowing smoothly across rock in a small water feature. The out-of-focus foreground plant is marsh marigold (*Caltha paulstris*).

Okay, so what's this bubbling rock? It's a large stone with a hole bored through it that's set over a reservoir with a pump creating a recirculating water flow that, in our yard, birds can't resist. Ours is a homemade job, highly cost effective. Hummingbirds hover to drink from the edge, bluebirds jostle with goldfinches for position near the "bubble," robins arrive in families to sip and splash, and juncos bathe in leisure, freshening up after their travels. The hubbub sometimes

Aquatic Plants for Submerged Pots

COMMON NAME	SCIENTIFIC NAME	COMMENTS	NATIVE, PLANTING ZONE
Broadleaf arrowhead	*Sagittaria latfolia*	1–4' tall, 1–3' spread; full sun; white flowers July–Sept; to prevent spreading, gather seeds	Most of US Zones 5–10
Water iris synonymous with **southern blue flag**	*Iris virginica*	1–3' tall, 1–3' spread; full sun; violet-blue flowers in June; ranked tried and trouble-free	Eastern US except ME, NH, VT, MA, CT, RI, NJ, DE, and PA Zones 5–9
Yellow marsh marigold	*Caltha palustris*	1–1.5' tall, 1–1.5' spread; full sun, part shade; yellow flowers Apr–June; spreads by rhizomes; ranked tried and trouble-free	NC, TN, MO, and all states north of these Zones 3–7
Aquatic milkweed	*Asclepias perennis*	1–3' tall, 1–1.5' spread; part sun, part shade; white flowers throughout summer	IN, IL, MO, KY, TN, and all states south of these Zones 6–9
Pickerelweed	*Pontedaria cordata*	2–4' tall, 1.5–2' spread; full sun; soft blue flowers June–Oct; grow plants in containers to avoid spread	Eastern US Zones 3–10
Swamp rosemallow	*Hibiscus grandiflorus*	6–10' tall, 2–4' spread; full sun to part shade; pale pink blossoms in late spring, early summer	FL, GA, AL, MS, and LA Zones 8–10
Sweetflag	*Acorus americanus*	2–3' tall, 1' spread; full sun to part shade; wheat-colored blossoms May–July; rhizomes medicinal	IA, IL, IN, OH, PA, and states north of these Zones 3—6

gives me a chuckle as I watch the little guys vying for a drink or a bath, lining up in pecking order to await their turns, or sometimes pushing their faces into the bubble.

Consider making your own bubbling rock or having one made. The required tools are minimal, the work not too intensive, and the supplies readily available. Choosing the perfect rock always turns out to be the toughest challenge. It should have texture. It must be light enough to pick up and move (for cleaning purposes). And it needs to fit the landscape. We've even stacked our "perfect" rock on top of others in order to elevate the water's fall, thus creating more of that attention-getting sound to entice the birds.

Our bubbling rock bubbles year-round, thanks to a thermostatically controlled submersible heater, available where pet or livestock supplies

A fall migrating Red-breasted Nuthatch (top) and Nashville Warbler stop at a bubbling rock for a drink. The sound of moving water draws birds in like a magnet.

are sold. For safety, both the heater and the recirculating pump are plugged into a GFCI outlet.

The following diagram provides the essential elements for an in-ground bubbling-rock water feature. The folks we know who have built their own—and there have been many—have modified details to suit their own vision of the ideal bubbling rock, one most appropriate for their own locations. The results have been delightful, attracting birds they never expected to see. It's an idea worth considering for birdscaping your own yard.

REVISITING THE YARD MAP

Based on whatever you plan to do about water sources, update your yard map now. Add the locations and label waterfront plantings. Make sure you're satisfied with the location of an added birdbath or—more significantly—an added water feature. Decide if already-existing vegetation or planned additions will serve birds well, neither concealing predators while birds drink or bathe nor leaving them stranded without sufficient protection close by. Plant—or replant—as necessary.

THAT'S IT!

Your yard map is complete. You're ready to plant, serving the birds a buffet they'll enjoy for years to come. Let's get planted! Step 5 is just ahead.

Closer Look at a Bubble Rock

Water pumped from reservoir up through stone spills over stone back into reservoir

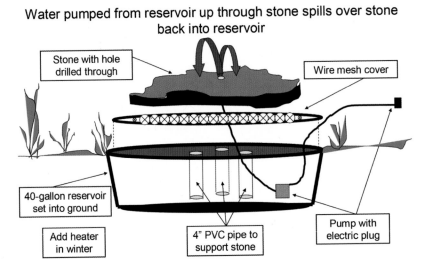

Stone with hole drilled through

Wire mesh cover

40-gallon reservoir set into ground

Add heater in winter

4" PVC pipe to support stone

Pump with electric plug

Reaching to gather nesting materials, a female Baltimore Oriole has her eye on wind-borne cottonwood seeds (*Populus deltoids*), perfect plant fibers for creating her hanging nest.

> *"We conserve only what we love; we love only what we understand; and we understand only what we have been taught."*
>
> —BABA DIOUM, Senegalese environmentalist and forestry engineer

Chapter 9
PUTTING THE PLAN IN ACTION

It's been an exciting journey. You completed an inventory and an evaluation of your yard, identified the assets and liabilities, and organized your yard map, choosing the plants you want to add. You have all the guiding details at hand: what you want to plant and where you want to plant it. This chapter will ease the way toward putting your plan in action.

Step 5: Put the plan in action.

REMOVING UNWANTED PLANTS

We recommended earlier that you implement your plan in baby steps, choosing only a section of the yard at a time to birdscape. Assuming you've made that choice, we'll proceed, assuming also that you'll repeat the steps later for other sections of your yard.

But first things first.

Perhaps in the course of your inventory and analysis, you discovered some plants that were not especially beneficial to birds. Maybe some were old, no longer attractive in the landscaping. Maybe some were nonnative. In fact, perhaps many were nonnative. In the course of thinking through the many options offered in previous chapters, you may have decided to remove some of these plants, perhaps because they're creeping into other parts of the yard or because you simply want to plant something else in that spot—something that will use the space more productively, providing more benefits to birds. For whatever reason, if you plan to remove any plants, now is the time, before you begin planting anew.

You will recall, however, that we focused especially on the necessity of removing any of the Disaster Dozen nonnative invasives: Bradford pear, princess tree, tree of heaven, bamboo, nandina, privet, Russian and autumn olive, burning bush, honeysuckle bush, Japanese honeysuckle, and winter creeper. Now is the time for action on that plan.

Eradicating Invasives

Since the Disaster Dozen invasives are particularly noxious, you probably suspect that many are difficult to eradicate. You're right.

When eradicating anything, however, invasive or not, always begin with the most benign methods—cutting back, pulling, or otherwise manually removing, and then treating any re-sprouts responsibly. When faced with persistent invasives, however, a more aggressive attack may be in order, perhaps with an appropriate herbicide. Contact a local expert, such as your county extension agent, for specific recommendations, and follow label directions to the letter.

Since troublesome nonnatives have a quirky tendency to leaf out earlier than natives, the early greening lets you take timely action to eradicate

them. If you've been advised that herbicide application is the only satisfactory route, you can probably apply it during this early greening without affecting natives that have not yet leafed out. Ditto with late-fall greenery, after natives have gone dormant. Again, check with local experts.

Some particularly resilient plants have extensive root systems that, if the plant is cut and not treated, will send up dozens and dozens of new sprouts around itself. The sprouts may resist a single herbicide treatment. In such stubborn cases, you may need to cut the plant to within a few inches of the ground and paint the cut edge and stem(s) or trunk(s) with herbicides prescribed for stump treatment. Again, a local expert can recommend what's best for your area. Be certain to follow label directions for safe and successful application. In addition, most herbicide labels include a toll-free number; give the company a call if you're uncertain about any part of this process.

Know that some of the most aggressive of the Disaster Dozen species will require repeated

Get rid of it! Highly invasive winter creeper, one of the Disaster Dozen, mostly smothers everything on the ground; but when it climbs trees or other structures and blooms, the berries, closely resembling bittersweet, attract birds that then spread the plant even farther.

treatment as new sprouts arise from far-reaching roots, sometimes several years later. Persistence is key to eradication.

Using Caution

In the process of eradicating invasives, keep in mind two cautionary notes: First, use caution spraying under tree canopies with an herbicide that, if it soaks into the ground, can kill roots, thus damaging or killing valuable, perhaps prized, trees. Second, some herbicides are highly volatile, and the vapor can damage or kill nearby tender plants. In short, herbicides are killers, so take care to target only the enemy. Above all, when using herbicides of any kind, read label directions carefully and always follow them exactly to assure safe and effective treatment. If in doubt, check with local experts such as your county extension agent, or call that toll-free number on the product label.

MOVING FORWARD

Eradicating the nonnative invasives will require keeping a regular eye out for seedlings and sprouts from remaining root systems. Just be prepared. Patience and persistence are in high demand for this operation.

Once the yard is rid of invasives, you're ready to move on. You can choose to replace the invasives with some of the suggested native alternatives below, or you can choose to alter your yard map to include other kinds of birdscaping plants—depending once again on space, budget, and time.

From Disaster Dozen to Delightful Dozen

We could probably come up with at least 100 suggestions for plants to replace any of the Disaster Dozen, so the following suggested native alternatives represent only a fraction of suitable options. Thus, don't hesitate to consider plants described in earlier chapters of this book. Most of the suggested native alternatives below appear on our plant lists, but don't shrug off those that do not. We can have only so many favorites on our lists, but all of the following are fine plants, equally suited to birdscaping.

Native alternatives to Bradford/Callery pear: Allegheny serviceberry (*Amelanchier laevis*), fringe tree (*Chionanthus virginicus*), green hawthorn (*Crataegus viridis*), yellowwood (*Cladrastis kentukea*)

Native alternatives to princess tree: northern catalpa (*Catalpa speciosa*), red mulberry (*Morus rubra*), but *not* Asian invasive white mulberry (*Morus alba*)

Native alternatives to tree of heaven: yellowwood (*Cladrastis kentukea*), pecan (*Carya illinoinensis*), butternut (*Juglans cinerea*), smooth sumac (*Rhus glabra*), fringe tree (*Chionanthus virginicus*)

Native alternatives to bamboo: arborvitae trees (*Thuja* spp.), especially tall narrow cultivars like 'Emerald Green', synonymous with 'Green Giant', or eastern red cedar (*Juniperus virginiana*) for a living screen

Native alternatives to nandina: Florida leucothoe (*Agarista populifolia*), yaupon (*Ilex vomitoria*), winterberry (*Ilex verticillata*)

Native alternatives to ligustrum privets: blackhaw (*Viburnum prunifolium*), devilwood (*Osmanthus americanus*), Carolina cherry laurel (*Prunus caroliniana*)

Native alternatives to autumn and Russian olive: silky willow (*Salix*

sericea), silverberry (*Elaeagnus commutata*), silver buffaloberry (*Shepherdia argentea*), bayberry (*Morella/Myrica cerifera*), American snowbell (*Styrax americanus*)

Native alternatives to burning bush: black chokeberry (*Aronia melanocarpa*), highbush blueberry (*Vaccinium corymbosum*), fragrant sumac (*Rhus aromatica*), Virginia sweetspire (*Itea virginica*)

Native alternatives to honeysuckle bushes: winterberry (*Ilex verticillata*), spicebush (*Lindera benzoin*), red osier dogwood (*Cornus sericea*)

Native alternatives to Japanese honeysuckle: scarlet/trumpet honeysuckle (*Lonicera sempervirens*), rock/American clematis (*Clematis columbiana*), American wisteria (*Wisteria frutescens*), but *not* Chinese wisteria (*Wisteria sinensis*), another invasive

Native alternatives to winter creeper: bearberry (*Arctostaphylos uva-ursi*), climbing hydrangea (*Decumaria barbara*), creeping blueberry (*Vaccinium crassifolium*), crossvine (*Bignonia capreolata*)

FINDING PLANT SOURCES

With your yard map and plant lists in hand, you're off to shop. Finding native plants at neighborhood nurseries currently remains a challenge in most places. But being the savvy business folks that they are, most nursery operators and horticulturalists recognize a market when they see one. The more we ask for specific native plants at area retail nurseries, the more the owners and managers will realize it's a market they can meet. They have at their command numerous wholesalers that specialize in native plants. Let it be clear: Native stock is readily at hand for retail outlets to purchase. Retailers simply have to be assured that they will sell what stock they order. Good marketing is always about meeting demand. Tell them which plants you want. Tell them you'll be buying. Better bet they'll be selling!

Virginia creeper, a berry-producing native vine, can be considered invasive because it spreads readily. However, its berries are highly prized by migrants, and the bright red foliage adds a lovely note to fall. Keep it if you can.

Since 96 percent of all songbirds, including Great-crested Flycatchers, feed their babies bugs, neonics destroy the very purpose we bird lovers have for planting.

Neonicotinoids
LONG-REACHING, LONG-TERM POISON

While you seek plant sources, also inquire about the use of neonicotinoids, usually shortened to neonics. It's too important not to revisit the issue here.

On plants, neonics work as a systemic insecticide so that every part of the plant—including stems, leaves, flowers, seeds, berries, nectar, and pollen—is toxic to whatever eats any of those parts. Thus, the plants are insect-free. The problem? Not all insects are bad. Think bees, butterflies, and caterpillars. What kills one insect kills all.

Research is ongoing. But many well-placed authorities report that bees nectaring on treated plants lose their sense of direction and can no longer find flower patches or their way back to the hive. They don't survive. Other insects, including butterflies and their caterpillars, that feed on nectar and leaves of treated plants also succumb. Some fairly solid studies, including over 200 reported by the American Birding Association, seem to verify the effect on birds. If they eat the seeds of treated plants or bugs, including caterpillars, that fed on treated plants, the birds do not survive. Nestlings, given their tiny size, need only minuscule exposure to neonics to cause death.

The problem with neonics is compounded by their very long half-life—from 2 to 10 years. In spite of the inherent dangers, some growers treat every plant—necessary or not—to keep them insect and disease free, lovely for the marketplace. Plant them in your garden, and you're adding long-term insect-killers to your plot.

The lesson: Always verify that the plants you purchase are free of neonics. Fortunately, most native plant growers understand that their plants support bugs. They tend to avoid insecticides. Still, be sure to ask.

Looking for Options

Meanwhile, until established commercial nurseries start regularly stocking native plants to meet our needs, look to the following options:

Online sources ship native plant seed, plugs, or dry-root plants. Be aware, however, that some growers stock plants specific to their own region. So, unless you live in that region, the plants may not be suitable for your planting zone. In other words, don't order native plants grown in Wisconsin for Wisconsin if you live in Georgia.

Local and state native plant societies typically post on their websites or blogs the names, addresses, and contact information for regional native plant sources, both retail and wholesale. Sometimes wholesalers will accept large minimum orders that you and your friends can place cooperatively.

Native plant societies at state and local levels often host plant sales. In general, you can be comfortable knowing the stock is reputable.

Master Gardeners often host plant sales that may include an assortment of native plants. Depending on their sources, the "native" stock may or may not be reliably native. Every organization handles these matters differently.

Choosing 6, 10, and 18 plants of 3 species makes better sense than choosing 2 each of 17 species.

Mom-and-pop businesses often cater to niche gardening interests and may special-order plants for you. Shopping local always helps the area's economy, and garnering a group of like-minded friends to place orders at a mom-and-pop business will generate additional local interest in planting native.

When all else fails, you may choose to raise your own plants by seed. You will find reputable native seed sources online. If you have the space and time to tend the seedlings and do the transplants, you will indeed save dollars. And maybe, given more seedlings than you can use, you can have your own plant sale, furthering the message about natives!

Reading the Labels: Native or Not?

Shopping specifically for natives or native varieties can turn into a hair-pulling challenge. As you roam nursery greenhouses, how do you check labels to make sure you get what you want? Let's assume by way of illustration that you're shopping for eastern purple coneflower. Your search leads you to a display of perhaps a dozen kinds of "purple coneflower." They're all different. Are they all natives? Highly unlikely. Are some of them native varieties? Maybe. Are some of them native cultivars? Possibly. Are some of them hybrids? It's a sure bet.

So how do you know?

Labels may help. But the bad news is that there's nothing standardized about labels. Each company, or grower, makes its own labels. If nurseries receive shipments unlabeled, or if they grow their own stock, they may purchase labels from stock companies. In any of these situations, the labels vary. They may include complete information—including common name, scientific name, and variety and/or hybrid name—or not. Mostly not.

But do look for possible clues:

The scientific name will let you check for native origin. So, for example, in the case of eastern purple coneflower, the scientific name should read *Echinacea purpurea.*

The abbreviation "var." indicates that the specimen is either a variety or cultivated variety (used interchangeably on most labels). So if a label reads something like *Echinacea purpurea* var. *arkansana,* you're good to go with this one.

The use of single quotation marks also indicates a variety or cultivated variety, with or without the "var." abbreviation, like this: *Echinacea purpurea* 'All That Jazz'. Probably good to go here, too—except that sometimes the hybrid name appears in single quotation marks.

The symbol × means the plant is a cross between, probably, two varieties;

in other words, a hybrid. So a purple coneflower hybrid label could read *E. purpurea* 'Magnus' × 'Kim's Knee High'. Probably should skip this one. It could be sterile, and there's no way to know. Worse, chances are that no one at the retail nursery or outlet can tell you.

Sometimes hybrids are not clearly marked. Sometimes the name in single quotation marks turns out to be a hybrid. Sometimes the label includes only a common name, period.

Given the range of plant-label information—or lack thereof—can you somehow verify what's what? Well, maybe. In the age of ready portable access to the Internet, you can shop with devices in hand and go online to the USDA Plant Database (www.plants.usda.gov) right at the retail business. A quick check of the maps answers all. While the database accepts both scientific and common names in its search engine, common names are less likely to turn up accurate results. Common names, after all, vary by region and by grower. Still, the search is worth the effort. There's nothing to lose but a few minutes' time.

I wish I had better news about this labeling business, but with no standards in the industry, we're left to our own wits. It's a truly "buyer beware" market.

PLANTING THE PLANTS

Once you're made your purchases, you're in the home stretch. You know what you want to plant where, so follow your plan. Most plants you can handle yourself, but trees and maybe certain large shrubs may present a separate issue: They may be too large for you to transport or handle. Thus, when you've made your final choices and purchased your large plants, decide whether you want to plant it/them or have a landscaper do the deed. Some nurseries accompany plant sales with short-term guarantees, but usually the guarantee

Plant labels, which have no standardization, range from a handwritten common name to colorfully printed details. Only with mobile Internet connection at hand while you shop can you sort out the poor, good, better, and best choices among these labels.

is effective only if the nursery's own personnel do the planting. The planting fee may be equal, or nearly equal, to the tree's cost. Consider your options before you decide.

Most plants require nothing more than following good planting practices: good siting, careful planting at the correct depth, and adequate water. Of course, always follow your nursery staff's advice about planting and watering, knowing that natives don't need fertilizers and, after they're established, little or no water. But getting plants established merits your TLC, making sure plants settle in nicely; watering them until they begin rooting, perhaps for three seasons; and protecting small plants from raiding rabbits, deer, raccoons, skunks, or other yard rascals.

Planting Vines

If you have chosen a vine for your birdscape, you no doubt know already how you want it to function. If it's to serve as a ground cover, perhaps twining over some unsightly part of the landscape, you have no pre-planting prep. On the other hand, if you want it to vine upward, you must provide suitable support. And that support must be permanently in place prior to your putting the vine in the ground.

Whether you purchase or build it, here are some considerations for a suitably strong supporting structure:

Wild grape vines feed and otherwise support many birds, including female Baltimore Orioles that use the shaggy bark for their pendulous nests.

> Regardless of construction material—wood, metal, or vinyl—the support structure must be sufficiently sturdy to support heavy vines. Consider whether the structure will bend, crack, sag, or break under, say, 20 pounds of tangled vine. Yes, vines can grow surprisingly heavy.

> Four-footed structures stand more firmly than two-footed structures. And the more widely separated the feet, the more stable the structure. Of course, the more windy the planting site, the more important the structure's stability.

> Joints should be fastened securely in order to withstand flexing in wind, under weight. If you can wiggle or twist the store model, reevaluate.

> Wooden trellises can rot unless made of rot-resistant or treated lumber. Paint or stain does not sufficiently protect wood long-term from rot.

> Metal structures can rust without suitable rust-preventative paint or sealant.

Any structure can topple in strong winds unless securely anchored, either on concrete piers or with sturdy metal stakes driven probably 2 feet deep. Trellis legs made of treated lumber can be set directly into the ground at similar depths.

FILLING IN THE BLANKS

Once your chosen plants are in place, stand back, take a look, and study the effects. Look for landscape gaps or spots you think would look better with some sort of filler or accent. Consider an additional clump or so of native ornamental grass. Or add a native fern. Maybe cluster a few more perennials. Consider which plants will increase the visual appeal while simultaneously improving bird habitat.

Beyond a few additional native grasses or ferns, consider additional accents in the form of containers. Almost any garden can benefit from strategically placed pots—large or small, tall or squat, formal or rustic, made of whatever suits your fancy. Using natives, you can create the formulaic pot planter: a thriller, a spiller, and a filler.

Using a sizable pot, begin with the thriller—that tall plant that spikes interest—maybe a long-blooming agastache like 'Purple Haze' (*Agastache* 'Purple Haze'), or maybe the thriller is one of the native ornamental grasses. Add a compatible spiller—the plant that drapes over the side—such as a small ground cover like trailing arbutus (*Epigaea repens*). Then add the filler—the plant (or plants) that provides the background for all the rest—maybe a bushy aster (*Aster dumosus*). Voila! A lovely pot next to a stone bench, that bit of hardscape in the corner of your bird-busy garden.

Consider other hardscape as well, maybe statuary, boulders, a decorative rain gauge, or other accents that suit your fancy. But before you settle

A fully mulched garden in spring eliminates weeding for the remainder of the season. Here, wood chips keep paths clearly delineated, while thickly spread shredded leaves keep the entire planted area weed-free.

back to bask in the glory of the task accomplished, you'll want to add one finishing touch: mulch.

MULCHING SAVVY

There's no denying you'd be pleased to have a (relatively) weed-free landscape. The miserable truth, however, is that unwanted weeds are sure to sprout—unless, of course, you wrestle them under your control. After years of working through the dilemma, I recommend mulching—the finishing touch in a garden. Not only does mulch dress up the appearance, it also helps retain moisture and shade delicate roots. Over the long haul, it also enriches the soil. But above all, it smothers the weeds that would love to rear their annoying heads.

In our yard, mulching is an annual rite of passage from winter into spring. After I clear away winter's debris, divide and thin big clumps of plants into sharable sections, prune the overgrowth, replace some old plants with new, and weed, I set myself up for a relatively work-free summer. I mulch. And I use lots of it. The best part of the mulch I use: It's free. Each fall, we gather bagged leaves from curbsides (and prevent bags from jamming the landfill), add them to our own, and shred the entire pile. Exposed to the weather all winter, the pile melts down and becomes a wonderful partly decomposed mulch by spring. Used liberally, it smothers summer weeds and provides birds leaf litter for yearlong gleaning.

Compared to other types of mulch, shredded leaves work exceptionally well as mulch because:

> Leaf mulch is 100 percent natural and 100 percent organic, readily available, and free.

> Leaf mulch is Mother Nature's nursery, cemetery, and breeding grounds.

> Leaf mulch harbors bugs in all forms—adults, eggs, and larvae. In winter and early spring, leaf mulch is the gold standard for housing essential protein for birds.

Breeding female birds need an abundance of calcium in order to produce eggshells, and they meet most of their dietary demand for calcium by foraging for small snails amid leaf litter—another reason to leave some leaves every fall.

> Leaf mulch harbors calcium-rich snails. Breeding female birds need huge amounts of calcium not only to produce eggs, but to produce eggshells stout enough not to crush under their weight.

> Leaf mulch naturally enhances the soil as leaves decompose and, literally, turn to soil.

> Using shredded leaves as mulch prevents bags of autumn leaves from overloading landfills.

Be certain, however, to avoid leaf mulch containing walnut tree leaves or debris. Walnut tree parts are toxic to most other plants.

If leaf mulch is not readily available, maybe pine straw is. Depending on where you live, pine straw may be more suitable—and more readily and reliably available—than is leaf mulch. It has most of the same attributes as leaf mulch, and it's lightweight, natural, and attractive.

Mulching Manners

Using just any mulch, however, is neither environmentally sound nor healthy for birds. A few guidelines:

> Using non-organic mulches defeats the purpose of creating bird-friendly habitat. Avoid non-organic mulches like rock or shredded rubber. They do not support bugs—or birds—and in summer increase the heat load on plant roots.

> Avoid using mulch containing anything unnatural, like dyes or other treatments. Colored mulch can contain arsenic from pressure-treated wood. As mulch from treated lumber deteriorates, it most likely contaminates the ground,

affecting the natural biodiversity you're trying to achieve in a bird-friendly habitat.

If neither shredded leaves nor pine straw is readily available, look toward natural hardwood mulch. It's usually either a by-product of the lumber and paper industries or made from tree-trimming debris.

While not as dense as shredded hardwood mulch, hardwood chips function nearly as well. Wood chips are almost always a by-product of the tree-trimming industry, so make sure the product is walnut-tree-free. Since light can penetrate the chips somewhat more readily than it can shredded mulch, a few weeds may work their way through. Still, as wood chips deteriorate, they enrich the soil, serving as Mother Nature's nursery and grocery store. Birds will forge through the layers, looking for bugs in all stages.

Using cypress mulch is environmentally unfriendly. Why cut down a vital tree to grind it in order to protect a few flowers? While cypress mulch supposedly has rot-resistant and termite-resistant qualities, only old-growth cypress contains the resistant qualities to any degree. Now that most old-growth cypress is gone, commercial ventures grind up any cypress they find, thus harvesting an important bird resource. The cypress trees in my yard are my go-to spots for watching spring warblers. Why would I want them cut down—anywhere—especially only to grind into mulch?

Having found an ample seed supply, an adult White-crowned Sparrow and a juvenile refuel after arriving on their winter range.

Oh, and one more thing: Termites are highly unlikely to find a home in mulch. They munch solid wood, not loose shreds.

THE DEAD STILL STANDING

Come winter, you'll want to leave standing the frost-killed plants. They're loaded with seed, and they offer protection against winter's elements. But wait—if you don't clean up your garden each fall, mustn't you worry about bugs in your garden? Contrary to popular belief, the answer is no. In our yard, we never use insecticides; we leave all our leaves, some whole and some mulched, and the bugs don't eat our plants. There's a simple reason: The birds, here in abundance, eat the bugs—in abundance. It's nature's balance. As the leaves enrich the soil, the birds enrich our lives.

So your Five-Step Plan is now complete. Well, at least phase one of your birdscaping plan is complete. Whether you have finished what your space, budget, and time allow or have several more phases in your master plan, it's time to evaluate what's what.

Give the new landscaping about a year to establish itself, go through the four seasons, and show off its results. You're then ready to move on, perhaps tweaking your master plan. Everyone who gardens know that it's always a work in progress.

GRASSY BENEFITS: REVISITING LAWN

With the plantings in place, you may want to turn your attention once again to lawn. Perhaps you've already reduced it with the just-completed plantings. But if any lawn remains, think about the following options.

Native turf can add a touch of magic and function to your yard. Yes, we've been openly critical of lawn, the second-most-desertlike habitat for birds—second only to pavement. But there's a huge difference between lawn and grass. Contemporary lawn turf has been developed with the use of exotic grasses, mostly from the Eastern Hemisphere. Virtually no "lawn" is native. And virtually every lawn demands fertilizers, pesticides, irrigation, frequent mowing and trimming, thatching, and reseeding, followed by additional fertilizing and irrigation. But more and more folks care about water conservation. They strive to reduce or eliminate pesticides and fertilizers that pollute waterways; and they aim to reduce or eliminate the gas-guzzling, pollution-emitting use of mowers and weed whackers. So conscientious folks are looking to eliminate useless and environmentally negative lawns and take advantage instead of no-mow or low-mow alternatives.

If you've decided to lose the lawn and are considering incorporating sedges, native turf, or flowering bee lawns, now's the time to take that next step. Again, though, start with a small section of the yard, see what works best, give it time to develop, and then move to the next section.

You'll never regret the one-section-at-a-time approach.

Lose the Lawn with Sedges

One up-and-coming alternative to lawn is sedges, and the *Carex* genus includes several natives suitable for eastern US yards. They include Pennsylvania sedge (*C. pensylvanica*), Baltimore sedge (*C. senta*), and Catlin sedge (*C. texensis*).

All have similar characteristics: They grow in dense mats of fine-textured leaves, reaching no more than 6 to 8 inches tall when left unmowed. Baltimore sedge tolerates deep shade; Catlin accepts part to full shade. All thrive best with little or no fertilizer or chemicals and far less water than traditional lawns—maybe none at all, depending on where you live. Some *Carex* species tolerate wet soils. All are best mowed only two or three times a year (yes, a year!) to a height of 3 to 4 inches, and all are best planted via plugs set out on 6- to 8-inch centers.

Lose the Lawn with Native Turf: Buffalograss

There's yet another alternative: The only truly native warm-season turf grass in the mid and southern US is buffalograss (*Buchloë dactyloides*), so named for its being buffalo's favored grazing grass. Having evolved on the Great Plains, buffalograss is a sod-forming efficient user of water. Short and fine-leaved, it does not tolerate shade or sandy soil. Instead, it's deeply rooted and thus tolerates drought.

Buffalograss turf can be planted as seed, plugs, or sod. If needed, it can be watered once a month to get established, and then be watered once a month later to prevent dry-weather dormancy. Or not. It's a personal choice. Once established, however, it spreads by seed or runners that take root to create new plants. Mowing depends on use. On a golf fairway, for instance, more frequent

A Chipping Sparrow finds bugs, one in its beak, in a bird-friendly flowering bee lawn. Although the dandelion and white sweet clover in this lawn are nonnative, similar flowering bee lawns can be developed using natives.

mowing may be necessary than in your yard—probably depending on nothing more than how you prefer your turf.

Currently about 15 buffalograss cultivars are available for regionally specific markets, from northern to transitional to southern regions. Check with local experts to choose the one best suited for your eco-region.

Either of these alternatives—sedges or native-turf buffalograss—will serve well as a substitute for lawn. But what do they offer birds? Any native grass supports native grassland insects like grasshoppers, katydids, and various beetles. Give some thought to yet another way to add native habitat to even the smallest yard.

Switch to Smart Lawns

Recent research from Michigan State University and the Bee Lab at the University of Minnesota recommends flowering bee lawns to support pollinators, many of which are in decline. The general principle is simple: You can mow and still maintain habitat where you mow by allowing turf to mingle with miniature flowering plants. Of course, the plan automatically precludes the use of any herbicides or other lawn treatments. Instead, to gain the full impact, you'll likely need to introduce the appropriate flowering plants into the turf. Suitable flowering species will, of course, vary by region, so check with your local county extension agent for advice about a suitable bee-lawn mix and the procedure for incorporating the flowers.

Many flowering bee-lawn seed mixes include introduced species like sweet clover (*Trifolium repens*) and creeping thyme (*Thymus serpyllum*), but the Bee Lab recommends four excellent natives: lanceleaf self-heal (*Prunella vulgaris*), ground plum (*Astragalus crassicaprus*), lanceleaf coreopsis (*Coreopsis lanceolata*), and calico aster (*Symphyotrichum lateriflorum*). All of these make fine native flowering options for a high-mowed lawn. Set the mower at 3 or 4 inches, thus providing the opportunity for small plants to blossom. When mowed, these plants, usually growing much taller, will form low, dense clumps—and keep on blooming. What an imaginative way to add biodiversity to the yard, support declining pollinator populations (which ultimately affect the bird populations), and still maintain a "lawn"—only this time it's a smart lawn!

As an added benefit to you, the flowering bee lawn increases your lawn's resilience to environmental pressures. And you'll enjoy the pleasure of the flowers.

MONITORING AND TWEAKING

As your native plants are becoming established, keep an eye on the habitat. Have you seen more pollinators? More butterflies, moths, and skippers? More birds? Which of your new plants host the most bees? Which plants attract birds to their seeds? Which plants are the best berry producers in each of the four seasons? Which plants attract the most hummingbirds?

You may wish to keep a journal, recording new sightings, their frequencies, and behaviors. My own journal tells me when bird species were first spotted in the yard—all the way back to 1973, the year a blizzard brought Snow Buntings to my yard for the first, and last, time. I also keep a garden journal, noting when which plants were set out where. In most cases, I've filed the labels as

Acadian flycatcher, dependent on bugs for survival, hunts from a perch in a black locust tree (*Robinia pseudoacacia*).

well. I don't often read these journals, but I often use them as a reference for names and sources. And I keep photographic records. The photos identify butterflies and skippers sighted in the garden. Photos of plants and their blossoms take up a few megs on my hard drive. And well, yes, of course, photos record the birds, too.

But along with monitoring the birds, bugs, and butterflies, you'll also want to keep an eye on what's growing. Are invasives creeping in? Are new plants showing signs of stress—from too little water, too much water, too little drainage, too much drainage, too much sun, too much shade? Are some plants sending up sprouts or multiplying by seed? Is that okay? If you prefer to keep plants more tightly contained, use a spade to cut off suckers and transplant seedlings, perhaps to share with others.

I'm betting that at the end of every growing season, you'll see something you want to change: a new plant that will attract a new bird, an old plant that nothing finds attractive—not even you. Maybe there's something you want to prune to keep it tame, or something you want to stake for support to keep it away from the front walk. Making at least a weekly trek past every plant assures me of the health and well-being of each—and gives me time to react in case something is awry.

JOYS OF BIRDS IN THE YARD

Indeed, we all love our feathered friends. They bring us song. They bring us color. They bring us joy. Returning habitat—native, life-giving habitat—to these tiny songsters will help save their lives. As climate change affects even more habitat, as some forests move north and west and others disappear altogether, and as the equilibrium of biodiversity hangs in the balance, every shrub we plant, every nectar source we encourage, every tree we support—all will matter in the life cycle of these feathered creatures that serve as a measure of our own quality of life.

So here's a challenge: After you've added as many natives to your birdscape as space, time, and budget allow, and after those plants have become established, consider your own year-long bird tally in your native bird-friendly habitat. I'm betting you'll have a dramatically improved count.

Of course, it's not about the numbers, but it *is* about what those numbers mean: As a result of your efforts, birds have a new shot at survival, and not only in your yard and garden. Just think: If everyone in your neighborhood—or county, or state—follows your footsteps, what a difference those footsteps will make. Visualize a diverse green corridor of native plants supporting a diverse bird population, aiding them on their breeding grounds, supporting them on their migratory routes, and fostering them during the four seasons. What an impact that would make!

Rest well, knowing you've done your part. May you and the birds in your yard live well.

This handsome male Northern Cardinal obviously found adequate native berries in order to produce his healthy, brilliant-red plumage.

References

American Bird Conservancy. "BirdScapes." www.abcbirds.org/birds/birdscapes.
———. "Glass Collisions." www.abcbirds.org/program/glass-collisions.

Baicich, Paul J., and Colin J. O. Harrison. *Nests, Eggs, and Nestlings of North American Birds*. 2nd ed. Princeton, NJ: Princeton University Press, 2005.

Burrell, C. Colston. *Native Alternatives to Invasive Plants: A Brooklyn Botanic Garden All-Region Guide*. Brooklyn, NY: Brooklyn Botanic Gardens, 2007.

Chicago Botanic Garden. "Gardens and Natural Areas." www.chicagobotanic.org/gardens.

Conner, Jack. "Not All Sweetness and Light: The Real Diet of Hummingbirds," October 15, 2010. Cornell Lab of Ornithology, All About Birds. www.allaboutbirds.org/not-all-sweetness-and-light-the-real-diet-of-hummingbirds.

Cornell Lab of Ornithology. All About Birds. www.allaboutbirds.org.

Deep Roots Garden Center. "Why Natives?" www.deeprootsgc.com/why-natives.

Epic Gardening. "Sixteen Invasive Species Sold at Garden Centers You Should Never Buy," July 29, 2014. www.epicgardening.com/invasive-species.

Glassberg, Jeffrey. *Butterflies through Binoculars—the East: A Field Guide to the Butterflies of Eastern North America*. New York: Oxford University Press, 1999.

Gorchov, David. Cited in Reis Thebault, "MU Professor Combats Invasive Amur Honeysuckle." *The Miami Student,* April 28, 2014.

Greenlee, John. "Sedge Lawns: A Sustainable Low-Maintenance Alternative to Grass," December 31, 2001. Brooklyn Botanic Garden. www.bbg.org/gardening/article/sedge_lawns.

Harstad, Carolyn. *Go Native! Gardening with Native Plants and Wildflowers in the Lower Midwest*. Bloomington: Indiana University Press, 1999.

———. *Got Sun? 200 Best Native Plants for Your Garden*. Bloomington: Indiana University Press, 2013.

Illinois Wildflowers. "Plant Identification by Habitat." www.illinoiswildflowers.info.

Lady Bird Johnson Wildflower Center. "Native Plants: Find Plants." www.wildflower.org/plants-main.

Lane, Ian, et al. "Flowering Bee Lawns for Pollinators." University of Minnesota Bee Lab. www.beelab.umn.edu/sites/beelab.umn.edu/files/floweringlawninfoenrtflogo.pdf.

Marzluff, John M. *Welcome to Surbirdia: Sharing Our Neighborhoods with Wrens, Robins, Woodpeckers, and Other Wildlife*. New Haven, CT: Yale University Press, 2014.

Missouri Botanical Garden. "Gardens and Gardening: Plant Finder." www.missouribotanicalgarden.org/plantfinder/plantfindersearch.aspx.

Morton Arboretum. "Trees and Plants." www.mortonarb.org/trees-plants.

National Audubon Society. "Plants for Birds." www.audubon.org/plantsforbirds.

National Wildlife Federation. "Garden for Wildlife: Create a Sustainable Garden That Helps

Wildlife." www.nwf.org/Garden-For-Wildlife
.aspx.

Palmer, Cynthia. "American Bird Conservancy
Supports Bill to Suspend Neonics," June 23,
2017. American Bird Conservancy. www.abc
birds.org/article/american-bird-conservancy
-supports-bill-suspend-neonics.

Riordan, Terrance. "Planting and Maintaining a
Buffalograss Lawn," April 4, 2012. Brooklyn
Botanic Garden. www.bbg.org/gardening/
article/planting_and_maintaining_a_buffalo
grass_lawn.

Rodewald, Amanda. Cited in Laura Tang-
ley, "Nonnative Plants: Ecological Traps?"
National Wildlife Federation Blog. http://
blog.nwf.org/2013/01/nonnative-plants
-ecological-traps.

Saeed, Abiya, and Rebecca Krans. "Smart Lawns
for Pollinators," January 2016. Michigan State
University Extension Smart Gardening. www
.migarden.msu.edu/uploads/resources/pdfs/
Lawns_for_pollinators.pdf.

Sarver, Matthew, et al. *Mistaken Identity? Invasive Plants and Their Native Look-alikes: An
Identification Guide for the Mid-Atlantic.* Delaware Department of Agriculture, November
2008. www.nybg.org/files/scientists/rnaczi/
Mistaken_Identity_Final.pdf.

Sibley, David Allen. *The Sibley Guide to Trees.*
New York: Alfred A. Knopf, 2009.

Sorenson, Sharon. *Birds in the Yard Month by
Month: What's There and Why and How to
Attract Those That Aren't.* Mechanicsburg, PA:
Stackpole Books, 2013.

Steiner, Rob. "Landscape Design Principles for
Residential Gardens." Originally published as
"Rules of the Game" in *Garden Design,* Early
Spring 2015. https://www.gardendesign
.com/landscape-design/rules.html.

Stokes, Donald, Lillian Stokes, and Ernest Wil-
liams. *Stokes Butterfly Book: The Complete
Guide to Butterfly Gardening, Identification, and
Behavior.* New York: Little, Brown and Company, 1991.

Tallamy, Douglas W. *Bringing Nature Home: How
You Can Sustain Wildlife with Native Plants.*
Portland, OR: Timber Press, 2007.

United States Department of Agriculture Forest
Service, Northeastern Areas, State and Private
Forestry. "Urban and Community Forestry."
www.na.fs.fed.us/urban/index.shtm.

United States Department of Agriculture Natural Resources Conservation Service. "Plants
Database." www.plants.usda.gov.

Veloz, Liz. "Why Are Plant Hybrids Sterile?"
Sciencing, updated April 24, 2017. https://
sciencing.com/plant-hybrids-sterile-5619428.
html.

Wile, Rob. "The American Lawn Is Now the
Largest Single 'Crop' in the U.S." *Huffing-
ton Post,* updated August 17, 2015. www
.huffingtonpost.com/entry/lawn-largest
-crop-america_us_55d0dc06e4b07addcb
43435d.

Acknowledgments

No one puts together a reference book like this without guidance and support. Because the subject matter ranges from wildlife biology to botany to ornithology and from landscaping to gardening to restoration, the knowledge of many supersedes the knowledge of one. So all of the folks who generously offered their time and expertise have made this work possible, including the following:

Paul Bouseman, Botanical Curator, Mesker Park Zoo and Botanic Garden, pursues his lifelong interest in native plants at his family's redeveloped farmstead. I owe him far more than I can ever repay, both for his friendship and his mentoring. His personal experience with thousands of plant species gives him unparalleled understanding of their behaviors and attributes. Genius in his suggestions for addressing potentially controversial matters, he showed me how to smooth the way for gently introducing readers to a complicated subject. From the book's initial plan and continuing to its completion, his wisdom is reflected throughout much of this effort. The stars in his crown must now surely be blindingly bright. Thank you, Paul, for your kindness, generosity, and devotion to the plant world—and to this project.

My hat is off to botanist Ellen Jacquart, retired Stewardship Director of The Nature Conservancy of Indiana and chair of the Invasive Plant Education Committee of the Indiana Native Plant and Wildflower Society. Years ago (we won't say how many, Ellen), her educational workshops gave me the initial nudge to plant natives to attract birds to my yard; and now, having critiqued the manuscript, she has kept me in line, returning me to the straight and narrow when I veered from accuracy. She corrected errors I would never have recognized and taught me along the way. Further, her encouragement regarding the need for this work lends credibility to the effort. Thank you, Ellen, for your gracious and far-reaching contributions. Any errors that remain are mine.

A gracious thank-you to Heath Hamilton, Wildlife Refuge Specialist with the United States Fish and Wildlife Service, currently focusing on restoration efforts at Patoka River National Wildlife Refuge and Management Area. He read the manuscript, offered encouragement, and recommended valuable additions and alterations. Since he also manages his own five-acre home refuge, planted in prairie, woodland, and pond edge and landscaped almost entirely with natives, I'm grateful for his tour around the property—an intense two-hour in-the-field education, identifying plants, their growing habits, and the wildlife they attract. The experience was an inspirational springboard into manuscript revisions. Thank you, Heath.

A kind and heartfelt note of thanks to Robin Wright Mallery, passionate and self-described as "needs-to-learn-more landscaper for the birds." She, too, read the manuscript with an eye (and ear) for this book's likely audience. Her encouragement helped me keep on keeping on, completing the rewrites in timely fashion.

A true friend, F. Jeanette Frazier, retired Indiana Accredited Horticulturist, earns my sincere gratitude for focusing her keen eye for detail on the initial manuscript, significantly aiding in the goal toward accuracy. She gave up precious time to talk me through a maze or two.

Cassie Janzen Hall, Director of Philanthropy for The Nature Conservancy and home native landscaper for the birds, also read with a critical eye for detail. Thanks to her for proofreading during a time of personal stress. I'm not sure which of us needed the other more at the time.

There were innumerable conversations with folks about those little technical details that, inaccurately presented, would have made the work less credible. While I've bent the ears of many, a few deserve special thanks for tolerating my endless questions:

Nancy Hasting, Purdue University grad horticulturalist and now owner and operator of Hasting Plants, explained the ins and outs and overall complications of plant labels—what they mean, what they don't mean, what they say, and for good measure, what they should say but don't. Thanks, Nancy, for helping me understand.

Entomologist John A. Shuey, Director of Conservation Science of The Nature Conservancy of Indiana, helped me get it straight about native bugs and their reliance on native plants. I hope I've honored his name by actually getting it right.

Ron Giles, American Orchid Society Trustee, Central American Orchids, and avid birder and Master Gardener, patiently explained the details of how hybrids differ from their parents and from their "cousin" cultivars, and helped me understand at least in general the scientific process by which new hybrids are developed and patented.

Thanks to Anne Butsch, who took time from her busy medical practice to redirect my initial plans for the book's organization. Because of her experience presenting native-plant seminars, she guided my vision, nudging me toward a step-by-step plan . She knows whereof she speaks!

A few years ago, Pam Locker introduced me to the rooftop prairie at Oaklyn Library, touring me through the plants, their quirks, and their joys. It was the first time I understood that, given the right conditions, a native-plant enthusiast really could plant a successful prairie in southwestern Indiana. Thanks to her for the inspiration and the effect she had on my own native plantings to attract birds (and butterflies) to my yard.

Fellow members of the Indiana Native Plant and Wildflower Society and the southwestern Indiana chapter have shared their ideas, their native plants, and their native plant seeds, helping me learn about more native plants than I would ever have discovered on my own. Thanks to all. You helped without ever knowing. And a special thanks to member Adam Hape for sharing insight into his gardening history, from his first native plantings through his struggles to re-landscape and pursue a now-successful grow-your-own approach.

Thanks, too, to my Facebook friends, many of whom I do not know personally but who nevertheless shared their native plant preferences and the results for attracting birds. I am grateful for your often long-distance contributions.

I'd be remiss without a nod to the many years of monthly, bimonthly, quarterly, and one-time publications I've devoured about birds and their lives—magazines, books, newsletters, web posts, and professional journals. Likewise, I can't possibly omit a nod to those authors and other members of the ornithological community who spoke at those many meetings and conferences—a lifetime of learning—all woven into the background and fabric of this effort.

Ultimately, Judith Schnell, Stackpole Books publisher, deserves the credit for finding excitement in the topic, seeing the work's potential, and directing it to fruition. Working as Judith's right-hand associate, Stephanie Otto took care of the day-to-day grind of managing the project's intricacies and answering my barrage of questions. Copyeditor genius Elissa Curcio trained her eagle eye on the manuscript's details, fixed them, and miraculously smoothed all the wrinkles. Amanda Wilson, whose design made it the lovely book that it is. Joanna Beyer who worked her magic to make the pages come to life. Roberta Monaco for her proofreading and indexing expertise, and Production Editor Alex Bordelon, the go-to guy for resolving all things complicated, employed his professional expertise to shepherd this project successfully to completion, keeping us all on track and on schedule. Hugs to you, every one of you, for your dedication to the task. You've made me look good in spite of myself.

Finally, the biggest hugs of all go to my husband Charles, in appreciation of his ongoing and ever-present support. My sometimes-disruptive projects limit our leisure time and throw the burden of usually-shared tasks on his tired back. Yet he sits beside me while we choose and edit photos, sort through the complexities of technical details to make them reader-friendly, and tweak the manuscript, deciding if the narrative covers the necessary details. For well over 50 years, he has been my sounding board, my support, my soul mate, my only true love.

May all of you benefit from the expertise of the many!

Index

blue stem goldenrod, 162
Blue-headed Vireo, 111
blueberry, 112, 123, 194; highbush, 194
bluebird, 24, 29, 31, 35, 76
Blue-gray Gnatcatchers, 26-27, 34
Blue-headed Vireos, 2, 4
bluestem, little, 178
blunt mountain mint, 166
Bobolinks, 12
Bohemian Waxwings, 24, 99, 114, 115
boneset, 169, 171
borers, 75
botanists, vi
bottlebrush grass, 64, 175, 178
Boutelous curtipendula, 178
'Bowhall' maple, 96
boxelder, 88, 93, 183
Bradford pears, 58; alternatives, 193
brambles, 4, 143-44
Brazil, 10
'Brilliantissima,' 124
broadleaf arrowhead, 187, 189
broadleaf evergreen shrub, 108
Brown Creepers, 34, 76, 90
brown-eyed Susan, 150
Brown-headed Nuthatch, 100
Brown Thrashers, 4, 33, 34, 37, 76, 90, 113, 136, 138, 139
bubbling rock, 71, 188-89
Buchloë dactyloides, 202-03
buffalo grass, 202-03
bugs, v; bird babies and, 4; nutrition and, 6
bull thistle, 37
'Burkil,' 105
burning bush, 59; alternatives, 194
bushy American aster, 159
bushy aster, 66
butterflies, 5, 21, 87, 89, 90, 100, 117, 137, 153, 156, 195
butterfly weed, 63, 154, 165, 173
butternut, 193
buttonbush, 39, 112-13, 124
button snake-root, 156, 168
button-willow, 112-13

cabbage white butterfly, 45
calcium, 22
calico aster, 204
Callery pear, 58; alternatives, 193
Callicarpa americana, 8, 25, 110-11, 123
Caltha paulstris, 187, 188, 189
camouflage, 22
Campsis radicans, 15, 142
Canadian goldenrod, 171
Canadian hemlocks, 104
Canadian serviceberry, 133, 135
candleberry, 111
Cape May Warbler, 2, 114
cardinal flower, 61, 164, 184
cardinals, 24, 25, 26, 30, 86, 87, 102
Carnus florida, 88
Carolina cherry laurel, 193
Carolina Chickadee, 17, 19, 22, 29, 88, 102, 115, 133, 147, 150
Carolina hemlock, 104
Carolina Wren, 19, 29, 33, 46, 88, 144, 147, 176
Carolina yellow jasmine, 138-39, 142
Carya illinoinensis, 1, 18, 193
Catalpa speciosa, 193
catbird, 30, 92
caterpillars, 5-6, 19, 20, 23, 36, 43, 44, 195
Ceanothus americanus, 65, 126
Ceanothus herbaceus, 126
Ceanothus microphyllus, 126
cedar, 30
Cedar Waxwings, 24, 26, 43, 58, 99, 114, 115, 116, 132, 133
Celastrus scandens, 24, 136, 141
Celtis occidentalis, 22
Celtis spp., 21
centipedes, 20
Cephalanthus occidentalis, 39, 113, 124
Cercis canadensis, 107, 116, 133, 135
Chaenomeles speciosa, 37
Chamaecyparis thyoides, 103, 183
cherry trees, 21
Chestnut-sided Warbler, 29, 89, 114, 138
chickadees, 26, 26, 31, 33-34, 35, 43, 76, 87
chickweed, 37

Northern Mockingbird, 24, 98, 107, 112, 114, 115, 116, 121, 136, 137
Northern Parula, 19, 22, 79, 89
Northern red oak, 85
northern white cedar, 84, 101, 103, 105, 130, 183
numbers, plant, 49
nuthatches, 31, 35, 46, 84, 91, 100
nutrition, 3, 8
Nyssa sylvatica, 94; 'Tupelo Tower,' 97

oak, 40, 60, 79, 82-86
oleaster, 59
olive oleaster, 59
options, native plant, 195-96
orange coneflower, 150, 160
orange-blossom crossvine, 70
Orchard Oriole, 2, 15, 138, 143
oriental bittersweet, 136
orioles, 30, 33, 86, 92
ornamental grass, 173-76; perennials, 173-76
Osmanthus americanus, 193
ostrich ferns, 64, 65, 66, 179
Ovenbird, 101
owl, 28, 29, 31, 35, 99, 102
Ozark witch hazel, 121, 129

pagoda dogwood, 134
Panicum virgatum, 64, 134, 174, 176, 178
Parthenocissus quinquefolia, 25, 142
Passiflora spp., 21
passion vines, 21
Paulownia tomentosa, 58
Pawpaws, 21
'Peabody,' 105
pearl crescent, 21
pears, flowering, trees, 57
peaty soil, 61
pecan, 18, 193; blossoms, 1
penstemon, 156, 167; *canescens*, 167; *digitalis*, 62, 65, 167
Penstemon canescens, 167
Penstemon digitalis, 62, 65, 167
perennials, 145, 184; array, 148; planning for, 70-71; seasons, 146-48

pesticides, 54
Phlox glaberrima, 168
Phlox maculata, 168
Phlox paniculata, 'David,' 167, 173
phlox, 156, 167, 168, 173
Phyllostachys spp., 58
Physocarpus opulifolius, 39, 65, 117, 126
Phytolacca americana, 170, 172
Picea, 100
Picea glauca, 103, 105, 183; 'Conica,' 105
pickerelweed, 189
Pileated Woodpecter, 19, 34, 87, 88, 101
pin cherry, 25
Pin oak, 85; 'Green Pillar,' 86
pine, 30, 100, 102-03
pine cone seeds, 17
Pine Grosbeaks, 100
Pine Siskin, 4, 18, 90, 91, 100, 101, 102, 110, 151
Pine Warbler, 100
pineapple sage, 16
pink pussy willow, 95
Pinus banksiana, 100, 103
Pinus resinosa, 103
Pinus rigida, 103
Pinus spp., 102
Pinus strobus, 103; 'Fastigiata,' 105
Pinus virginian, 102
pipevine swallowtail, 21, 137, 138
pitch pine, 103
Planatus occidentalis, 33
plant(s): planting, 197-98; plug, 47; removing unwanted, 191-92; sources, 194; vines, 198-99; zone, 81
Platanus occidentalis, 5, 29, 95
pokeweed, 170; American, 172
polydamas swallowtails, 21
Polystichum acrostichoides, 65, 179
pond cypress, 94, 183
Pontedaria cordata, 189
Populus deltoide, 7, 191
possum haw, 116, 126
possumhaw, 116, 120, 128
pot-and-patio gardens, 64, 66; deciduous alternatives, 95-97; deciduous cultivars, 95-97;